The First Oregonians

An Illustrated Collection of Essays
on Traditional Lifeways, Federal-Indian Relations,
and the State's Native People Today

Edited by
Carolyn M. Buan and Richard Lewis

Designed by
Jeanne E. Galick

Oregon Council for the Humanities
Portland, Oregon
1991

Typeset in Berkeley and Garamond Condensed

Printed in the U.S.A.

ISBN 1-880377-00-4

Library of Congress Catalog Card Number 92-60562

First Printing 1992, Second Printing 1992

PREFACE

This book is the culmination of a three-year program focus on the native peoples of Oregon. Based mainly on a special grant from the National Endowment for the Humanities, that focus had three principal parts.

The first was a series of grants from the Oregon Council for the Humanities to the nine federally recognized tribal communities, allowing them to undertake heritage-recovery work within their tribes. Archival research, oral histories, and videotaping were the principal recovery activities, which in many instances have led to further heritage work. Second was a statewide public conference of native people, teachers, and the general public. This two-day event was called "The First Oregonians" and featured workshop presentations by Indians describing their own history, language, and culture. The conference drew more than 400 people, including representatives of all the tribal groups.

The third element in our focus on Oregon's native peoples is the publication you are about to read. It looks outward from the tribes to the general public, with essays drawn from 18 writers and scholars. The publication is aimed at teachers and students, at those who work with Oregon's native people, and at the general public. Its purpose is to offer as full and varied a set of perspectives on Oregon Indian experience as that experience deserves. We hope that it will be read widely and carefully and will enrich the state's understanding of these remarkable people.

When the idea of a publication was first proposed, we envisioned a tabloid-style reader that could be issued in great numbers. As the project went forward, the sheer scale and importance of the subject changed our minds and moved us to undertake this fuller treatment in a more durable format. We hope that both native and non-native people will agree that this was the right decision.

A Note About Variant Spellings: *Inconsistencies in the spelling of Indian names are part of the historical record. Individuals who took down information about various bands and languages did not know how to convey the sounds of the unfamiliar words in English. This fact, combined with the vagaries of nineteenth-century spelling on the frontier and elsewhere, resulted in multiple spellings for the same words. The editors have chosen the form Athabaskan rather than Athabascan, Athapaskan, or Atapascan for use throughout this publication.*

ACKNOWLEDGMENTS

It would be difficult indeed to offer adequate thanks to all the individuals who have contributed in so many ways to the development of this publication. First, of course, are our writers, who have worked closely with the editors and waited patiently for the finished product.

Before the writers began their work, we relied on an advisory board to establish the publication's broad outlines and to suggest both content and writers. Members of that group included Doug Hutchinson, executive officer of the Oregon Commission on Indian Services; Louie Dick, vice-chairman of the Confederated Tribes of the Umatilla, Cayuse, and Walla Walla Indians; Gordon Bettles of the Klamath Tribe's Cultural Heritage Committee; Bill Ray, who serves on the Oregon Commission on Indian Services; Minerva Soucie, chair of the Burns Paiute Tribe's Heritage Committee; Kathryn Harrison, chair of the Heritage Committee for the Confederated Tribes of the Grand Ronde; Sherri Shaffer, tribal manager of the Cow Creek Band of Umpqua Indians; Mary S. Viles and Cynthia Viles, members of the Cultural Committee, Confederated Tribes of Siletz Indians of Oregon; Floy C. Pepper, Creek Indian and specialist with the Portland Public Schools; Stephen Dow Beckham, professor of history at Lewis and Clark College; Theodore Stern, professor of anthropology emeritus at the University of Oregon; Yvonne Hajda, anthropologist; David French, professor of anthropology emeritus at Reed College; Marilyn Couture, adjunct faculty in anthropology at Linfield College; Rick Minor of Heritage Research Associates in Eugene, Oregon; and Laura Rice, then chair of the Oregon Council for the Humanities.

For assistance in securing photographs and other illustrations for the book, we wish to thank photographers Lawrence Johnson, Tony Neidek, and Chuck Williams, a Grand Ronde tribal member, and Jack T. Lee; Klamath Culture and Heritage Specialist Gordon Bettles; authors Marilyn Couture, Stephen Dow Beckham, Yvonne Hajda, George Wasson, Jr., Kathryn Toepel, Minerva Soucie, and Deward Walker, Jr.; anthropologist Kathrine French; visual anthropologist Joanna Cohan Scherer at the Smithsonian Institution; Columbia River Inter-Tribal Fish Commission editor Laura Berg; Umatilla Office of Fisheries Director Gary James, the staffs of the Coos County Museum, the Lincoln County Historical Society Museum, the Photographs Department of the Oregon Historical Society, the Bandon Historical Society, the Whatcom Museum, the Denver Public Library, and the Smithsonian Institution; James Fox at the Special Collections Department at the University of Oregon's Knight Library, Patty Krier at the University of Oregon's Museum of Natural History, JoAnne Cordis at the Central Oregon Community College Library, Ellen Waterston of Waterston Productions in Bend, Bernyce Courtney at the Warm Springs Reservation, *The East Oregonian*, and Nan Cohen at the University of Washington Archives; and Mary Slick and Esther Lev for directing us to additional photographic sources

We are grateful to Jeff Zucker for allowing us to draw on the visual materials in *Oregon Indians: Culture, History & Current Affairs* and to Bruce Hamilton of the Oregon Historical Society's Western Imprints for permission to reproduce maps and drawings from that book. For permission to reproduce petroglyphs from *An Introduction to the Natural History of Camp Hancock and the Clarno Basin, North Central Oregon*, our thanks to Michael C. Houck and the Oregon Museum of Science and Industry. To Joe Poracsky at Portland State University, our appreciation for providing the base maps used on pages viii and 121 and to Portland State University, our thanks for producing them.

For word processing and review, our thanks to Meg Larson. For photo research and editorial assistance, our thanks to Paula Hammer. For reviewing the introductions, thanks to Gordon B. Dodds and Robert Keeler. Thanks also to Lee Sitter at J.Y. Hollingsworth for expediting the typesetting, to Ron and Harry at Camera Graphics for their meticulous reproduction of old photographs, and to Diana Bradbury and Print NW for their care and generosity in printing this book.

Major funding for the book was provided by the National Endowment for the Humanities. Indeed, the book could not have been produced without the Endowment's substantial support. Additional support was provided by the Jackson Foundation. Funding for other aspects of the Oregon Council for the Humanities' three-year focus on Oregon's native peoples was also provided by the Rose Tucker Charitable Trust, the Oregon Community Foundation, the Collins Foundation, the Clark Foundation, the OCRI Foundation, and the S. S. Johnson Foundation.

TABLE OF CONTENTS

The woka gatherers' boats and pole

INTRODUCTION

The Oregon Council for the Humanities is proud to present this tribute to the dignity and character of Oregon's native peoples. *The First Oregonians* speaks of their ancient habitation, of their historical lifeways—and the brutalization of those lifeways by Euro-American settlement and federal policies—and of their continuing role in the state. It also describes something of the vigorous heritage-recovery work that today's tribal councils are engaged in, recording the knowledge of elders and documenting traditional sites and activities.

The book is funded principally by a special grant from the National Endowment for the Humanities, and its overriding purpose is to give the native heritage in Oregon greater public attention. Such attention is overdue. It is not possible to give back to the tribes all that has been taken, but certainly greater understanding and respect can be given. Those of us who are not Indian can, for example, better recognize that these tribal peoples are not simply a minority within a larger population, but sovereign communities, with inter-governmental relations with other governments. And we can acknowledge that these native peoples embody the human history of Oregon in a special way, that we have attached our history to theirs, and that our love of this land rides on their long, long presence here.

Richard Lewis
Executive Director, Oregon Council for the Humanities

This publication is the result of a project that began with a meeting in the early part of January of 1988. In format, content, and proportion, this work varies greatly from the original concept. But that is all right. For the real product desired of this long undertaking is neither the very successful "First Oregonians" conference nor this publication itself.

Beginning with the very lively debate that characterized the first project meeting more than three years ago, the involved scholars, Indians and non-Indians, have focused their efforts on the message rather than the vehicle. By whatever means, they hoped to offer the general public an insightful appreciation for the unique values represented by the history, customs, and traditions of each of Oregon's nine federally recognized tribal groups.

Although much of message arrives filtered through the writing of non-Indians, the cooperative atmosphere of this project offers assurance that the voices and visions are mostly those of the Indians themselves.

With the project completed, it is now hoped that the readers will heed the advice of author John Folk-Williams, and ". . .learn to listen to the rhythms of a different people. . . . "

Elwood Patawa,
Chair, Oregon Commission on Indian Services
August 30, 1991

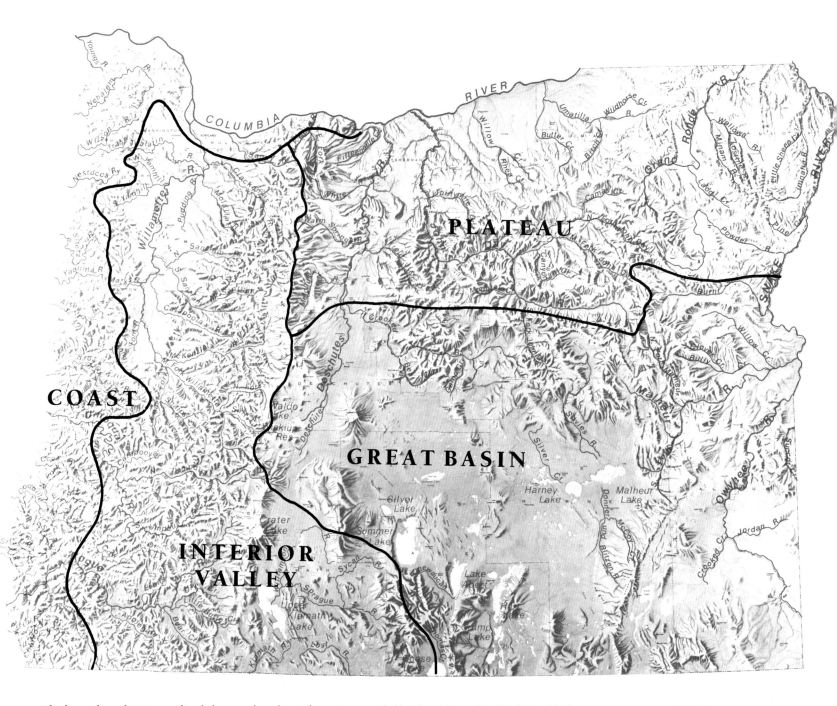

The four culture divisions outlined above are based on information provided by the authors of the Traditional Lifeways essays on pages 2 - 26. It is important to realize, however, that culture areas often overlapped. In particular, the Celilio Falls area on the Columbia River and the Klamath area in southern Oregon have sometimes been configured differently or been given separate cultural designations. For the first Oregonians, gathering, hunting, trade, and social activities took individuals bands across any dividing line scholars may devise. Indeed, the Indians of "Oregon" roamed beyond the borders of the present state and often shared traits with many other groups, encountered through trade and travel.

Traditional Lifeways

Oregon has supported human life for thousands of years—
some scientists now say for 15 thousand years or more.
In the following section, our purpose is not to examine that ancient past nor
to review theories about how Oregon's first people reached the Northwest.
Rather, we are concerned with the period just before Euro-Americans arrived
to explore, trade, and "settle" the land.

In discussing the traditional lifeways and languages of Oregon Indians,
we have focused on four geographic regions: the Coast, the Columbia Plateau,
the Interior Valleys, and the Great Basin.
Other scholars and publishers have preferred to talk about three, five, or even six areas.

Any of these organizational schemes has its drawbacks, however, for Oregon
was home to dozens of individual bands, all with their own traditions,
language peculiarities, and ways of life. Theirs is a complex story of skillful adaptation
to the land, sophisticated solutions to the problems of social organization,
and thoughtful views of the world and their place in it.

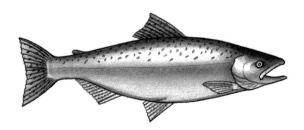

THE OREGON COAST

BY STEPHEN DOW BECKHAM

*Their land was washed by the sea, bathed in fogs and mists,
covered with towering forests, and filled with dense underbrush.
It was broken by mountains jutting into the ocean, cut by river valleys lying
in isolated east-west directions, and fronted by the vast Pacific Ocean.
In this rain-soaked region the estuaries served as the food-rich places of livelihood,
while the margins of bays provided secure village sites and access
to the resources needed for daily life.*

*Here, in Oregon's coastal region, life was rich but perhaps a bit lonely.
Communication north and south was difficult, and visits to the east
necessitated journeys through dark forests and over the Coast Range.
As one writer has observed, Oregon's coastal Indians lived in the quieter back eddies
of the swifter currents of Northwest Coast culture.*

VILLAGES AND SHELTERS

The Indians of coastal Oregon had little need of an extensive seasonal round such as that found in other regions of Oregon. Nature provided most resources, especially an abundance of food close at hand. The various groups lived in permanent villages usually at the mouths of rivers, favoring sites with good drainage, visibility up and down the bay, a nearby source of fresh water, and abundant firewood. In time these people built up a thick layer of broken shell, fire-cracked rock, charcoal, and other debris that has made it possible for archaeologists to identify the early village sites.

In addition to the year-round or permanent villages, coastal Indians established berry-picking camps in the foothills of the Coast Range, as well as at blueberry bogs or huckleberry patches on the margins of lakes. Often in the fall these people journeyed upriver to take freshwater mussels and the last lamprey eels from the spring run and to hunt for elk and deer. Some people lived all year at these remote sites, but many more probably resided at the mouths of rivers or within a short distance of the Pacific Ocean, the great giver of resources.

These Indians erected a variety of structures, including semi-subterranean, plank-slab houses. Constructed over a shallow pit in the earth, framed with poles, and covered with large planks of cedar, these lodges might shelter a single family or several families. Tastes in design varied. The Tillamook, for example, used a shed roof of a single-pitch, while other groups used a two-pitch gable roof. The Coos constructed some dwellings almost entirely underground, while the Tututni and Chetco built theirs nearly at ground level. Some of the peoples, especially those on the southwest coast, constructed sweat lodges where heated rocks sprinkled with water produced soothing sauna baths to cure illness, prepare a man for hunting, or bring good luck in gambling.

Other structures in the villages included windbreaks to quell the incessant north winds of summer and shelters for woodworking, basketmaking, or firewood. Dwelling units were often too dark or smoky for toolmaking and basketmaking, while lean-to shelters enabled craftsmen and women to work in better light, protected from the elements.

SUBSISTENCE

At low tide the coastal Indians' table was set. The food-rich intertidal zone abounded in mussels, chitons, snails, cockles, clams, and crabs. With prying and digging sticks, women and children eagerly worked the beaches to gather basic foods, while the men took salmon by spear, net, gaff, hook and line, and trap. They also constructed massive weirs of poles, literally damming the rivers and forcing the migrating schools of salmon, sturgeon, steelhead, and eels into their traps. While the weirs were often difficult to maintain and to repair after winter freshets, they proved their usefulness again and again.

The men used bow and arrow or nets to hunt ducks and geese on the bays and coastal lakes. The Tillamook even employed a unique basketry decoy covered with feathers to look like a duck. A man slowly stalked his prey by putting the decoy over his head,

Coastal Indians lived in permanent villages during the winter—usually at the mouth of a river where fresh water and firewood were readily available. Their houses were covered with large planks of cedar.

wading into the estuary, grabbing the duck's feet, and pulling it silently beneath the water until it drowned. Getting dinner was a wet, cold, but often productive experience.

The men and boys also pursued a number of mammals. Deadfall—a log trap—carefully baited and mounted with rocks, might ensnare and crush a bear, or pits dug on the far side of a log on game trails might trap unwary elk or deer, which would be impaled on sharpened stakes at the bottom.

During the course of the summer, the women and girls picked many baskets of berries—salmonberries in May, then thimbleberries, blackberries, and finally huckleberries and blueberries. To preserve the berries, the women dried some, such as salal, and packed them into cakes for later use. They also dug camas in the coastal meadows or in the uplands of the Coast Range.

Nature also provided some items that held special value for the Indians. For example, men and boys avidly hunted the pileated woodpecker for its bright red topknot, which they prized as a symbol of wealth and as a decorative item. They also sought rare albino deer and hunted sea otters for their lustrous fur.

Nature yielded generously for those who worked. Life was not easy, but starvation was a remote prospect in a place that held so many riches.

CLOTHING

From northern California to the great fjords of southeast Alaska, the cedar was the tree of life to the Indians. In the spring of the year as the sap rose, Oregon's coastal Indians stripped the cedar bark, shredded it into strands, and wove capes and skirts. While women wore a fringed, hula-like skirt for everyday labors, they might put on a tanned leather sheath dress, cape, or wrap-around skirt for special occasions. They decorated these garments with tassels of bear grass, shells, and even projectile points tied to buckskin thongs. They also used pounded cedar bark (the silky inner cambium layer) for baby diapers.

Lodges sheltered several families and provided room for sleeping, cooking, food drying, and storytelling. Tool and basketmaking often took place in lean-to shelters, where better light was available.

For the men, clothing was simpler. Part of the year they went naked or wore a leather breechclout wrapped over a belt around the waist. In colder, wetter weather, they wore a leather shirt, either open or laced across the chest, and put on leather leggings which they tied to their belts.

Men usually were bare headed, while the women and girls often wore a woven basketry cap. On special occasions both men and women donned headdresses containing short, vertical feathers that extended across the forehead but did not have the dangling eagle-feather piece used by Plains Indians. Because leather shoes were impracticable in the wet environment of coastal Oregon, the people seldom wore moccasins.

Like Indians in other locales, the men might bedeck themselves with body paints, favoring red ochre which they obtained from quarries like that near Cape Perpetua and which they bonded with salmon eggs and saliva. Along the southern Oregon coast the women tattooed their chins in puberty, usually with three vertical lines marked with indelible willow-bark charcoal, which fixed the design for life. On the northern coast (and along the lower Columbia River), Indians of high status bound their infants in cradle boards, applying slow but steady pressure to the skull to shape it into a distinctive, flat shape with a straight line from the tip of the nose to the crown of the head. Only slaves, they observed, had ugly round heads. Head-flattening extended into Alsea country but was rare south of the Siletz estuary.

TECHNOLOGY AND ARTS

The Indians of Oregon's coastal zone exhibited skills in woodworking, bonecarving, weaving, and stone-tool manufacturing. Unlike their distant cultural cousins, who lived hundreds of miles to the north along the same Pacific shore, they did not carve totem poles, masks, elaborate houseposts, screens, or partitions in their dwellings. Their skills were able but simple.

Men drew the assignment to manufacture dugout canoes, wooden scoops for use as bailers, spear handles, sinew-backed bows, and housing. Using their skill at lashing, they constructed pole frames for drying fish and meat, erected plank dwellings, hollowed out wooden bowls for cooking or holding foodstuffs, and wove eelpots for catching lampreys in late spring. The men also made arrow shafts by steaming slender poles of wood (to make them straight and true) and sanding them with sandstone, or by scouring rushes. To manufacture projectile points, knife blades, fleshers, and scrapers, they employed pressure flaking; to make hammers and other heavy tools they pecked and abraded hard stones.

Coastal women were skilled at weaving. From the margins of lakes they gathered tules, which they sewed together to make rain capes and matting for partitions and floor coverings in their lodges. They also used spruce root and shredded hazel bark as basic materials for weaving a wide variety of baskets. Their nimble fingers produced basket hats, storage containers, baby cradles, drinking cups, cooking baskets, serving trays, and large clam baskets with heavy handles. The women often decorated these wares with overweave of bear grass (white), maidenhair fern stems (black), or materials dyed with alder bark (red). They preferred geometric designs, but the Chinookans sometimes wove animal or human-like figures into the outsides of their baskets.

SOCIETY

Oregon's coastal Indians lived in a stratified social world in which there were three classes of people: free, rich upper-class families; free, but poor and exploited lower-class families; and slaves, who counted for little and were ruthlessly exploited.

For Indians of the Oregon Coast, slavery was an unpleasant but real part of life. While the institution was not widespread and certainly not as widely practiced as it was farther north, it existed. Slaves included children, kidnapped from distant villages or language groups, and captives, seized during warfare or "won" through gambling. Slaves worked constantly, suffered from cold and abuse, and lived lives that had no quality.

The poor classes eked out an existence in pole-frame dwellings covered with woven rushes or matting when they could not afford plank houses. The wealthy sometimes preyed on them, demanding a good-looking daughter in marriage or services to support their interests. Tension often existed between rich and poor.

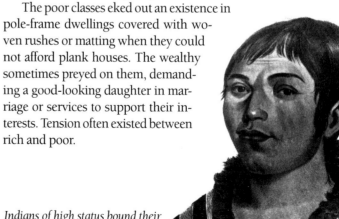

Indians of high status bound their infants in cradleboards to shape their heads into a distinctive flat shape, seen here in an early illustration of a Chinook boy.

For everyday labors, women wore a fringed, hula-like skirt and cape. On special occasions, men wore a feather shirt and shell beads. Both men and women donned feather headdresses like the one worn by Coos Chief Doloose Jackson (right) in 1905.

The rich possessed power and insured their wealth with strategic marriages and payment of a "bride price." They measured wealth in dentalium shells, dugout canoes, house planks, privileges of telling certain tales or of holding political power, or—on the southern coast—in woodpecker scalps and obsidian display blades. The rich man who had ability served as the "headman." The village of a dozen to 40 or more people constituted the "tribe," though this body had no overarching political authority or tribal government.

Among the Coast Indians there was little evidence of social mobility. Slaves were absolutely trapped in servitude and were likely to be traded north into even harsher circumstances. While the poor might aspire to gain wealth, they had little opportunity to do so, except through hard work and luck. Even then, they might fall victim to the intrigue of the wealthy, who viewed them as "upstarts," fit victims for the malice of a shaman or for murder on a dark night.

LANGUAGES

The linguistic complexity of the Oregon seaboard mirrored long residency of many Indian groups. Major language stocks, from north to south, included:

Chinookan Family (Penutian)—Clatsop
Salishan Linguistic Isolate—Tillamook, Siletz
Yakonan Family (Penutian)—Yaquina, Alsea
Siuslawan Family (Penutian)—Siuslaw and Lower Umpqua
Coosan Family (Penutian)—Hanis, Miluk
Athabaskan-Eyak—Upper Coquille, Tututni, Shasta Costa, Chetco.

Even the languages in the various groupings exhibited differences. Hanis and Miluk speakers, for example, both occupied Coos Bay, yet their languages were so different that communication was virtually impossible. Similarly, the Athabaskan languages of southwestern Oregon had started to differentiate.

The Penutian language stock was perhaps the oldest in coastal Oregon. The Chinookan, Yakonan, Siuslawan, and Coosan speakers thus might lay legitimate claim to deep ancestry in the region. They had been hard pressed, however, by two different groups. The Salishan-speaking Tillamook resided on the north-central coast. Either they were oldtimers who had been shoved back from the mouth of the Columbia, or they were newer arrivals. Linguists are certain that the Athabaskan-speakers of southwestern Oregon's lower Rogue River and Curry County coast were, indeed, newcomers. Their language tied directly to that of the Apache and Navaho, from whom they split off perhaps 2,000 years ago.

WORLD VIEW

The short days and dark nights of winter, the pall of fog and rain, and the vast, unknown virgin forests were inhabited by many spirits—so believed Oregon's coastal Indians. These beings were both good and evil and might bring misfortune, even death, to the hapless person who encountered them. Signs of the spirit world were all around: terrible smells in the forest, ravaged rotten logs where wild creatures had fought or jostled for food, even sounds in the night. The trick was to stay clear of—or, if necessary, secure the proper skills for communicating with and managing—these supernatural companions.

This was best done by right behaviors. At puberty, most boys and many girls went on a spirit quest. Prepared by an upbringing of awareness that they faced a rite of passage at 12, 13, or even 14, the young people knew that they would have to go out alone at night to retrieve marked sticks from distant places—their first tests. Ultimately each would go to a vigil site, often a lonely promontory overlooking the river or the sea, and prepare to gain a spirit helper.

These young people, quite alone, had to endure several days and nights of seclusion. They were prohibited from eating and were instructed to fast, pray, and dance. Above all, they were to wait. Even if they became scared, cold, and sick, they were to wait until the spirit world spoke. Ultimately, perhaps in the fourth or fifth day, each gained a "spirit helper." These helpers might be animate or inanimate: otter, grizzly bear, bluejay, fir tree, or even flint, the stone from which some men made projectile points. Once a young person knew this "helper," he or she was free to return to the village to perform a dance and a short song that revealed the guardian spirit's identity.

Those who had particularly strong "helpers," or who aspired to become professional communicators with the spirit world, might go on successive quests or vigils. By gaining more "helpers," they increased their abilities to cure the sick, bring good luck, or hire out to bring death or misfortune through their powers and incantations.

Right or correct behaviors ordered Indian life. These people observed "first salmon" rites. They believed ritual observances insured the bounty of the annual migrations of fish. Some groups, such as the Athabaskan-speakers at the entrance to the Rogue River, reportedly burned the hillsides near the river's mouth each year in the belief that this action would compel the fish to return. The world view of the Indians along the shore included deference to the wealthy, respect for elders, and acceptance of the world where myth and reality blended to create a sense of place and belonging.

ORAL LITERATURE

Oregon's coastal Indians had a rich oral literature. Melville Jacobs, who made the most ambitious effort to record what remained of this literature in the 1920s and 1930s, estimated that at Euro-American settlement in the 1850s more than 10,000 tales were in the literature of these people. Tragically, less than one-tenth of those accounts were recorded. Untold works—poems, epics, tragedies—vanished when the last speakers of the coastal languages died in this century.

The literature focused on how the land came to be and why things were the way they were. The tales mixed past and present. Some were set in a Myth Age, a time when only animals (who acted much like humans) occupied the earth. Others were set in a Transition Age, when animals and near-humans interacted. The near-humans, however, were sometimes incomplete, lacking fingers or even mouths. Then there was the Historic Past, the epoch when humans alone occupied the earth in an era that was bonded with things past. Time was a continuum along which things past seemed to flow into the present and in which modern realities were inextricably linked to the past.

Coyote, the "trickster," appeared in a number of the oral traditions. He created things, caused trouble, got involved in many sexual escapades, and somehow always escaped the fate that would have overtaken a mere man. Coyote seemed human at times but was very clever. He and other supernatural heroes populated the literature and imaginations of Oregon's coastal peoples.

CONCLUSION

The Indians of the Oregon Coast lived well but had a hard life. They were exposed to the elements in a world filled with spirits and class conflict. Theirs was an isolated existence, with coastal trade made difficult by a rugged shore.

While some groups may have experienced little change over the centuries, others were affected by new coastal dwellers. The Miluk-speaking Lower Coquille, for example, were undoubtedly under pressure just prior to Euro-American contact from the incursion of Athabaskan speakers; and the Upper Coquille had shoved through the Coast Range from the Umpqua Valley and taken over most of the upper drainage of the Coquille River. Change, some of it unpleasant, occurred and life at times was troubled.

On the other hand, the land was rich and yielded a steady supply of foods. Subsistence demanded work, correct behaviors, understanding of the spirit world, and participation in society. Those who accepted these conditions coped well; those who did not were at odds with their world and faced an uncertain fate.

THE PLATEAU SEASONAL ROUND

Mariposa Lily
Calochortus macrocarpus

Bulrush
Scirpus acutus

Gray's Lomatium
Lomatium grayi

Chum Salmon
Oncorhynchus keta

Mountain Whitefish
Prosopium williamsoni

Indian Hemp
Apocynum cannabinum

Pacific Lamprey
Entosphenus tridentatus

Bitterroot
Lewisia rediviva

Mule Deer
Odocoileus hemionus

Townsend's Ground Squirrel
Citellus townsendii

Huckleberry
Vaccinium membranaceum

Arrowleaf Balsamroot

Balsamorhiza sagittata

Sage Grouse
Centrocercus urophasianus

Fall Chinook
Oncorhynchus tshawytscha

Blueberry
Vaccinium, sp.

Bare-stemmed Lomatium

Lomatium nudicaule

Gooseberry
Ribes, sp.

Spring Chinook
Oncorhynchus tshawytscha

Yellow-bellied Marmot

Blueback Salmon
Oncorhynchus nerka

Marmota flaviventris

Chokecherry
Prunus virginiana

Golden Currant
Ribes aureum

Camas
Camassia quamash

Indian Potato
Claytonia lanceolata

Bitter White Dogwood
Cornus stolonifera

DECEMBER

JANUARY

NOVEMBER

FEBRUARY

OCTOBER

MARCH

SEPTEMBER

APRIL

AUGUST

MAY

JULY

JUNE

2

THE PLATEAU

BY EUGENE HUNN

*The culture area we call the Plateau spans a vast region that includes portions
of what is now British Columbia, Montana, Idaho, Washington, north-central and
northeastern Oregon, and sometimes the Klamath Lake basin.
The region straddles the Columbia River and follows its tributaries.*

*Here, seasonal temperatures vary greatly, as the Cascades cut the Plateau off
from the moderating effect of marine air and leave a semidesert embraced
by forested uplands. For the Indians who came to live in the Plateau,
these seasonal extremes of temperature posed daunting challenges, but—
as if to compensate—the Columbia River system provided great runs of salmon
and other fish, which enriched the natives' lives.*

THE SEASONAL ROUND

The Plateau encompasses a variety of habitats, beginning near sea level along the Columbia River and rising to the Cascades' volcanic summits. The region has six major life zones, each characterized by dominant plants that grow and mature in stages each year, beginning in the low elevations and moving gradually into the higher ones. The Plateau Indians took advantage of this complex habitat and its long harvest season by following a highly mobile "seasonal round" as they gathered their food.

The seasonal round of a family from the John Day River, for example, would begin during the winter, when "home" was a tule mat "longhouse" in a village containing several such houses. Each house contained several families, two of whom shared each hearth or fireplace. Explorers Meriwether Lewis and William Clark described a cluster of these villages opposite the mouth of the Umatilla River containing 5, 15, and 24 houses respectively, with 32 persons

Opposite. *The Plateau Indians took advantage of a complex environment that began at the Columbia River and stretched south to the Klamath basin and east to the Blue Mountains. The Indians' annual "seasonal round" began in the winter, when they remained in their winter villages making tools and weapons and subsisting on foods gathered during the year. In spring few foodstuffs remained and small groups set out in search of Indian celeries (Gray's lomatium) and spawning suckers and eels. In April the women established camps in nearby canyons and harvested bitterroot and other lomatiums. May brought Chinook salmon runs and families moved to fishing sites at Celilo Falls. Then began a series of moves south and eastward to catch various types of fish from July through October; pick berries in mountain meadows; hunt; and gather Indian hemp, bulrushes, and tules with which to make tools, clothing, and shelters.*

counted in one house. They estimated the collective population of that village to be 1,500.

Winter villages typically were established near the Columbia or on the lower reaches of its major tributaries, sheltered from the wind and located near a source of driftwood, which was used for fuel. In this season, opportunities for hunting, fishing, and gathering were severely limited and people relied for sustenance on dried stores of roots, fish, and berries. During the long winter months they manufactured and maintained their tools, recounted myths, held spirit power dances (which were sponsored by Indian doctors), and paid social visits.

The winter's fast was broken in late February as the Indians harvested Indian celeries and in March as they caught spawning suckers, both of which could be found near the winter villages. In April the women might establish camps a few miles from the river in tributary canyons and, from these, climb adjacent ridges seeking bitterroot and various tuberous lomatiums—key starchy staples. Back at the village, they would dry supplies of these roots for storage.

In early May, spring Chinook salmon runs peaked and families with claims to fishing sites at Celilo Falls might move there for the duration of the runs. John Day families then dismantled their winter lodges and began a series of moves southward, camping successively at Rock Creek, Olex, Condon, Fossil, and Spray—then moving east to Monument, then south again, climbing to the camas meadows in the Fox Valley, and then (after white settlers arrived) going on to John Day town for the Fourth of July celebrations. When they returned to the river, these families would be laden with food to be stored in special pits at the winter village site.

In summer, people focused on salmon and steelhead, intercepting successive runs that began with blueback salmon in July, peaked with fall Chinooks in early September, and ended with silver and dog salmon in October. Many families left the river during the heat of late summer to go on berrying expeditions in mountain meadows, which were kept open and productive by intentional burning. While the women gathered and dried quantities of huckleberries, the men hunted.

In late October 1805 Lewis and Clark found the Indians of the mid-Columbia hard at work drying spawned-out salmon. These final preparations assured an adequate winter food supply, bringing the seasonal round full circle. At this time the Columbia River Indians provided virtually all their own food, shelter, tools, and medicine by harvesting local wild plants and animals. For Sahaptin-speaking Indians (those who lived east of The Dalles), these included 35 species of edible roots, 30 of fruits and nuts, 8 of edible greens, 21 of fish, 37 of birds, and 31 of mammals. In addition, Plateau Indians recognized well over 100 species of medicinal plants. Other plants—foremost of which were Indian hemp and tules (a species of bulrush)—were used in making tools, clothing, and shelters. Each species was named and its harvest seasons and preferred habitats well known, as were techniques of harvest, preparation, and storage.

For the Indians of the Plateau, edible roots were the primary sources of food energy, in contrast with neighboring regions, which emphasized seed, acorn, bison, game, or fish. The Plateau was also characterized by strong seasonal contrasts that required substantial food supplies to be dried for winter use. Within the region, however, subsistence strategies varied. West from The Dalles were the Chinookan peoples, who controlled trade and exchanged their surpluses of dried salmon for upland products, allowing the people to remain on the river throughout the year. These Indians ranged as far west as the Pacific Ocean and were, in some ways, similar to coastal Indians. On the eastern edge of the

Plateau, Nez Perce and Cayuse peoples laid greater emphasis on hunting deer, elk, and bison.

CLOTHING, TECHNOLOGY, AND THE ARTS

Plateau peoples survived in the face of a harsh climate by means of their detailed knowledge of ecology, but also by virtue of their technology. They had implements—digging sticks, bows and arrows, nets and fishing spears, and dugout canoes—made of various local woods, hemp, obsidian, and other natural materials. They also had carrying bags and baskets, tule mats and mat-covered lodges, and clothing of softened hides. The knowledge of how to manufacture, employ, and repair each item was passed from generation to generation by precept and example.

The largest portion of the Plateau Indian toolkit was made of plant materials. Indian hemp, for example, was essential for making string for bindings, for knotting fish and rabbit nets, for twining carrying bags and a special Plateau hat, and for making a woman's "time ball," her personal record of the important events of her life.

Tules were cut, dried, and sewn into mats to sit and sleep on or to eat from. Because their cylindrical stems are filled with a cellulose matrix that traps air, tules make wonderful insulation. For this reason, lodges with tule-mat walls could keep out the sub-zero cold of a Plateau winter.

The elegant Klickitat baskets for which Plateau Indians are famed were woven of cedar root and decorated with bitter cherry bark and the leaves of bear grass.

Deer and elk were prized for their meat but were perhaps more important for their skins. These were softened by being soaked in a fatty solution of deer brains and sturgeon heads, then carefully scraped and stretched, and finally cut and sewn for clothing. Moccasins, leggings, shirts, a woman's ceremonial full-length dress—plain or highly decorated—were the products of this craft. The decorative designs were traced in porcupine quill, shell, and natural dyes.

ORAL LITERATURE

The creative talents of the Plateau Indians were most fully expressed in the verbal art of storytelling. In 1976 during the winter—the customary season for myth telling—Elsie Pistolhead, a 67-year-old Columbia River Indian, told from memory in Sahaptin nearly 70 Coyote stories, a full 16 hours on tape. Elsie's remarkable recitation of her people's oral literature is testimony to the importance of that literature in the culture of the Plateau.

The stories, all of which feature Coyote as the central figure, are myths in the sense that they tell of a primordial time, a myth age in which animals were fully human and the present humanized world was ordained. Here, Coyote is frequently described as a trickster and a fool, but he is much more than that. He is Everyman, acting out our fantasies and fears and inspiring moral behavior, while making the world safe for "the [Indian] people who are coming soon," to use the characteristic Plateau myth refrain.

The mythology of the Plateau Indians is an oral tradition, properly appreciated at once as dramatic performance (ranging from burlesque to tragedy), as poetry, and as sacred text—the "Indian

In this region, edible roots were the primary sources of food energy. The women gathered them using pointed digging sticks fashioned from strong woods and crafted with handles of stone, antler, or wood.

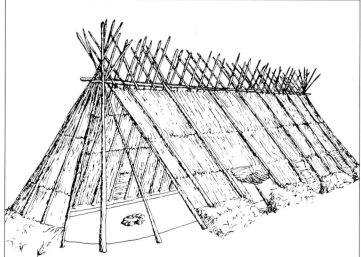

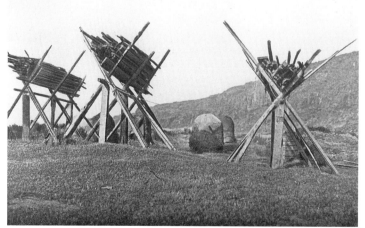

In the winter, Plateau Indians lived in longhouses covered with tule mats. Each house was home to several families, and a village contained many houses. Tule-mat walls could keep out the sub-zero cold of a Plateau winter. Raised caches were used for storing food or summer housing material.

bible." Some of the stories have been preserved in written form, but much is lost in this translation, not least of which is the wealth of common experience and cultural values that informed the traditional audience's appreciation of the tales' humor and dramatic power.

PEOPLES AND LANGUAGES OF THE PLATEAU

Celilo Falls, on the western edge of the Plateau, was the meeting place of two distinct Indian cultures. At and east of the falls lived speakers of Sahaptian languages, while to the west—as far as the Pacific Ocean—Chinookan speakers were found.

Sahaptian speakers included those who spoke the related languages of Nez Perce and Sahaptin—a complex of mutually intelligible dialects spoken in Oregon by the Umatilla, John Day, Celilo, Tenino, and Tygh Valley peoples. Judging by the internal diversity of this language family and its contiguous distribution, Sahaptian speakers must have occupied the Columbia River basin above The Dalles for many centuries.

In the Blue Mountains, after the winter snows melted, Umatilla and John Day people mingled with their Cayuse and Nez Perce relatives and friends, gathering, fishing, and hunting on the upper reaches of the Umatilla, Walla Walla, Grande Ronde, and Powder rivers.

The Cayuse were regarded by whites as fierce warriors. However, their numbers were always small and their terrain lay off the main rivers. The Nez Perce lived in the Wallowa Valley, tributary to the Grande Ronde.

On the southern marches of the Plateau lived parties of Northern Paiute or Shoshone, who raided northward on horseback or simply pursued their own seasonal rounds on the headwaters of the Columbia's southern tributaries. Their presence drove a wedge between Sahaptians on the Columbia River and the Klamath, whose language was similar.

PLATEAU SOCIETY

Plateau society countenanced no kings. The right to lead one's own life was highly prized, and the exercise of power was distrusted. We cannot imagine how a society can function without judges, courts, police, or executive officers, yet Plateau society succeeded for millenia without such institutions of social control.

Throughout the region, people were linked by ties of reciprocal moral obligation among kin, trading partners, and friends. These obligations were established and maintained by exchanges of gifts in the form of food, valuable manufactured items, or services. For example, marriages were cemented by a series of formal gift exchanges among corresponding kin of the bride and groom and by the groom's bride-service for his parents-in-law. Such exchanges continued periodically throughout the life of the marriage and if one partner died, they were carried on by means of the levirate and sororate (preferred marriages of a widow or widower to a sibling or cousin of the deceased spouse).

Among the people of the Plateau, social control and leadership were in the hands of several individuals, whose functions were respected. Children had their first taste of discipline from "whippers," and each village was home to one or more "chiefs," a status often—though not invariably—passed from father to son. Chiefs did not command, but led by example and by rhetorical inspiration, their

A detailed knowledge of ecology and technology helped the Plateau peoples survive. For fishing, they crafted long dugout canoes.

speeches amplified and broadcast by a "herald," who helped sustain the dignified reserve expected of chiefs.

These chiefs were rarely if ever shamans—Indian doctors whose extraordinary spiritual powers were harnessed to the work of curing. Rather they might be individuals distinguished as warriors, salmon chiefs, or leaders of root-digging or hunting parties, depending on their personal character and ability. The shamans themselves were revered but might also be feared because of the deadly potential of the powers they controlled.

The people of the Plateau also held war captives from northeastern California, who were captured and sold by Klamath intermediaries or taken on raids by war parties along the Columbia. Among the Chinookan peoples on the Columbia, slaves were apparently quite numerous and were roughly treated, but among Sahaptian peoples they were rare and most often were treated as if they were "family."

Extended family ties remain at the core of Plateau Indian social life today. Traditional kinship usage, in which cousins and siblings are equated, is still evident in the common use of the terms "aunt" and "uncle" to include the first and second cousins of one's parents. Also, funerals and memorials continue to be important occasions for reaffirming the overriding importance of traditional kinship ties.

RELIGION

In everyday Plateau life, "religion" did not exist as a separate sphere of belief and practice set apart from the "secular." Rather, spirit power was thought to be manifested in all things—a form of belief called "animism."

Children were sent questing until a spirit revealed itself to them, taught them a song, and promised a lifelong alliance. Once such revelations occurred, individuals revealed their spirit powers only in an indirect way—in their character and achievements and at winter spirit dances—for to speak of those powers was to lose them. Thus, the relationship between individual and spirit was intensely personal and private. In the case of shamans, their extraordinary healing power came from several especially powerful spirit allies.

Animism also involves the belief that plants, animals, and other natural forces possess will and intelligence, a belief that establishes a moral community which transcends human society and strongly sanctions respect for nature. This attitude of respect was reinforced in Coyote stories and in periodic thanksgiving feasts.

In historic times the focus of Plateau Indian religious expression shifted from the relationship between individuals and their spirit powers to communal worship, whether Christian or distinctively Indian. The "Sacred Dance" Religion (also known as the "Longhouse Religion," "Seven Drums Religion," or "Dreamer Religion" and closely allied with the "Feather Dance Religion" still practiced on the Warm Springs Reservation) is the dominant Indian church in the Plateau today. This religion may have roots in pre-contact communal dance ceremonies, such as were witnessed by David Thompson at the John Day River in 1811.

For men, porcupine quills, shells, fur-wrapped braids, and moccasins were part of traditional ceremonial dress. Later, beads and other Euro-American items were incorporated. A woman's ceremonial fringed leather gown is elaborately decorated with porcupine quills. Her basketry hat and corn-husk bag are typical Plateau dress.

The specific, modern forms of these religions owe much to a series of revelations by Plateau "prophets" prominent in the nineteenth century. Of these, Smohalla of Priest Rapids, Washington, is best known, but others also experienced miraculous resurrection, returning from death's door with instructions for the proper conduct of communal worship as a means of personal expiation and communal salvation. Sacred Dance worship now focuses on respecting indigenous "sacred" foods, on public testimonials, and on reinforcement of social ties at funerals, memorials, and name-giving rites—which in many respects are similar to coastal "potlatches."

It has been suggested that nineteenth-century Plateau prophecy was an example of cultural revitalization in response to the profound shocks following depopulation due to epidemic diseases such as smallpox and measles, which were introduced by white settlers. In the face of these new diseases, which tore at the heart of Plateau social fabric, the traditional curing of Indian doctors was ineffective.

In traditional Plateau religion the dead were a danger to the living, and showing appropriate respect to the dead was essential for the health of those still living. This remains true today, when the ghosts of deceased relatives are still thought to cause serious illness. We can scarcely imagine the despair Plateau peoples must have felt during the great epidemics of the early

Plateau technology made wide use of plant materials such as hemp, tules, cedar root, and bear grass. Basketmaking was an important skill for which Plateau Indians were famous.

nineteenth century, when the dead outnumbered the living. During those trying times, Sacred Dance worship gave the people of the Plateau the will to survive.

THE LONG SWEEP OF LIFE ON THE PLATEAU

Archaeologists find abundant evidence of human occupation in the Plateau throughout the past 10,000 years. Well-documented early sites include Wakemap mound, at the site of the easternmost Chinookan village of Nixluidix, and Windust and Marmes rock shelters on the lower Snake and Palouse rivers. Evidence from these and other sites suggests that for the peoples of the Plateau, key resources—salmon, roots, fruits, and deer—were always important, though in varying proportions as climate and technologies changed. The stability of Plateau cultural ecological patterns was only altered—and radically so—by the spread of Spanish horses from the Southwest (after about 1730) and later by the importation of guns from the expanding fur-trading frontier in the Plains and by the spread of smallpox and other Old World epidemic diseases (after about 1775). Remarkably, however, many of the Plateau lifeways are kept alive today, as other chapters in this publication attest.

THE WESTERN INTERIOR

BY KATHRYN ANNE TOEPEL

*Though not gifted with lands as rich and productive as either the coastal region to the west
or the Columbia Plateau to the northeast, the peoples of the interior valleys of western Oregon
enjoyed a hospitable and varied environment of floodplains, foothills, and mountains.
Reliable plant foods could be found throughout the valleys, along with the game
that the lush prairies, oak savanna, and forests supported.
Life seemed to proceed at a predictable and unhurried pace,
flowing with the rhythms of the seasons
and remaining largely unchanged
until the arrival of the whites.*

15

The Kalapuya Indians occupied most of this region for thousands of years, inhabiting the expansive Willamette Valley and spilling south into the Upper Umpqua basin. A number of distinct bands unrelated to the Kalapuya lived in smaller valleys in southwestern Oregon, including the Upper Umpqua, the Rogue River, and the Klamath Lakes basin in the Cascade Mountains. Sandwiched between coastal peoples to the west of the Coast Range and Plateau groups east of the Cascades, the Indians of western Oregon shared some similarities with these neighboring culture areas, while developing their own unique adaptation to the rain-drenched drainages of the Interior.

SUBSISTENCE ROUND

A diverse environment composed of prairie and oak savannas, oak and fir groves, forests, marshes, and lakes produced an abundance of foods for the Indians of the Interior Valleys. Their annual subsistence round was divided into two general seasons: summer

Deer were numerous and an important food source in the Interior Valley. Above, a hunter disguised in a deerskin stalks game .

and winter. The summer months, from about March to October, were spent in temporary open camps, moving about the valley floors and foothills to harvest roots, nuts, seeds, and berries as they ripened. Before the winter rains began in earnest, though, the people returned to permanent villages.

Among the plants they collected were acorns, wapato ("wild potato"), hazelnuts, ipos, arrowroot, sego lily, tule, cattail, and a variety of berries. One of the most important harvests involved camas, similar in appearance but not in taste to onion. The small camas bulbs were first harvested in March or April when most tender, but collection for winter storage did not begin in earnest until June, when camas was harvested in great quantities, roasted in below-ground rock ovens, and prepared for winter storage.

Another staple food, the tarweed seed (similar to a sunflower seed), was ready for harvesting by late summer. Then, tarweed plants were set afire and the seeds beaten from the stalks into basketry or buckskin platters. These seeds were parched, ground into flour, and sometimes mixed with mashed cooked camas and hazelnuts.

Game, waterfowl, and fish supplemented this plant diet. Deer were numerous, and elk were available both on the valley floor and in the upland forests. In addition, birds (wild goose, grouse, duck, quail, pigeon) and small mammals (squirrel, rabbit, raccoon, beaver) were trapped and cooked by roasting or boiling. (To boil food, hot stones from the fire were placed with wooden tongs into a water-tight basket containing a stew or soup.)

Eels, crawfish, freshwater shellfish, trout, suckers, and salmon were also caught from rivers and lakes, and the fish were roasted, boiled, or dried for winter storage. In addition, large quantities of dried salmon were obtained through trade along the Columbia River.

Although agriculture was an unnecessary pursuit in such a rich environment, the early inhabitants were able to increase the abundance of the prairie plants upon which they depended. In the fall they frequently set fires on the valley floor to maintain vast areas of open prairie. This burning served not only to make seed harvesting much easier, but to roast grasshoppers (a delicacy) and clear out undergrowth between trees, thus making berry picking and acorn harvesting easier.

SOCIAL GROUPS AND VILLAGES

The winter village was the basic social group for the Indians of the Western Interior. Each village consisted of related males (such as a man and his sons and grandsons) and their wives and children. Suitable marriage partners were found outside the village group during foraging trips, trading forays, or social visits with relatives. Once married, a woman usually joined her husband's village.

Clusters of closely related villages, recognized as bands, shared a common territory (usually a particular river basin). Each village had its own rights of access to some resources (such as a particular tarweed patch), but other resources such as camas or game animals were considered to be available to all villages within the band.

In each village, leadership roles were filled by the most qualified people. Some social distinctions were made on the basis of wealth, with the wealthiest member of a village often known as the head

For the Klamath Indians, situated at the conjunction of the Interior Valley and Great Basin regions, wokas (water lily seeds) were an important food. This Klamath woman is grinding the seeds.

Marshes and lakes produced an abundance of food. A man in a dugout boat hunts for ducks among the cattails and tules.

Sweat lodges were an integral part of village life. They were often built of layers of earth covered with planks.

chief. Although wealth was gained or lost with relative ease, the distinction between freemen and slaves was never confused. While the origin and extent of slavery in western Oregon is unclear, it may have been a relatively recent practice, playing a particularly important role among those groups living near the trading centers of Oregon City and the Columbia River, and among the Klamath, who were frequent visitors to these centers. Slaves were usually captives or their descendants, taken from neighboring groups and traded throughout the region.

Villages and camps were constructed to fit the needs of the season and were occupied in accordance with their place in the subsistence round. Winter lodges were built at permanent village sites and usually consisted of a semi-subterranean or earth-banked structure with a bark roof and a central fireplace. They were rectangular, up to 60 feet on a side, and often housed more than one family.

During the warmer months, the winter village splintered into smaller groups for increased mobility. While these groups were hunting or on the move from one food gathering place to another, temporary camps were set up under oak or pine trees or sometimes in the open. Often no shelter was built, but if need be, windbreaks of boughs, brush, or grass could be quickly constructed when the weather required it.

Sweathouses, used for purification purposes, were often erected next to rivers or streams near camps or villages. These small round structures, large enough for a few individuals, consisted of bent hazel sticks with a covering of fir boughs and dirt. Inside, fired stones provided the heat for steam baths.

CLOTHING

Relatively few descriptions of Western Interior dress and adornment exist, but it is apparent that the amount and type of clothing varied with the seasons. The basic dress throughout the year included leather moccasins and leggings for the men and a leather or grass apron or skirt, sometimes with leggings and moccasins, for the women. Botanist David Douglas, who visited the Umpqua Valley in June 1826, observed the dress of the Yoncalla Indians he had met:

> *The dress of the men is skins of the small deer undressed, formed into shirts and trousers, and those of the richer sort striped and ornamented with shells, . . . The women, a petticoat like that worn by Chenook [Chinook] females, and a sort of gown of dressed leather, in form differing from the men's only by the sleeves being more open.*

When the weather turned colder, both men and women wore caps of fur or basketwork, along with heavier shirts, trousers, or gowns. Fur cloaks or robes were sometimes made of gopher, squirrel, or deer hides sewn together with deer sinew.

Social status was often reflected in an individual's personal adornment. For example, designs were tattooed on arms, legs, and faces with a sharp piece of bone and blackened with cinder from the fire, not just as a mark of beauty but also as an indication of social status. Natural pigments of red, white, or green were often used as ornamental face paint. Both men and women were also fond of necklaces, arm bands, and nose and ear plugs fashioned from beads made of salmon backbones, marine shells, bone, trade beads, feathers, porcupine quills, and strips of otter skin.

Like the Chinook and northern coastal groups, the Klamath-Modoc and the northern Kalapuya groups practiced head-flattening of infants, accomplished in the cradleboard. The Klamath regarded an undeformed head with derision, saying it was "slave like," while they admired deformed, or flattened, or "good heads." However, many groups in the interior of western Oregon did not practice head-flattening.

MATERIAL CULTURE

In much of western Oregon, little remains of the native inhabitants' technology. Although archaeological excavations have un-

During the Wilkes Expedition of 1841, Joseph Drayton drew this sketch of Indians fishing on spring boards with dipnets at Willamette Falls.

earthed an ever-growing collection of native artifacts, these consist mostly of stone tools, because organic materials do not remain preserved in the acidic valley soil. However, we do have a few sporadic descriptions of material culture in the literature of the early Euro-American arrivals.

Before the introduction of historic trade goods, tools and utilitarian items were fashioned of locally available materials such as wood, grasses, stone, bone, shell, and skins. After about 1750, however, Euro-American trade items, including glass and metal beads, trinkets, and other metal items, became increasingly important.

Woodworking was a largely undeveloped art, although canoes were built by all groups in western Oregon for water transport. Because horses were not available until sometime after 1800, land travel was accomplished by foot.

Spears, clubs, and bows and arrows were basic hunting equipment, as were an array of snares, traps, and decoys. Fishing was accomplished by many means, including spears, detachable harpoon heads, line and hook, clubs, lures and bait, basket traps, and rock dams. Items frequently used in daily activities included cordage, basketry, stone mortars and pestles, digging sticks for root gathering, knives, and scrapers.

Basketry materials of grasses and bark were twined into both soft and rigid items. In western Oregon the basketry of the Klamath-Modoc Indians is the best known. They used tule, cattails, and swamp grasses to twine bowls, hats, gambling or sifting trays, and circular baskets. Burden baskets and storage baskets were made of a more open twine weave. Rigid loop containers included seed beaters, ladles, and winnowing baskets. Other basketry items included trays, two-handled baskets, fish traps, cradles, and twined flat bags. Water baskets were made by coiling rather than twining. Less durable weavings of tule and grasses were made as bedding and house coverings. Cordage was often fashioned from nettle bark and flax fibers and made into nets. Rope was made of willow bark or twisted hazel sticks, or braided from grasses, tule, hide, and nettle fibers.

Unlike the well-known and gifted woodcarvers in the heart of the Northwest Coast culture area, the people of the Western Interior expressed their artistic bent in a mundane fashion. Everyday items, such as grinding tools and basketry, were often subjected to a decorative touch. Small anthropomorphic sculptures called *henwas* were used by Klamath-Modoc shamans and were often artfully decorated. Rock art, though not often found in western Oregon, served as an aesthetic, and presumably a religious, outlet. To a great extent, the people expressed a sense of art in the manner in which they tattooed and arrayed themselves.

LANGUAGES

With the exception of enclaves of Athabaskan speakers in southwestern Oregon and near the lower Columbia River, the Western Interior was occupied by speakers of the Penutian stock of languages. This language stock was composed of the Kalapuyan Family (including three Kalapuyan languages), the Siuslawan Family (Siuslaw and Lower Umpqua languages), and the Molala, Klamath-Modoc, and Takelman languages (which are believed to have no close relationships to any other surviving languages).

The presence of these diverse but distantly related language families in western Oregon strongly suggests that Penutian speakers were in the region for thousands of years.

In western Oregon, the language distribution appears to have centered on river basins, following "natural" boundaries of mountains and drainage breaks. This seems particularly the case for the Kalapuya, who spoke a number of dialects within their three language groups along the entire length of the Willamette Valley. These three groups were:

• *Tualatin-Yamhill*, spoken in a small portion of the Lower Willamette Valley upstream from the falls at Oregon City;

• *Santiam*, which included dialects in the Middle and Upper Willamette Valley; and

• *Yoncalla*, whose speakers occupied the Upper Umpqua drainage basin south of present-day Cottage Grove.

A Klamath woman carries a load of wood.

WORLD VIEW

Among the Indian people of western Oregon, the world was reflected in a rich mythological heritage. Various animals and supernatural beings inhabited the myths, recounting in part how the trickster Coyote created the world, Willamette Falls, sickness, and the technique of net fishing for salmon and how he engaged in a number of amusing adventures and misadventures along the way. Winter was the traditional time for telling stories, which served to convey morals to the youngsters as well as to while away the long cold days.

The animals and beings represented in mythology also had a real existence for the Indians in everyday life. Many of these beings were guardian spirits or spirit powers, who guided individuals through their lives and provided them with luck, strength, and protection. To acquire one or more powers, children approaching puberty were sent alone to a mountain place to seek a vision. After several days of fasting and little sleep, questers were often rewarded with a visit from a spirit power or dream power.

Sometimes during vision quests, a spirit seeker would mound or stack stones as part of the path to a prophetic dream. The remains of these vision quests are still found in the upland regions of western Oregon today.

Men and women who acquired strong spirit powers were known as shamans and served as highly respected healers and ceremonial leaders. Shamans were primarily responsible for curing diseases and wounds, but they also acted occasionally to recall lost souls, control the weather, foretell the future, and locate lost or stolen objects.

CONCLUSION

Archaeological research has established that the lifeways practiced by the hunters and gatherers of the Western Interior were in existence for a very long time. A number of archaeological sites—including Cascadia Cave in the western Cascades, the Marial Site in the Rogue River Valley, and several localities along the Long Tom River west of Eugene—have been radiocarbon dated to between 6,000 and 10,000 years old. Stone tools and charred plant remains indicate a long-standing way of life focused on hunting and root gathering. Both linguistic evidence and the emphasis on root crops suggest that the early peoples of the Western Interior may have migrated into the area from the Plateau many thousands of years ago.

These peoples found an occasionally arduous but generally comfortable life in the fertile valleys and hills of the Western Interior. Hard work and group efforts were required each season to gather sufficient food to survive the winter. Spirit powers aided in the flow of life by providing strength, guidance, and protection to individuals in their quest for food, shelter, and village harmony. By maintaining a balance with the spirit world and generally peaceful relations with their neighbors, villages flourished through the centuries—aided by the productivity of the land.

THE KALAPUYA YEAR

The Kalapuya year was divided into 12 lunar months, beginning with the first new moon in late August or early September.

Month names reflect the annual growing cycle and the importance of particular foods.

September. *First month of the Kalapuya year.* Small groups are still living in their summer camps scattered across the valley, collecting acorns, berries, and camas roots. Prairie burning begins for tarweed seed harvesting.

October. *Month when "hair [leaves] falls off."* Wapato harvest time begins in the northern Willamette Valley, and the northern Kalapuya groups move to camps close to the lakes where the wapato grows. Groups in the southern Valley complete their camas harvesting.

November. *Approaching winter.* The Kalapuya prepare their winter houses for the coming cold weather.

December. *"Good month."* The weather becomes colder but is still mild. The Kalapuya settle into their villages for the winter.

January. *Month of "burned breast."* The winter becomes cold and the old people sit so close to the house fires that their chests get

Images of the Kalapuya people are rare. This drawing of an unidentified Kalapuya boy is taken from Pickering's The Races of Man.

singed. The Kalapuya spend much time in their winter houses, feeding the fires .Winter dances begin.

February. *"Out of provision month."* The end of winter finds the Kalapuya short on stored provisions, and it is a lean time. Hunters spend more time in the woods trying to find game.

March. *First spring.* People begin to leave the winter village, making short camping trips to gather food, including the first shoots of camas, which are only finger high at this time.

April. *"Budding month."* The Kalapuya make more trips onto the valley floor to gather roots as the camas grows higher.

May. *"Flower-time."* The camas begins blossoming as the Kalapuya leave their winter houses to camp out for the summer. The spring runs of salmon head up the Willamette River and its tributaries.

June. *Month of camas harvesting.* The camas becomes fully ripe. The women begin to gather and dry camas bulbs for the following winter, an activity pursued until September or October. The people also "catch all sorts of fish." Berry picking begins.

July. *"Half-summer-time."* Weather is hot and dry. The Kalapuya begin to collect hazelnuts and caterpillars.

August. *End of summer.* The weather remains hot as the people continue to gather a variety of berries, nuts, and roots in preparation for the winter.

4

THE GREAT BASIN

BY C. MELVIN AIKENS AND MARILYN COUTURE

*The aboriginal lifeway of Oregon's Great Basin Indians was rooted deep in the land
and in ancient traditions shared with cultures throughout the desert west.
Today's Burns Paiutes are a remnant of a group that formerly occupied Harney Valley in southeastern Oregon and are representative of the Northern Great Basin
cultural tradition. For thousands of years the Indians of the Great Basin lived
and maintained a balance with the land, for the earth was their mother
and her seasons the rhythm of their lives.*

THE TRADITIONAL LIFEWAY

Residents of the Burns Paiute community interviewed during the 1930s drew on their knowledge of local tradition to recount the annual "seasonal round" of the Wada Tika band of Northern Paiutes.

In aboriginal times, they said, the Wada Tika ranged a broad territory around Malheur Lake, congregating for the winter along the shore in clusters of conical, pole-framed lodges covered with tule mats, made from a species of bulrush. They favored this area because even when cold weather limited travel, they could depend on being able to take some fish, waterfowl, small game, and marsh plants to supplement the foods prepared and stored during the warm months of the year.

In April the first green shoots of spring appeared, and by May "Indian potatoes" (Tsuga and bitterroots) were ready to be dug in the hills 40 miles north and east of the lake. Camas was harvested in the lowland meadows as well. At the same season, salmon were starting to run in the headwaters of the Malheur River not far beyond the root grounds. While companies of women dug and dried roots for storage, men went on to set up salmon traps in certain streams or to spear the salmon. With the root harvest completed, all joined in catching and drying the fish, an activity that continued through June.

During July and August, small household groups scattered widely, from the high country near John Day on the north to the Alvord Desert beyond Steens Mountain in the south. There, they gathered seeds, hunted deer and grouse, caught marmots, and collected crickets that could be pounded into cakes and dried for storage. In suitable places they fished or harvested chokecherries, huckleberries, and buck berries.

In the fall, women might wander along stream banks in search of chokecherries, which they picked from stems, washed, and crushed between a hand stone and a flat grinding stone. The cakes were then formed by hand, dried in the sun and wind, and stored in

buckskin bags. Before using the cakes the women would soak them overnight in water, boil and strain out the crushed seeds ("the bones weren't good"), and thicken the mixture to make a pudding.

In September the wada, a low-growing plant with an abundance of tiny seeds, began to ripen along the alkaline shore of Malheur Lake. The Wada Tika, whose name means "Wada Eaters," came back together at this season to gather and store large quantities of the seeds for the approaching winter. They also gathered the seeds of saltbush, pigweed, and other species.

A rabbitskin robe was a luxuriant garment that would keep its wearer warm, even in the snow.

In October and November the plant harvest was completed and the people turned to hunting bighorn sheep, deer, antelope, and jackrabbits. They stalked sheep and deer in the surrounding highlands, and drove bands of antelope and hundreds of jackrabbits into more open country. They trapped the antelope—or surrounded and shot them—and drove the jackrabbits into 300-foot-long nets made of plant fiber cordage. Meat from the hunt was dried for winter stores, while hide, sinew, gut, and bone were used to make clothing, containers, and tools. December saw people once again at the pivot point of their annual cycle, settled into winter encampments around the lake.

Other Paiute bands—the Elk Eaters, the Yapa Eaters, the Salmon Eaters, and others—ranged their own territories throughout Oregon's Great Basin. In fact, groups related by language and custom lived everywhere in the vast intermontane desert of Oregon, southern Idaho, Utah, Nevada, and eastern California. The "eater"

names by which many of these bands were called drew attention to the resources of their individual territories, but when circumstances dictated, communities shared in one another's abundant resources. Such exchanges were facilitated by a web of kinship maintained by intermarriage. Kin ties could reach across hundreds of miles, giving members of any band access to the resources of a vast region—a great help when local foods were scarce.

In the spring, reunions would take place at the annual root camp, where people from all over the region congregated to catch up on the news and to trade, gamble, arrange marriages, and dig roots. The root camp represented a sacred and spiritual experience for all of the people.

Though the specifics varied according to local landscapes and resources (symbolized by the "eater" names of particular bands), the wide-ranging, cyclical lifeway of the Wada Tika was characteristic of all Great Basin societies. For all, altitude, soil, and water dic-

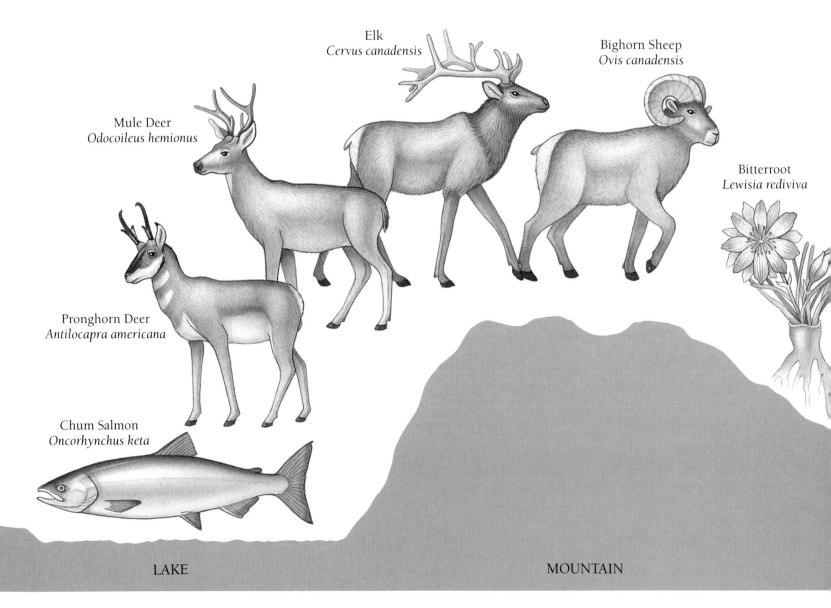

Elk
Cervus canadensis

Bighorn Sheep
Ovis canadensis

Mule Deer
Odocoileus hemionus

Bitterroot
Lewisia rediviva

Pronghorn Deer
Antilocapra americana

Chum Salmon
Oncorhynchus keta

LAKE

MOUNTAIN

22

tated where particular plants and animals could be found, while the time of year determined the schedule of hunting and harvesting.

This pattern of life, evolved by the Indians to fit their landscape, emerged thousands of years ago, as a later archaeological example will show. It continues today as Burns and Warm Springs Indians hunt, fish, and gather such traditional foods as bitterroot, biscuitroot, and camas lily bulbs. Now, however, the broad range of wild foods that once served as staples are eaten primarily as delicacies, or used at special celebrations of traditional heritage.

GREAT BASIN SOCIETY

In Great Basin society the roles of women and men were clearly defined. Women cared for the children and gathered plants for food, medicine, and the manufacture of useful items. They prepared the food, built shelters, tanned hides, made clothing, and wove baskets, cradleboards, and mats.

Men hunted deer, big-horn sheep, and antelopes. They fished for salmon along the "Drewsey River" (the middle fork of the Malheur River) and for trout in the streams. They also manufactured tools of wood, stone, and bone; duck decoys of tule and cattails; and drums, rattles, game pieces, Indian-hemp rabbit nets, and ceremonial headdresses.

Men and women participated in some activities jointly. Both joined in salmon fishing, and either men or women could stalk groundhogs (marmots) in rocky areas with a dog and stick. Men, women, and children also participated in the rabbit drives. The women and children usually held the rabbit net or walked along beating sticks together to chase the animals into it.

A rabbitskin robe was a luxurious but essential work of art. Fifty rabbit pelts were required to make one robe, and rabbits were captured during the winter, when their fur was rich and thick. After the rabbits were snared, they were immediately hit on the head, for if

The Wada Tika seasonal round encompassed a broad territory around Malheur Lake and stretched from the present-day community of John Day to the Alvord Desert beyond the Steens Mountain. Altitude, soil, and water dictated where particular plants and animals could be found, while the time of year determined the schedule of hunting and harvesting.

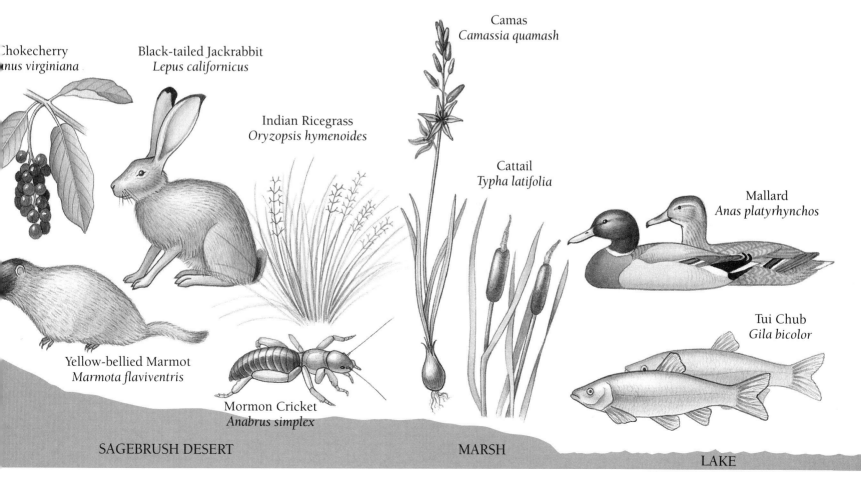

Chokecherry
nus virginiana

Black-tailed Jackrabbit
Lepus californicus

Indian Ricegrass
Oryzopsis hymenoides

Camas
Camassia quamash

Cattail
Typha latifolia

Mallard
Anas platyrhynchos

Tui Chub
Gila bicolor

Yellow-bellied Marmot
Marmota flaviventris

Mormon Cricket
Anabrus simplex

SAGEBRUSH DESERT   MARSH

LAKE

Illustration of a feather head-dress worn by Paiute men.

they were allowed to struggle, the meat would "taste tired." That meat was stored for future use.

To fashion a rabbit robe, the maker would place an obsidian blade between his or her teeth, hold the pelt taut against it, and cut in a spiral pattern to produce a long strip of hide with fur attached. Each strip was stretched to dry, causing it to curl and produce a hollow inside, which undoubtedly helped insulate the robe. The lengths of pelt were then sewn together with two-ply twined plant fiber to make a luxuriant robe that would keep the maker warm, even in the snow.

Men built sweat houses in which to purify themselves. Each small structure was closed and tightly made—well-insulated with pine bark from dead trees. Just outside the door a fire was built to heat rocks. These were carried inside and placed in a central pit, where water was sprinkled on them. Two or three people would enter, to steam themselves and talk before taking a dip in a nearby stream.

WORLD VIEW

The Paiute people of the Great Basin had beliefs similar to those held by Indians of the Coast and Columbia Plateau—beliefs in animism, the spirit world, respect for the dead, spirit quests, and shamans. For them there was good and bad power: the power to make people love you, to cause misfortune, to bring sickness or death, and to heal. There was power to lead an antelope drive and power to charm a snake as big as a log.

According to Beatrice Blyth Whiting, who interviewed Burns Paiute Indians in the mid-1930s, sorcery was a form of social control, needed to maintain peaceful relations within the band by instilling a fear of sorcery or accusing individuals of sorcery. (A sign of a sorcerer was the failure to conform to customs, for conformity was considered essential to the welfare of the group.)

LANGUAGE, ENVIRONMENT, & CULTURAL HISTORY

The speech of Oregon's Northern Paiutes belongs to the Numic family of languages, which includes Bannock, Shoshone, Comanche, Ute, Gosiute, and Southern Paiute. The sister languages these Indians spoke are about as closely related as the Romance languages of Italian, Romanian, Spanish, Portuguese, and French.

Numic-speaking people in historical times occupied the entire Great Basin and extended eastward to the edge of the Plains. Similarities in grammar and vocabulary show that all their languages are descended from a single ancient speech community whose homeland was probably the central-southern Great Basin. The major

Numic languages appear to have radiated from that area, spread by a migration—the Numic Expansion—which carried Numic speakers throughout the Great Basin and western Plains.

Efforts to date this migration from linguistic evidence are controversial, but a recent archaeological study suggests that the Numic Expansion caused Northern Paiutes to replace western Nevada's Lovelock Culture about 1,500 years ago and the Shoshone, Utes, and Southern Paiutes to replace the Fremont and Anasazi cultures of Utah and northern Arizona about 700 years ago. Written records show that even in early historic times, Numic speakers were still pushing out their territorial borders, and archaeological data suggest that Northern Paiute people may have taken over from earlier Klamath and other residents within the last few hundred years.

These people, who lived around Lake Abert in south-central Oregon, may have been ancestors of the Yahuskin band of Paiutes, who are now legally incorporated into the Klamath Tribe. The Wada Tika of the Malheur Lake region would also have been part of this great movement, replacing an unknown people who had previously gathered, fished, and hunted there.

Why did the people of the Great Basin move such distances? One likely answer is that in the rigorous desert landscape, where good hunting and gathering sites were widely scattered, the Numic speakers had to be extremely mobile to survive. On the other hand, the groups they replaced occupied richer areas in the foothills and mountains, where food was readily available and they were able to establish more permanent villages. However, when the climate became dry, these Indians might have moved into higher, moister country, where they could maintain their accustomed lifeways—allowing the Numic speakers, who were accustomed to arid conditions, to replace them.

Such fluctuations of Great Basin climate over the centuries may have caused repeated expansions and contractions in the home

Among objects found at Roaring Springs and Catlow caves are well-preserved tiny sandals. These sites were occupied 6,000 to 8,000 years ago.

ranges of culturally different native communities. It may be that the Numic Expansion is only the most recent in a series of ebbs and flows that recurred throughout Great Basin prehistory.

PREHISTORY

Evidence gathered by archaeologists suggests that people have lived near Malheur Lake in the northern Great Basin for at least 10,000 years. Excavations at Roaring Springs and Catlow caves show that those sites were probably occupied beginning 6,000 and 8,000 years ago, respectively. Among the objects found at the caves are sagebrush bark sandals, rabbitskin robes, twined baskets, soft bags, nets, mountain mahogany digging sticks, grinding tools, and weapons such as bows, arrows, and projectile points.

Other evidence from Blitzen Marsh, south of Malheur Lake, shows that people camped there often over the last 2,500 years. The bones of ducks, geese, suckers, chubs, and various mammals are evidence of their hunting activities, while traces of a hard-packed floor and fireplace suggest that a substantial house stood there.

Ethnological and archaeological evidence attests to a traditional Indian culture in eastern Oregon that was finely attuned to the Great Basin environment and endured there for millennia. The Numic Expansion of recent centuries brought a new people up from the south, but they too were Great Basin natives of long standing. They came from no extreme distance, and the way of life they brought—though different in some details—was nevertheless part of a basic tradition shared in ancient times across the length and breadth of the Great Basin.

In a special tule-mat and cattail-twined house, a young woman labored. As she knelt clinging to an erect post, two midwives encouraged her, comforting her and massaging her abdomen in downward strokes. Nearby lay two newly tanned buckskin hides—payment for the women's assistance.

A small hole lined with grass and sagebrush bark received the child, whose umbilical cord was tied with sinew and cut with an obsidian knife. The cord was wrapped in rabbit skin and tied to the cradle, while the placenta was carefully buried. Following delivery, the woman remained on a bed of juniper boughs in the tule house, where she and the infant girl were nestled under a robe of rabbit fur. The mother would be denied meat and fish for a month.

Soon the child, dressed in a buckskin shirt and sagebrush bark diapers, would be placed in a cradle board, or *hupa*, and suckled until she was able to walk. (In case of a rare twin birth, the twins would be separated and one given to an auntie or grandma to rear.) The child would remain in a cradle until past walking stage, occupying up to five cradles in graduated sizes, provided by close female relatives. Each buckskin-covered willow frame would have an extended twined willow shade, from which trade shells dangled to amuse the infant. The front would be covered with intricate beadwork designs, and the shade decorated with cross-stitch embroidery (for a girl) or diagonal stitches (for a boy).

Personal care would also extend to beautifying the child, whose mother would bind it tightly, then gently massage its nose to shape, narrow, and beautify it. Soon her tiny ears would be pierced with a greasewood thorn, but tattooing would be postponed until puberty, when the girl herself would administer ash with a porcupine quill, piercing the skin on her left forehand. (Unfortunately, resultant infection would often determine the final design.)

The child would be named when she began to walk and talk, often for something she had done while little. As she grew, she would enjoy playing with her siblings and pets. She might tie a

The Wada Tika spent the winter in conical willow-framed lodges covered with tule mats made from a species of bulrush. These houses were clustered around Malheur Lake.

string on a groundhog, leading him in and out of the house, while her brothers adopted a pair of baby hawks that would eventually follow grandma on her errands, circling and lighting on nearby posts as they accompanied her.

When the child reached the age of five or six, she would help with chores, watching and learning from her mother and other women. By the time she was eight, she would be old enough to dig roots, often with a baby sibling strapped to her back in a cradleboard. Meanwhile, her brothers would learn from their father how to hunt and stalk an animal.

Throughout her life, the girl would rely on the teachings of her grandmothers to guide her. She would learn from them to gather tule and cattails and to make a tule bag. She would accompany them to the Silvies River to collect the strong, supple wands of red willow that grew along the banks. Later, her grandmother

would show her how to split the willows in thirds lengthwise, discard the core, and wind the split willows into coils for later use in making baskets or cradleboard shades. As she learned, she would be carrying on a technique handed down for hundreds of generations.

This child, like other Paiute children, would be taught to respect all living things, to love and obey her parents, to stand up for siblings, to be pleasant to outsiders, and not to be aggressive toward her family or others. She would be cautioned not to wander away, or *huuna* (monster) would get her. If she disobeyed, the fear of losing support and help—even being accused of sorcery and punished accordingly—would help control her behavior.

One of the girl's favorite pastimes, as she grew older, would be to hear her mother tell stories of the past. "Keep telling me you're awake, and I'll keep telling you a story," her mother would say, and then the story would begin.

Long ago some Indian groups fought and killed one another. The Bannock Indians at Fort Hall were out gathering horses in our area. One of our hunters went with his son into Crowcamp Hills in search of groundhogs. (A place was always named for a plant, animal, or important feature or event associated with it.) They searched for the little animals in the rock cliffs. Suddenly they heard noises in the distance and saw a band of Bannock Indians approaching. The hunter had a leather string of groundhogs tied to his waist, which slowed his pace. Scurrying for shelter, he was wounded by an arrow. He and the boy took refuge in a rock shelter and waited silently. He talked to his son and explained what to do. Handing him his bow and arrow, he told the boy to watch for whoever was coming and then to shoot. The boy took steady aim, and as the chief and his band closed in on the pair the boy fired, striking the chief in the eye and making the boy a hero.

"I'm still awake, Mama," the child would say, and the stories would continue:

Once long ago at the root camp, the "witch doctor" Kadatwa sent his son to fetch some little baby woodpeckers who were nesting high in a juniper. The boy climbed high into the tree and when he put his hand in the hole, he was bitten by a rattlesnake. His hand swelled up and, stranded, he remained there. He was found dead four days later, hanging by his hand. The angry witch doctor cried all summer long, mourning the death and blaming his own tribe for the tragedy, even though he had sent the boy to his death. In the fall, when the people had gathered together by the banks of Malheur Lake to collect the tiny black wada seeds, the "mean old witch doctor" declared that he would destroy all his people. After his curse, most of the people lay dying. He repeated the curse the following year, determined to destroy the rest of his tribe. Captain Louey's parents were destroyed in the second death while he was still an infant sucking on his mother's breast. The few people remaining decided to destroy the mean old witch doctor and tried to kill him with arrows, but he ignored them and didn't die. They took after him, captured him, and put him on a huge sagebrush fire. He refused to burn right away and just curled up; finally he burned to death. *

*Captain Louey died in 1928 at about the age of 100. Co-author Marilyn Couture, who has collected many oral stories from the Burns Paiutes, believes that this one coincides with, and is an explanation of, the malaria epidemic that occurred and spread along the Columbia River and the Willamette Valley between 1830 and 1833, decimating the native populations.

5

LANGUAGES AND THEIR USES

BY DELL HYMES

Oregon has been rich in languages.
Traveling down the coast 200 years ago, starting from the Columbia,
one would have found a different variety of language at almost every river mouth along the way:
Clatsop at the Columbia, then Tillamook and Siletz, Yaquina and Alsea, Siuslaw and Umpqua,
Hanis and Miluk, Coquille, Tututni, Shasta Costa, and Chetco.
In all, there were six families of languages, none intelligible to the others.

Clatsop is one of three Chinookan languages found from the mouth of the Columbia to The Dalles. Tillamook and Siletz are Oregon outposts of the great *Salish* family of languages found throughout much of Washington, Idaho, Montana and British Columbia. Yaquina and Alsea are a separate family, known today by the name of the *Alsea.* Siuslaw and Umpqua are a separate family, known today by the name of the *Siuslaw.* Hanis and Miluk are yet another family, *Coos.* Coquille, Tututni and Chetco are varieties of the farflung family known as *Athabaskan,* related to many of the languages of Alaska and northwestern Canada, on the one hand , and to Navajo and Apache, on the other.

Starting upriver from the mouth of the Columbia to The Dalles, one would have found mostly varieties of *Chinookan,* some three distinct languages in all: Clatsop and Shoalwater across from each other at the mouth, known today collectively as *Chinook* or *Lower Chinook*; Kathlamet, Wahkiacum, and Skilloot on both sides of the river between Astoria and the mouth of the Cowlitz, known collectively as *Kathlamet*; and groups known collectively today as *Upper Chinook,* including Multnomah at Sauvie Island and thereabouts and similar varieties at the Cascades, Hood River, and The Dalles, with Sahaptin and its relative, Nez Perce, to the east.

Along the Willamette River, the Indians spoke another variety of Upper Chinook—Clackamas—near what is now Oregon City, and on the west bank and south a series of three languages—Tualatin, Santiam, and Yoncalla, known collectively as *Kalapuyan.* If one pushed further south, there would be Upper Umpqua, Galice, and Applegate, other varieties of *Athabaskan,* the first probably a separate language, the last two in amongst the Takelma. Heading east, there would be the closely related Klamath and Modoc.

Heading north from there along a trading trail and down the Deschutes, one might encounter four languages, Molale, Cayuse, Paiute, and Sahaptin.

All in all, a great many local dialects and varieties, some 18 mutually unintelligible languages, and, so far as has been established with certainty, almost as many separate families, some 13.

HOW THE LANGUAGES DEVELOPED

The first languages of Oregon knew no empires or plantations. Each community was independent. Language change went on unforced, a result of the variation and local adaptation present in every community. Considering the changes that must have occurred to bring about so many different families, the languages must have been in Oregon a long time.

To be sure, a few of the languages may have come fairly recently. The Clatskanie in the northwest corner; the Coquille, Tututni, and Chetco of the southern coast; the Upper Umpqua, Galice, and Applegate inland all are branches of the Athabaskan family. The ancestors of the Athabaskan languages probably were the last migration into the New World across the Bering Strait, and those who moved south into the present United States probably did so within the last 2,000 years. The Tillamook and Siletz belong to the great Salish family of languages, whose other members lived adjacent to each other over large parts of Washington, British Columbia, and northern Idaho and Montana. It is hard to say whether the Clatsop and Shoalwater Chinook came between the Tillamook and the rest, taking over the mouth of the Columbia, or whether the Tillamook themselves moved. In eastern Oregon the Paiute are connected to the Bannock, Shoshone, Ute, and other members of the Uto-Aztecan family whose center of gravity is to the south (it includes Hopi and Aztec) and may have expanded into the area in recent times.

Certainly the locations and boundaries of all the groups changed over time. Still, it is likely that most of the languages have been more or less where they are for many centuries and that most are related, as members of a single family that has been given the name *Penutian.*

CHINOOK JARGON

One Oregon language—Chinook Jargon—was created in quite recent times. (This relatively new language should not be confused with the Indian language from which it takes the name.) Like other "jargons," or pidgin languages, Chinook Jargon was a simplified form of speech that grew up between people who did not speak one another's language. Much of its vocabulary was Chinookan in origin, but stripped of that language's grammatical complexity. Other words were borrowed from Nootka of Vancouver Island, French (because of the French traders and missionaries), and English.

During the nineteenth century, Chinook Jargon spread rapidly and was used from Alaska to northern California and the Rockies as a means of trade and, indeed, missionary instruction. Evidently it could be learned as a separate language with some rules of pronunciation and a word order of its own.

The Nootka words and records of early visits by trading ships have made it seem that Chinook Jargon started on Vancouver Island after contact with non-Indians. However, long before whites came, Chinookan peoples had slaves—usually Indians who had been captured or traded and who spoke other languages. In such situations, the slaves would have had to learn just enough of their owners' language to carry out commands. Therefore, it seems almost certain that some simplified form of Chinook would have existed well before the first whites arrived at the Columbia, as would simplified forms of the languages of other Northwest Coast peoples who held slaves, including the Nootka. Since Indians themselves traded over large distances, some words may have been shared. Early trading ships encountered these trade jargons, and the nineteenth-century influx of whites caused "Chinook" to flourish. Toward the end of that century it declined, to be replaced by English as a *lingua franca*, yet many people retained some knowledge of the Jargon well into this century.

The most likely picture of the early history of language in Oregon is one of settlement by communities that spoke varieties of Penutian. With their speakers settled in different places, the changes taking place in one community would be independent of those taking place in another. As the differences accumulated, first in vocabulary and pronunciation and then in grammar, speakers of one community would no longer be able to understand those of another. As a rule of thumb, this result usually takes about a thousand years. The differences between, say, Hanis and Miluk Coos or Kathlamet and Wasco Chinook must be at least this old. Still, the relationship between them remains evident. Relations can be traced in many details, even after 6,000 years. For it to become difficult to recognize a connection, as is the case with the separate families of Oregon, a long history is needed indeed.

One day it may be possible to demonstrate what is now a reasonable hypothesis: that Tillamook and Siletz (Salish), Paiute (Uto-Aztecan), and the Athabaskan languages apart, the languages of Oregon are related as members of a single family.

The Penutian families in Oregon are Chinookan, Sahaptian and Molallan, Cayusan, Lutuamian, Kalapuyan-Takelman, Alsean, Siuslawan, and Coosan. Other Penutian families are found in central California (Wintuan, Maiduan, Yokutsan, Constanoan), and in Alaska (Tsimshian). If these are indeed all related, Oregon is very likely the center from which they spread.

Before Chinook Jargon (see sidebar), many factors encouraged Indians to learn one another's languages. Their communities were small and often situated near villages where other languages were spoken. A wife from another community could be a source of prestige and would bring another language with her. Trade was important to obtain resources from other localities, and travel by canoe along waterways and the coast was easy and frequent. An individual might establish an enduring relationship with a partner in another place. Thus, people would learn at least some of another language and take up words with new sounds as names for new places, persons, and objects. These eventually would enter their own speech. Also, the pronunciations of others would be imitated for amusement sometimes, and tellers of myths might have a character say something in another language.

Such multilingualism is probably the source of one striking similarity among the Indian languages of the North Pacific Coast, including Oregon. Their grammars and vocabularies are largely different, but they are largely alike in their sets of sounds. They have few vowels but many consonants, including some unfamiliar to European languages.

A SPECIAL KIND OF GRAMMAR

One of the most interesting things about languages is the way their grammars develop to make it easy for speakers to express themselves in ways the culture considers important. Speakers of Klamath, for example, seem to have been interested in repetition and intensity and to have enjoyed repeating parts of words. One kind of "reduplication" conveys that the main action is by a single actor on several objects, by a single actor on a single object over a period of time, by several actors on a single object, and by several actors on several objects. Another kind of reduplication expresses persistent emotional and bodily conditions, such as feeling bad or having a burning sensation in the mouth, and repeated states of activity, such as twinkling, flickering, or wiggling the buttocks around. A third kind of reduplication expresses an especially intense, habitual, or continuous condition or action (keeps swimming around and around underneath).

Speakers of Takelma seem to have taken great interest in specifying spatial relations and locations and, in the process, have made unusually elaborate use of names for body parts. The names can simply refer to body parts and their owner ('head-my,' 'mouth-my'). But these body parts can also suggest a *location*. 'Head' can have the sense of *over* or *above*; 'mouth, lips' can convey *in front*; 'ear' can suggest *alongside*; 'leg' can mean *under, away from view*; and 'eye' has the sense of *to, at*. When these new meanings are intended, 'over the house' is literally *head* plus *house*, and 'under water' is literally *leg*

INDIAN LANGUAGES

□ PENUTIAN PHYLUM
░ UTO-AZTECAN FAMILY
▨ ATHABASKAN FAMILY
▨ SALISHAN FAMILY
■ SHASTAN FAMILY

This map, showing the Indian language groups in Oregon, is adapted from a map in Oregon Indians: Culture, History & Current Affairs *by Zucker, Hummel & Hogfoss (Western Imprints, 1983) with cartography by Jay Forest Penniman. Each language group is further divided into a large number of languages and dialects, depicted in the chart on page 30.*

plus *water*. Or the word for 'leg' may be incorporated in a verb that means 'he washed his legs' and also in a verb that means 'they put (food) away' (i.e., under platforms away from view).

Speakers of Sahaptin have evolved a language that offers great attention to the way in which an action is accomplished. Verb stems commonly have two parts. The second part names the act, while the first part identifies a means or manner. When asked how one says "cross the river," an elder at Warm Springs responded, "How do you want to go? Cross by swimming, cross by wading, cross by riding?" One would not just say i-wáicha ('he went across'). One would choose between i-shúu-wáicha ('he swam across'), i-yáwash-wáicha ('he waded across'), i-xásu-wáicha ('he rode horseback across'), i-wishá-wáicha ('he went across in a canoe'), or something else. Other simple word elements can specify time, very general (rather than specific) modes of movement, and rather involved actions that in English would require several words ('with the hand,' 'push with the hand,' 'thrust, wield, push,' 'with the teeth or mouth,' 'pull, lift with the hand,' 'with an implement,' 'with the hands,' 'throw, place, lie down,' and also 'on the knees,' 'involving the head,' 'involving the ear,' 'with the eyes,' 'on hands and feet,' 'with the foot,' 'on the buttocks or bottom side,' 'creep on all fours,' 'hop or limp,' 'sit up,' 'jump,' and a number of others). Thus, it is possible to say, in one word, 'eating, he died,' 'seated, he sang,' and so on.

In Chinookan, the gender of a word usually bears no relation to the object it names, except in the case of persons and large animals.

The term for 'horse' is the noun-stem- kiutan. With the feminine prefix, it designates a mare (a- kiutan); with the masculine prefix, a stallion (i-kíutan). But the word for 'mosquito' always has a feminine prefix: a- p'únachikchik. When asked if it was possible to use the masculine prefix instead, an elder speaker replied, "How could you tell the difference?"

These formal prefixes are far from irrelevant, however. There is an unusually large number of them, making several precise distinctions, as in the following Wasco forms:

n-	*'I'*
nd-	*'two of us'* (excluding you)
nsh-	*'we'* (more than two, excluding you)
m-	*'you'* (just one)
md-	*'you two'*
msh-	*'you'* (more than two)
tx-	*'we two'* (just you and I)
lx-	*'we'* (more than two, including you)
ch- or i(y)-	*'he, him'*
g- or a-	*'she, her'*
L-	*'it, someone'*
sht-	*'two of them'*
t-	*'they'* (more than two)

Moreover, such person-marking prefixes define the four parts of speech.

The verb is often the most complex kind of word in an American Indian language. In Chinookan an element that means 'say' or 'tell' or 'give' cannot be said by itself. It has to be part of a word that begins with an element that indicates something about time (future, present, or a degree of distance in the past). And the word has to have at least one person-marker to indicate who is doing or experiencing something (*the subject*). To say 'she said,' the one word has to have all three elements: igágim ('she said, a little while ago')(ig- immediate past, a- she, -gim, 'to say').

A verb can have two person-markers. The second marker indicates who or what is affected (*the direct object*). Some verbs, such as that for 'to tell' have to have both. In Chinookan, 'you told him (a little while ago)' is one word with four main elements: igmiúlxam (ig- immediate past, m- 'you,' i- 'him,' -lxam 'to tell'). (U- has to be there, but has no translatable meaning.)

Some verbs can or must have three person-markers. The third indicates a different kind of object (*indirect object*). One way in which two kinds of object are used is to signal a difference between a means of doing something and who or what is affected by the doing. An English equivalent would be "I will give it to her." In English we say this with six words. In Chinookan languages one says it with one, but the one word, of course, has several parts. In many languages it is reasonable to think of pronouns as substitutes for nouns, but in a language such as Wasco Chinook the opposite is true: nouns are adjuncts to pronouns. In fact, a verb can be a complete sentence: one doesn't need a noun or separate pronoun. We must keep in mind that these languages were used face to face by people who knew a great deal about one another and the situation they were discussing.

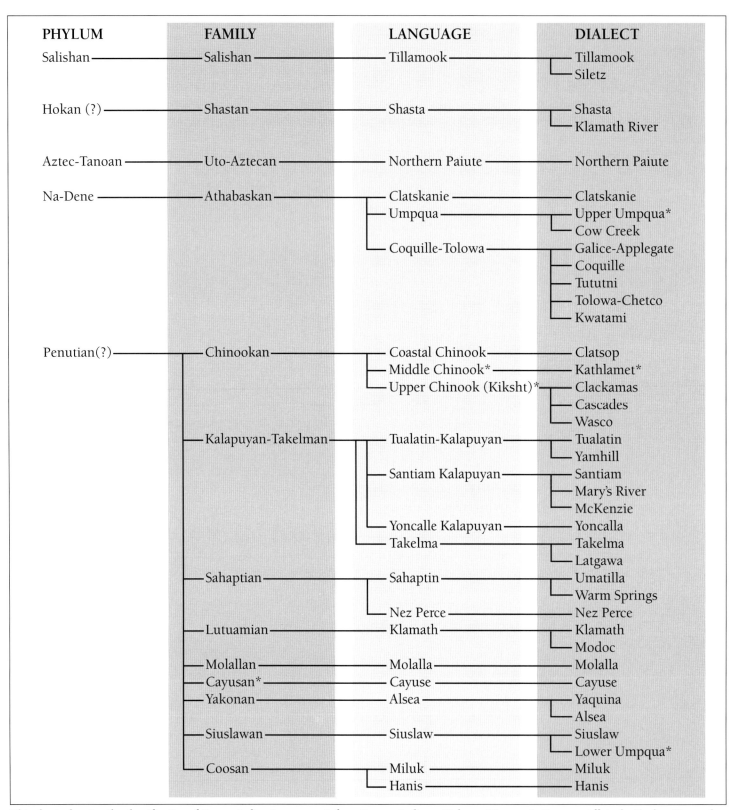

PHYLUM	FAMILY	LANGUAGE	DIALECT
Salishan	Salishan	Tillamook	Tillamook
			Siletz
Hokan (?)	Shastan	Shasta	Shasta
			Klamath River
Aztec-Tanoan	Uto-Aztecan	Northern Paiute	Northern Paiute
Na-Dene	Athabaskan	Clatskanie	Clatskanie
		Umpqua	Upper Umpqua*
			Cow Creek
		Coquille-Tolowa	Galice-Applegate
			Coquille
			Tututni
			Tolowa-Chetco
			Kwatami
Penutian(?)	Chinookan	Coastal Chinook	Clatsop
		Middle Chinook*	Kathlamet*
		Upper Chinook (Kiksht)*	Clackamas
			Cascades
			Wasco
	Kalapuyan-Takelman	Tualatin-Kalapuyan	Tualatin
			Yamhill
		Santiam Kalapuyan	Santiam
			Mary's River
			McKenzie
		Yoncalle Kalapuyan	Yoncalla
		Takelma	Takelma
			Latgawa
	Sahaptian	Sahaptin	Umatilla
			Warm Springs
		Nez Perce	Nez Perce
	Lutuamian	Klamath	Klamath
			Modoc
	Molallan	Molalla	Molalla
	Cayusan*	Cayuse	Cayuse
	Yakonan	Alsea	Yaquina
			Alsea
	Siuslawan	Siuslaw	Siuslaw
			Lower Umpqua*
	Coosan	Miluk	Miluk
		Hanis	Hanis

This chart, showing the classification of Oregon Indian Languages is from Oregon Indians: Culture, History & Current Affairs *by Zucker, Hummel & Hogfoss (Western Imprints, 1983). They note that "the phylum level of classification is questioned by many linguists and is particularly hypothetical for Penutian. Language families which contain only a single language are now called language isolates (e.g. Waiilatpuan & Lutuamian) and are included here for convenience. This chart omits sub-family divisions and lists only major dialects. Each village probably had its own dialect—a language area may be seen as a continuous chain of related dialects." Author Hymes made changes to the original chart where the asterisks appear. He also believes that work now being done will prove the phylum classification for Penutian to be correct.*

30

Naming Things

Indian languages were also a copious source of names. Their speakers, who traveled by foot and canoe and depended on land and water for food, had an intimate knowledge of their environment and were attentive to each change in contour and vegetation, to each sign of animals or birds. To those who know only the names of highways and cities and recognize only kinds of things—trees, birds, flowers—a landscape may seem unvaried, almost empty. To an Indian community, however, a landscape was thronged with all the thousands of names by which the inhabitants knew their world.

How Indian Communities Got Their Names

Different communities might have different styles of naming, to be sure. Along the Columbia River, speakers of Chinookan languages named communities after some special thing to be found among them. "Wasco" comes from the Wasco word for 'cup,' and in their language their name would properly be Ga-thla-sqo, 'the ones who have a cup' (literally, 'the ones-their-cup'). The word refers to a natural stone bowl in which water once bubbled up for drinking (until it was destroyed in the building of the railroad). "Clackamas" comes from a word for 'vine maple.' "Kathlamet" and "Clatsop" come from the same kind of name: 'the ones-their-mat' and 'their-tsap' (-tsap was a prized mixture of huckleberries and salmon; what -mat was is not known).

Other groups were named by their neighbors. "Klamath" is a Chinookan name, referring of course to Klamath Lake. Chinookan speakers who lived across from The Dalles came to

Two modes of everyday speaking, humor and advice, should especially be noted. Where humor is concerned, the stereotype of the silent, stolid Indian is false. People might be quiet in strange situations or among strangers but among friends, conversation full of humor was, and is, common indeed. Often the butt of a story includes the one telling it: not "Didn't she look silly!" but "Didn't we look silly!" Advice-giving is also common, especially from elders and parents to young people. Youngsters become responsible at an early age, due in part to their elders' frequent advice about values and conduct.

The modern pattern of a pair of names—a first name and a continuing family name—is, of course, only a few centuries old, even in English and the other European languages. 'Millers' go back to someone who was once "so-and-so the miller," 'Johnson' to someone who was actually a "son of John," and 'Newtons' to someone who was "so-and-so from Newton (new town)." For Indian people in Oregon, family names came about in the nineteenth century. Officials assumed everyone must have one. Sometimes a father's English first name was given to a family (Dick, Pat, Charley). Sometimes an Indian name was adapted (Simtustus, Suppah, Kuckup, Tufti, Wallulatum). And of course many English names were adopted, in some cases through marriage.

be known as "Wishram," a word in their neighbors' Sahaptin language. "Chinook" itself is a name applied to one group of Chinookan speakers near the mouth of the Columbia by their Salish-speaking neighbors. And along the Columbia, Lewis and Clark learned a name for the Paiutes of the Deschutes River that meant 'enemies' to those who used it. Sometimes, a group was known by several names—some rather generic. Often it was enough to speak simply of 'upriver people' and 'downriver people.'

Soldiers, governments, and scholars, however, wanted a single name for each group and a general name for as many as could be classed together. If it was discovered that languages were related, the fact usually was seized upon. Thus, communities on the Columbia with related languages were christened with a Salish name for one of them, "Chinookan." People who lived on the west side of the Willamette along the Tualatin, Santiam, Yoncalla, and other streams were all called "Kalapuya." Klikitats, Yakimas, Teninos, and others were christened "Sahaptin."

History itself also has an effect. The Sahaptin-speaking peoples on the Warm Springs Reservation are known as "Warm Springs," for their long residence there. "Wasco" has become a common name for the Chinookan-speakers from various points along the upper Columbia. In general, the names one sees in maps and books today often were not known or used that way 200 years ago.

How Individuals Were Named

Indian personal names had a different role than English personal names do. Often one's name was not for casual use, but functioned like a title. It had belonged to an ancestor and was given to honor the previous bearer and to promise that the new bearer deserved and perhaps would increase the honor.

Only family members could call a person by name, and everyone was expected to know it, for to ask would be improper. After the bearer died, the name could not be used again for a certain number of years, and one would certainly not name the dead person with it. Family members might change their own names rather than be pained by hearing a name their loved one had used for them.

In everyday life the title-like name was not much needed, for people knew one another and often were related. Instead, people used terms of kinship, in part to be polite—even to people who were not relatives. Thus, one might say "Grandmother" to an old woman, "Nephew" or "Younger Brother" to a younger man, and so on. Myths and other stories are full of such usages.

In face-to-face conversation, pronouns also served very well. In speaking of oneself and others, one might distinguish economically between a 'we' that included the person spoken to and a 'we' that did not.

SPEAKING PROPERLY

An important activity might give rise to a way of speaking not open to everyone. When men of the lower Rogue River went out to sea for fish or seals, they did not mention land animals or women. Anyone who broke the taboo had to be thrown overboard to save the rest from the anger of sea creatures. And the steersman, in giving directions, would speak as if a game were being played against the ocean. He would not say, "Paddle in that direction," but (if the game agreed upon was *shinny*), "Hit the ball over that way." The uninitiated would be at a loss.

Some had an ability to understand that others did not. The Tillamook, Chinookans, and perhaps others considered infants to be born with a language of their own, which some had the power to interpret. Understanding was important, for each child was precious and it might go back to the world from which it had come if its wants were not understood. Some could interpret what particular animals said as a warning, perhaps, or an omen. These gifts were usually acquired through success in a guardian-spirit quest.

In general, any of the activities of life—from winter spirit dancing to salmon fishing, naming, or trading—might have a way of speaking somewhat its own.

Also, in Indian communities there were things one should and should not say. Probably all the people avoided the ordinary name for grizzly bear and rattlesnake, using instead a respectful term such as "Grandfather" or "Ancestor." Nor did one speak the exact name of a person who had died.

RECOUNTING MYTHS

Myths were part of the sacred winter season as well and for practical and spiritual reasons were not to be repeated at any other time. One could quote them. Seeing a coyote, one might say something the Coyote of the stories would characteristically say, such as "I'm hungry." But to tell myths outside of winter might bring rattlesnakes or other misfortune.

Myths themselves were not merely stories, but dramatic performances, often told by an older person who might be specially invited to come to a house for several nights and be presented with gifts. Against the enclosed light of a smoldering fire, the narrator would develop a story using different voices for the various characters, highlighting their characteristic turns of expression, underlining foolishness and pathos with tone of voice, imparting emphasis with gestures. One or more of the audience would be expected to respond at intervals, perhaps after every verse, with the equivalent of "yes" or "indeed." A child who fell asleep might be made to go bathe in a frozen river; but if all response ceased, clearly it would be time to tie off the story for the night.

Performance did not stop with the end of the story. There would be a formal phrase to signal "the end," then a phrase invoking good weather, and then perhaps instruction to the boys and the girls to find something associated with spring. These conventions suggest that the winter telling of myths was a world-renewal rite.

The language of myths would include some standard words, often related to a community's pattern for the repetition of important acts, such as rituals. Along the Columbia River and down the Willamette Valley, the pattern centered on the number *five*. Among many other groups it was four. In stories in which a scene was repeated, as when the last of several sisters succeeds, there would be five sisters and five scenes in the one case, and four in the other.

Traditional stories drew upon a set of underlying possibilities for giving shape, for arousing expectation and satisfying it, again and again, as the story progressed. Where the pattern number was five, sequences of three were also used for this purpose. Where the pattern was four, pairs were also used. That was the ordinary way. When intensity was wanted, stories that ordinarily organized what happens in sequences of five and three might resort to pairs. And stories organized in sequences of two and four might resort to threes. These kinds of patterning were found at every level of a story, from the smallest units (sequences of lines and verses) to the largest (sequences of scenes and acts).

All this allowed a narrator to shape a story in the course of telling it. Though each story must have a certain series of incidents, there were options for organizing them. One part might be elaborated with what characters say, another not. One repetition of a scene with another brother might be spelled out in full, another repetition shortened. The whole would have satisfying form as long as what was said followed the patterns.

Today much of the art of telling myths has been lost but much remains. There are stories—some comic, some tragic, some stirring—rich with reflection on human nature and its needs. And such patterning is not limited to formal story telling. Speeches and formal explanations display it. Everyday reports of experience and the giving of advice can have rhetorical form—a touch of verbal art—as well.

A few examples (pages 34-35) illustrate different kinds of discourse and the main kinds of rhythm. Two—a Takelma invocation and a Paiute account of the true beginning of the earth—proceed in rhythms of two and four. Another, a personal statement in Kalapuyan, proceeds in rhythms of three and five; and a fourth, a Klamath statement of advice, consists of a series of five pairs. Stories in Nez Perce often proceed in rhythms of three and five, but the morning speech given here uses two and four; it has four sections, each of which pairs an opening statement with three lines that amplify it, for four lines in all.

The rich variety of Oregon Indian languages mirrored a complex indigenous population.

CONCLUSION

Many of the first languages of Oregon are no longer spoken, especially those of the western part of the state, which was early swept by disease. Some of the languages still are known, and a number of communities—such as those of the Confederated Tribes of Warm Springs; the Confederated Tribes of the Coos, Lower Umpqua, and Siuslaw Indians; and the Klamath Tribe— are making efforts to preserve and teach them. A great deal remains to be done to make earlier records of the languages available to these communities and to learn from the languages what can be learned about history, tradition, and verbal artistry.

A TAKELMA INVOCATION

When a new moon rose, the Kalapuya, Takelma, and others would shout to it. Here is a Takelma invocation, as given by Frances Johnson:

"I shall be blessed,
I shall go ahead.

Even if people say of me,
'Would he were dead,'
I shall do just as you,
I shall still rise.

Even if all kinds of things devour you,
Frogs eat you,
Everything,
Lizards,

Even if they eat you,
Yet you shall still rise,
I shall do just as you from this time on—
'Bo————!'"

A NEZ PERCE CRIER'S SPEECH

Many communities had a "crier," someone to go about a camp at the beginning of the day, hailing the others and giving advice. Here is one such speech from the Nez Perce (written down in English, but reflecting the Nez Perce pattern):

I wonder if everyone is up!
It is morning.
We are alive,
So thanks be!
Rise up!
Look about!
Go see the horses,
A wolf might have killed one!
Thanks be that the children are alive!
And you, older men!
And you, older women!
Also that your friends are perhaps alive in other camps.
But elsewhere,
there are probably those who are ill this morning,
and therefore the children are sad,
and therefore their friends are sad.

KLAMATH ADVICE FOR CHILDREN

Among the Klamath, as among other groups, parents and elders instruct children and young people on many occasions. Such advice is essential to success in life. Klamath storytellers make use of three- and five-part patterning, and these two examples of advice, although in English, have five parts. The first is from a young mother to her four-year-old daughter:

I am going to teach you.
At home, you can wear any kind of clothes.

Save your new clothes for when you go out.
Patch your old clothes up.

Everybody should learn to put his clothes away just right.
If people see you doing that, they know you are doing all right.

You have to learn how to cook.
Everybody has to learn how to cook.

You have to be busy and work.
When you have nothing to do, that's when you get into trouble.

The second example is from an elderly father to a forty-year-old son.

If you want people to think well of you,
stay away from bad companions.
People say bad things about anyone who gets into trouble.

I say to you: Drinking is not good and costs lots of money.
When a man saves his money, people say he is steady.

When those men say, "Let's drink,"
you say to them, "Give me the money instead of the drink."

Then there's no trouble for anybody.
Then everything is right.

If there is no trouble, then everybody thinks good.
This is good advice.

In the course of recounting the history of his people, the Mary's River (Pinefu) Kalapuya, William Hartless said this about himself:

I am the only one now,
　I've been left alone,
　　all my people have died.
The only one now,
　I stay on.
Once I am dead,
　my tribe will indeed be gone.
My country—
　I am Kalapuya,
　　at Corvallis my country,
　　　the Indian people name my country
　　　　'Pinefu' - my tribe.
So I am now indeed the last,
　I in my country.

A PAIUTE ACCOUNT OF THE EARTH'S BEGINNING

Traditions and traditional ways of speaking have continued to be used to address situations brought about by the coming of whites. A Paiute doctor, Sam Wata, connected the old and new laws in this way:

One time this was all water but just one little island.
　This is what we are living on now.
Old Man Chocktoot was living on top of this mountain.
　He was living right on top of this mountain.
In all directions the land was lower than this mountain.
　It was burning under the earth.
Numuzoho was under there,
　and he kept on eating people.

The Star was coming.
When that Star came,
　it went up into the sky,
　　and stayed there.
When that Star went up,
　he said:
　　"That is too bad.
　　"I pity my people.
　　"We left them without anything to eat.
　　"They are going to starve."

This Star give us deer,
　an antelope,
　　and elk,
　　　and all kinds of game.

They had Sun for a god.

When the Sun came up,
　he told his people:
　　"Don't worry,
　　　come to me.
　　"I'll help you.
　　"Don't worry,
　　　be happy all your life.
　　"You will come to me."

The Sun and the Stars came with the Water.
　They had the Water for a home.
The Indian doctor saw them coming.
　He let his people know they were coming.
There were many of them.
　The little springs of water are the places from which the
　　silver money comes.
　It comes from the Sun shining on the water.

The first white man came to his land
　and saw that silver
　　but he lost himself
　　　and didn't get to it.
Finally white people found this place
　and they came this way looking for the silver.
Those white men brought cattle,
　sheep,
　　pigs,
　　　and horses.
Before they came,
　there were no horses in this land.

The Sun told his people,
　"Deer belong to you.
　They are for you to eat."
These white men don't know
　who put the deer and other animals in this land.

I think it is all right for me to kill deer,
　but the white men say they will arrest me.
Whenever I see cattle or sheep,
　I know they don't belong to me,
　　I wouldn't kill them.
I feel like going out and killing deer,
　but I am afraid.
　　I am getting too old.
Maybe the white people don't know about
　the beginning of this earth.

Euro-American Contact

They came in search of wealth and the means to attain it—
wave upon wave of explorers, traders, and settlers from Europe and the eastern United States.
The first men to search the Pacific shore were Spaniards and Englishmen, who were drawn
by rumors of a waterway across the continent that would provide an easy trade route to Asia.
These explorers included Juan Rodrigues Cabrillo and Bartolome Ferrelo, who came as early as 1543,
followed by other Spaniards whom some coastal place names recall. It is unlikely that these men
actually landed on the Oregon shore, although in 1707 one Spanish trade vessel,
the San Francisco Xavier, wrecked on the north coast, far from its southern trade route.

It wasn't until the last quarter of the eighteenth century, however, that exploration began again in earnest.
Among others, Spanish explorers Bruno de Hezeta and Juan Francisco de Bodega y Quadra
and Englishmen James Cook, John Meares, and George Vancouver searched for a passage
at various times between 1775 and 1792. In this period, the mariners began to attempt landings
and to establish contacts with native dwellers in the area north of California and south of Alaska.

One impetus for Spanish exploration in the last quarter of the eighteenth century was the news
that Russian mariners Vitus Bering and Aleksei Chirikov had sailed to Alaska from Kamchatka
and that the Russians were interested in acquiring furs there. During this period,
traders from Russia and Britain began to acquire furs from the native population
and to trade them in the Orient.

This idea appealed as well to the competitive instincts of American merchants.
The first Yankees to establish trade with the Indians were Captains John Kendrick
and Robert Gray, sailing out of Boston. They had with them
buttons, beads, cloth, and metal for the Indians, from whom they secured
sea otter pelts for Chinese markets. The American fur trade in Oregon had begun.
As the Indians traded pelts for Euro-American goods,
their way of life began to change.

From the visitors, the Indians also contracted diseases for which they had no resistance.
In 1805, only a few years after Captain Robert Gray's second voyage,
explorers Meriwether Lewis and William Clark ended their overland expedition
at the mouth of the Columbia River, where they found many of the Indians suffering
from venereal disease. In later years, other outsiders, including the American settlers,
introduced new diseases, such as smallpox and measles,
that quickly decimated the native population.

In 1811 Fort Astoria was established and parties were sent out to explore and trade
with various groups from the Columbia Plateau to the Coast.
After the fort was acquired by the British in 1813, brigades of employees
were sent into Oregon's interior to establish new trade relationships with tribes further south and east.
And although much of the British presence was benign, thanks to the efforts of the fur-trading
Hudson's Bay Company's chief factor John McLoughlin,
the reach of the Euro-Americans was nevertheless expanding.

In the 1830s a new group of visitors came, whose purpose was not trade but the salvation of souls.
In answer to a request for religious instruction from a delegation of Indians,
several American missionaries journeyed to the Oregon Country.
Once there, they found their attempts to convert the Indians thwarted by a variety of factors,
including the need to spend a great deal of their time merely surviving from day to day.

In the contacts between missionaries and native dwellers, the clash of cultures was painfully evident.
To the missionaries, the Indians' way of life, personal habits, and beliefs were incorrect
and sure to lead to perdition. To the Indians, the missionaries' God was arbitrary
and the ministers' internal squabbles clear evidence of their hypocrisy.

At Dr. Marcus Whitman's mission near present-day Walla Walla, Washington,
good intentions on the part of the religious emissaries ended in a tragic massacre
by several Cayuse Indians. The attack has been traced in part to the Indians' distress
at Whitman's efforts to bring settlers to the Oregon Country—
but more directly to their belief that the minister was using his medical knowledge
to save his own people from disease, while allowing their people to die.

By 1847, when the Whitman mission was attacked,
the Indians of the Plateau had watched vast numbers of wagons
pass through their territory or settle on their land.
There and in other parts of Oregon their lives had been irrevocably altered.

6

FEDERAL-INDIAN RELATIONS

BY STEPHEN DOW BECKHAM

The story of the United States' relationship with Oregon Indians is a tragic chapter in American history.
Fear, greed, cultural differences, exploitation, and racism shaped these relations and dictated
the consequences. The original federal intent appeared noble. It was summed up in the assurance of
"utmost good faith" in the Northwest Ordinance (1787), a philosophy of dealing with Indians
that was later extended across the Trans-Mississippi West:

"The utmost good faith shall always be observed toward the Indians;
their lands and property shall never be taken from them without their consent;
and in their property, rights, and liberty, they never shall be invaded
or disturbed unless in just and lawful wars."

Unfortunately, later lawmakers, government officials, and citizens did not live up to these assurances.
The hunger for Indian land and resources proved too alluring. The presumption of Euro-American
cultural superiority shaped too many attitudes toward Indians.
In consequence, the pattern of exploitation and dislocation of the colonial period
continued across the continent in the wake of pioneer settlement.

EARLY FEDERAL LAWS

The source of federal authority in Indian affairs stemmed from the "Commerce Clause" of the Constitution (1789). In five simple words—"and with the Indian tribes"—Congress presumed to have complete authority to deal with American Indians, and it did so. These words were considered to give Congress "plenary authority" to ratify and abrogate treaties, create and disband reservations, recognize and terminate tribes, and take other actions. The Constitution did not lay out this authority, but over time Indian affairs worked in this manner.

In 1823 the U. S. Supreme Court ruled that the "doctrine of the right of discovery" had dispossessed Indian tribes. The court arrived at this decision in part by accepting the erroneous idea that Indians were nomads and therefore had a "mere occupancy right" to the soil. According to the Court's logic, the Indians' right was less than that of the Euro-Americans, who had "discovered" the lands in question.

Later, in an 1831 decision, the Court softened its attitude by ruling that tribes were "domestic dependent nations" and, as such, possessed some sovereignty or power but were subordinate to the United States. The Court also found that the federal government had a "trust responsibility" for Indians, observing that the tribes

stood as a "ward to his guardian" and that as guardian, the government had certain obligations in dealing with the native peoples. In 1832 another case introduced an additional complication. The Supreme Court decided that in "Indian Country," tribal—not state—law prevailed! Indians had always assumed this, but the decision proved disturbing to trespassing pioneers and other Euro-Americans.

These Supreme Court decisions of 1823, 1831, and 1832 eventually had a bearing on the Indians of Oregon. So, too, did the Indian Trade and Intercourse Act of 1834—a law later extended to Oregon. The trade law further defined all Indian lands not covered by a ratified treaty as "Indian Country." While these turning-point decisions and laws thus set the stage for the loss of Indian lands and reduced tribal sovereignty, they also helped support modern realities for tribes. Today the "trust" responsibility of the federal government for Indian lands and welfare, as well as the limited authority of the state on reservations, can be traced to these early federal laws.

THE FIRST FEDERAL POLICIES IN "THE OREGON COUNTRY," 1846-1850

The beginnings of federal dealings with Oregon Indians took place in an atmosphere of rapidly changing lifeways, population dislocation, fear, and confusion as several thousand emigrants

In 1823 the U.S. Supreme Court ruled that the "doctrine of the right of discovery" had dispossessed Indian tribes of land. The Court used the Indians' seasonal food gathering expeditions to argue that they were nomads and therefore had less right to the land than did American settlers.

poured into Oregon between 1843 and 1845, setting the stage for competition for resources and a scramble for Indian land. Armed only with stone-age technology, weakened by new illnesses brought by the settlers, and forced to cope with a swift flood of cultural changes, the Indians needed special care and consideration.

These were the challenges that confronted the federal government in 1846, but Congress did nothing. It took no steps to set up a territorial government nor to deal with the Indians. However, a bloody attack by several Cayuse Indians on a mission operated by Marcus and Narcissa Whitman near present-day Walla Walla, Washington, provoked specific action by Congress. On August 14, 1848, that body passed the Organic Act, a law that created the Oregon Territory and laid out new federal policies for dealing with those who lived there.

Section 1 of the Organic Act acknowledged Indian land title:

nothing in this act contained shall be construed to impair the rights of person or property pertaining to the Indians in said territory, so long as such rights shall remain unextinguished by treaty between the United States and such Indians.

Section 13 of the Act appropriated $10,000 for presents to the Indians to preserve the "peace and quietude" of the country and Section 14 extended the "utmost good faith clause" of the Northwest Ordinance of 1787 to Oregon. The Organic Act thus established a four-part philosophy for dealing with the Indians in the Pacific Northwest:

1. The federal government recognized Indian title to all of Oregon Territory.

2. Indian affairs were to be administered in the field by a superintendent and such staff as he might need.

3. Indians were to be treated with the "utmost good faith;" protected in their lands, rights, and privileges; and not invaded unless in just and lawful wars.

4. Congress from time to time would appropriate money to assist the Indians and to further peace and friendship.

Within the next two years, however, more than 10,000 Euro-Americans were living in western Oregon. Thousands of these people had staked lands and filed provisional land claims, anticipating that Congress would soon pass a law which would make those claims their legal property. In July 1849 the Oregon territorial legislature endorsed a memorial that would make Congress aware of the settlers' problem. In the memorial the legislature pointed to what it considered the immediate need to extinguish Indian land title and to provide for the Indians' "early removal from those portions of the Territory needed for settlement, and their location in some district or country where their wretched and unhappy condition may be ameliorated." Many Oregon residents favored moving all Indians to the more arid lands on the Columbia Plateau or into the northern Great Basin.

On June 5, 1850 Congress somewhat belatedly responded by appropriating $20,000 to fund a treaty commission to negotiate with the Indians west of the Cascades and by passing a law that

- called for the Indians to cede their lands and move east of the mountains,

- created the post of Superintendent of Indian Affairs separate from the office of governor,

- provided for three agents, and

- extended to Oregon the Indian Trade and Intercourse Act of 1834—a measure that defined "Indian Country" as that region not ceded to the United States and under tribal law and custom.

In other words, federal law in 1850 declared all of the Pacific Northwest to be "Indian Country" and stipulated that the Indians must sign treaties agreeing to abandon their homelands before the settlers could have title to their provisional land claims.

However, before the treaty commission set out for Oregon, Congress acted again—and in contradictory fashion—to encourage Indians to cede their lands. On September 27, 1850 it passed what was popularly called the Oregon Donation Land Act—a law that authorized the government to give away hundreds of thousands of acres of Indian land to settlers. This Act stipulated that white men and women, "American half-breed Indians included," and immigrants who had filed for naturalization were entitled to free lands. Before the law expired in 1855, a total of 7,437 settlers had filed on over 2.8 million acres in Oregon—doing so before any of the treaties had been ratified.

In light of the way Congress so easily disposed of Indian lands, which for centuries had sustained the first Oregonians, the promises of "utmost good faith" seemed hollow.

THE ILL-FATED TREATY PROGRAM, 1851-1865

What followed passage of the Donation Land Act was a tragic comedy of errors. First, the Oregon Treaty Commission left for Oregon. Next, on February 27, 1851, before the Oregon Treaty Commission even began its work in western Oregon, Congress revoked the commission's powers. However, in April and May the commissioners (who did not know their powers had been taken away) assembled hundreds of survivors of the Kalapuya bands from the Willamette Valley in treaty councils at Champoeg on French Prairie. Over a period of days and repeated arguing—serving food, and talking about the "Great White Father in Washington"—the commissioners attempted to persuade the Indians to give up their lands and move.

In almost every case the Indian leaders refused to relocate, pleading that they had always lived in the valley, that they were at peace with the settlers, and that their ancestors were buried in these lands. The commissioners, feasting on oysters, canned strawberries, and champagne, easily expended the $20,000 appropriated for the treaty progam but obtained only six treaties. In none did the Indians agree to leave the valley.

These treaties failed to gain Senate ratification, for the commission no longer had treaty powers and, above all, none of its treaties provided for removals east of the mountains. The Indians had agreed to the treaties in good faith, but months—then years—passed while more settlers moved in and shoved them off their lands. The promises of the treaty commission remained unfulfilled.

During the summer of 1851, troubles erupted between gold miners headed to and from California and the Indians of the Rogue River Valley. When bloodshed occurred, Governor John Gaines rushed south to quell the fighting. Ultimately, he negotiated a treaty with the Takelma in the Rogue Valley, but because he had no authority to do so, Congress ignored it.

In 1851 Anson Dart became Oregon's first full-time Superintendent of Indian Affairs. That summer he launched his own ambitious treaty program with tribes near the mouth of the Columbia River in Oregon and Washington, holding councils at Tansy Point in Clatsop County and at Port Orford on the southwestern coast.

Dart's Tansy Point treaties provided for a variety of "reserved rights," including catching fish, taking whales from the beach, grazing livestock, and cutting firewood. Unfortunately, none of Dart's treaties gained ratification either. As with the treaty commission's work, none of the agreements provided for Indian removal to land east of the Cascades. Thus, more promises and hopes were fixed; but while the Indians waited patiently, only more settlement and dislocation occurred.

While Dart lobbied unsuccessfully in Washington, D.C., for action on his treaties, the superintendency passed to Joel Palmer, who in September 1853 initiated a new treaty program in the mining region of southwestern Oregon, where a gold discovery had led miners to drive the Indians from their nearby villages. Competition for land and food resources, unprincipled miners who murdered Indians, and disruption of the ecological balance were all factors that led Palmer to the potentially explosive region of

Joel Palmer was doggedly determined to terminate Indian land title. Between 1853 and 1855 he secured a number of agreements in which tribes ceded much of western Oregon and parts of the Columbia Plateau.

southwestern Oregon. To some extent, Palmer was successful. On September 10, 1853 he secured a treaty with the Rogue River Tribe (the Takelma) and on September 19 with the Takelman-speaking Cow Creek Band of Umpqua. These agreements ceded hundreds of square miles to the United States for approximately 2.3 cents per acre. Palmer did not have treaty-making authority and, before the Senate would act, had to return to obtain amendments to these treaties, again signed by tribal leaders. These two treaties, ratified in 1854 and proclaimed in 1855, were the first approved with Indians in the Pacific Northwest.

Joel Palmer's treaty philosophy differed dramatically from that of Anson Dart or of Governor Isaac I. Stevens in Washington Territory after 1853. Palmer did not believe in reserving rights for Indians. Only those treaties with the Umatilla and the Warm Springs, negotiated in conjunction with Stevens' Walla Walla Treaty Council of 1855, confirmed Indian fishing and gathering rights. Doggedly determined to terminate Indian land title in Oregon, Palmer mounted a program which led to a number of agreements.

These treaties all gained ratification and ceded much of western Oregon and parts of the Columbia Plateau south of the Columbia River. Palmer's treaty with the Tualatin Band of Calapooia (March 25, 1854) and with the tribes and bands along the entire Oregon Coast (August 11-September 8, 1855) remained unratified. In spite of the failure of the Senate to act, the government presumed that those Indian lands had passed into the public domain.

Various means were used to encourage Indians to give up their land. Around 1858 Father Jean Pierre de Smet persuaded several chiefs to surrender at Fort Vancouver.

The treaty program with Oregon Indians terminated with Palmer's administration and remained on hold until June 9, 1863, when the government persuaded some Nez Perce to sign a treaty ceding millions of acres, including the lands of Joseph's band in northeastern Oregon. That treaty became a critical issue in the subsequent Nez Perce War of 1877. On October 10, 1863, the controversial treaty of "peace and friendship" at Ruby Valley, Nevada, with the Western Shoshone appeared to confirm Indian title in southeast Oregon. However, the government subsequently claimed it ceded Shoshone lands.

J. W. Perit Huntington negotiated the treaty of October 14, 1864 with the Klamath, Modok, and Yahooskin Band of Snakes (Northern Paiutes), ceding much of south-central Oregon but reserving the Klamath Reservation. On August 12, 1865 the Woll-pah-pe Band of Snakes (Northern Paiute) agreed to cede lands in the Harney Basin. On November 15, 1865 the tribes of the Warm Springs Reservation signed a treaty ceding their off-reservation fishery. Almost immediately they denounced the ratified agreement as fraudulent and continued to exercise their reserved, off-reservation fishing rights.

In 1871 Congress suspended the formal treaty program, though for many years thereafter the House and Senate jointly approved "agreements" with Indian tribes which had treaty status. The Oregon treaties ceded millions of acres for paltry sums and token gifts. Only the Columbia Plateau treaties contained provisions of "reserved rights." The treaty era drove Indians from their old homes and left them almost landless.

WARFARE & DESTRUCTION OF TRIBAL LIFE, 1851-1878

Pioneer settlement, the faltering steps of the treaty program, the gold rush, and the actions of unprincipled persons plunged Oregon

JOEL PALMER'S TREATIES, 1853-1855

Date	Tribe or Band
September 10, 1853/ November 11, 1854	Rogue River Tribe
September 19, 1853	Cow Creek Band of Umpqua
November 15, 1854	Rogue River Tribe
November 18, 1854	Chasta, Scoton, Grave Creek Band of Umpqua
November 29, 1854	Umpqua and Calapooia
January 22, 1855	Confederated Bands of Kalapuya
June 9, 1855	Walla Walla, Cayuse, and Umatilla
June 11, 1855	Nez Perce
June 25, 1855	Tribes of Middle Oregon
December 21, 1855	Mol-lal-la-las or Molel Tribe

In exchange for the loss of their land, the U.S. government offered blankets, tents, and clothing to poverty-stricken tribes. Here, agent Heinlein issues goods to Paiutes.

Nez Perce Indians arrive at an 1855 treaty meeting that confirmed their reservation of 7.6 million acres. Soon thereafter, gold was discovered in their territory and white settlers and miners moved in.

Indians into warfare in the 1850s. The most bitter and prolonged troubles erupted in southwestern Oregon in the drainages of the Rogue and Umpqua rivers and along the nearby coast. Between 1852 and 1856 the region was beset with conflicts, many fomented by self-styled Volunteers who attacked the Indians. These men, operating without legal standing, acted as vigilantes to avenge alleged wrongs. A petty theft might provoke them to hang Indian men and—on occasion—even children.

In August 1853, for example, Martin Angel rode into the gold rush town of Jacksonville screaming: "Nits breed lice. We have been killing Indians in the valley all day." "Exterminate the whole race," he shouted. Within minutes the rabble, a mob estimated at 800 men, had hanged a seven-year-old Indian boy. These events, multiplied many times, fostered a determination of some Indians to fight to the finish. Others gave up all hope and gathered on the Table Rock Reservation on the north side of the Rogue River Valley. Even there they were not safe. In October 1855 a mob attacked and massacred eight men and 15 women and children. This incident provoked the final Rogue Indian war, which lasted until June 1856.

In a series of engagements in the spring and early summer of 1856, the combined efforts of several companies of the U.S. Army and the Oregon Volunteers defeated the Indians. The survivors fled deep into the canyon of the Rogue River, where in June they finally surrendered at the Big Bend.

As early as January and February of 1856, the Bureau of Indian Affairs (BIA) began removing the refugees over a long "trail of tears." The scattered remnants of the Indian bands of southwestern Oregon were marched nearly 200 miles through the snows of winter to the Grand Ronde Reservation on the Yamhill River. The army took others, either by steamboat from Port Orford or by trail along the coast, to the new Siletz Reservation.

During the 1860s conflicts between the Northern Paiutes and the U. S. Army erupted several times in central and southeastern Oregon. During this period the army moved into the region and established military posts, including Fort Harney, Camp Warner, and Fort Klamath. For many years, Indian leaders eluded the troops and sustained an Indian presence that deterred cattlemen and settlers.

In 1873 the Modoc War broke out along the Oregon-California border. While the Modocs had attacked emigrant parties on the Applegate Trail in the early 1850s, the retribution of settlers from Yreka, California was barbaric. They massacred Modocs and mutilated the bodies, collecting fingers and ears. A bitter legacy of these events was lingering distrust. The government's unwise efforts to compel the Modocs to move to the Klamath Reservation only renewed the potential for conflict.

Overall, the Modoc War proved costly and brutal. The Modocs attacked the Peace Commission and killed General E. R. S. Canby, the only American general to die in an Indian war. After the Modocs surrendered in June 1873, the government hanged Captain Jack and other leaders and sentenced two to life imprisonment at Alcatraz Island. That fall the government shipped 153 Modoc prisoners to the Quapaw Agency in Oklahoma. In 1903 a few returned to the Klamath Reservation.

Another tribe, the Nez Perce, occupied the lower Snake River drainage, including the beautiful Clearwater country along the western flanks of the Bitterroot Mountains in Idaho. Their 1855 treaty confirmed a reservation of 7.6 million acres, but the discovery of gold in their territory led to widespread invasion of their reservation and pressures to disinherit them. An unratified treaty in 1861 opened part of the reservation to trespass. On June 9, 1863, some tribal leaders agreed to a treaty reducing the reservation to but 1.1 million acres.

Chief Joseph

The lands of Joseph's band of Nez Perce residing in the Wallowa Valley of northeastern Oregon were swept into the public domain with the 1867 ratification of the treaty, though in 1873 the band temporarily obtained a reservation in the Wallowas. In frustration, Old Joseph tore up his New Testament. By 1877 his son and others, embittered by what they saw as a sellout by the Protestant-Presbyterian Nez Perce who accepted the 1867 treaty, were drawn into war. In a vain effort to escape into Canada, Joseph, Looking Glass, and White Bird led their people on a 1,800-mile journey across the Rocky Mountains. Some survivors were imprisoned in Oklahoma, and Joseph's band eventually was removed to Nespelem on the Colville Reservation but never permitted to settle among the Nez Perce in Idaho.

RESERVATIONS

By treaties in 1853, the Bureau of Indian Affairs created reservations at Table Rock in the Rogue River Valley and on Council Creek in the South Umpqua Valley. It constructed houses for chiefs, held out the prospect of allotments of land to individual Indians,

Inidan scouts of the Modoc War. The Modoc War in 1873 was one of the most brutal conflicts between settlers and Indians that occurred in Oregon. Indian leaders—angered by the loss of their land, a massacre of their people, and repeated attempts to place them on the Klamath Reservation—fought a short but bitter war. At its conclusion, many Modoc leaders were executed and 153 prisoners were removed to the Quapaw Agency in Oklahoma.

began programs of instruction in agriculture, and garrisoned troops at Fort Lane to help confine the Indians to the reservations. In 1854 it also created the Umpqua and Calapooia Reservation in the Umpqua Valley, and in 1855 the treaties of the Walla Walla Council reserved lands for the Umatilla and Warm Springs reservations on the Columbia Plateau. The Nez Perce retained much of northeastern Oregon in that council and, by executive order of June 16, 1873, they secured designation of the Wallowa Valley as a reservation.

The 1856 Rogue River Indian War persuaded the Bureau of Indian Affairs to remove all Indians from southwestern Oregon and the Willamette Valley. The bureau therefore abandoned the reservations at Table Rock, Council Creek, and the Umpqua Valley and began colonizing Indians on the Siletz and Grand Ronde reservations. In the 1870s pressures from ranchers who desired the lush meadowlands of the Harney Basin persuaded the president to revoke the orders creating the Malheur Reservation. In these matters the federal government presumed to exercise supreme authority, and on a number of occasions it did so—hardly ever considering the needs, wishes, and rights of the Oregon Indians.

In the nineteenth century the reservation system was premised on removal and residency. Indians were compelled to give up their seasonal round, abandon traditional villages, and surrender to the control of the Bureau of Indian Affairs. Colonized on the reservations, they were subjected to many constraints. The army established Fort Umpqua, Fort Hoskins, and Fort Yamhill to surround the Siletz and Grand Ronde reservations. It garrisoned troops at Fort Dalles to monitor the Warm Springs Reservation and others at Fort Walla Walla to watch the Indians at Umatilla. During the Civil War it established Fort Klamath to play a similar role at the Klamath Reservation and sent troops to Fort Harney.

The BIA segregated Indians from the surrounding Euro-American communities. Sometimes, when starvation threatened, the Indians could obtain work permits to leave the reservation. The goal, however, was to isolate them from evil influences and to prevent them from returning to their old homes.

On the Columbia Plateau those efforts ultimately led to the much-disputed treaty of November 15, 1865 with the Confederated Tribes of Warm Springs. By this ratified agreement the tribes were compelled to relinquish their off-reservation fishing rights at their "usual and accustomed stations" on the Columbia River. The Indians subsequently claimed deception and fraud and bitterly contested their confinement. Finally in 1888 Commissioner J. D. C. Atkins observed, "I think it highly improbable that the Warm Springs Indians would have relinquished their rights in these valuable fisheries for the mere asking."

Over several decades the reservations were subjected to abolition by executive order, sale because of termination by Congress, opening to public entry by statute, and allotment with sale of "surplus" lands. Reservations were created by executive order, act of Congress, or treaty, or subsequently by the BIA taking land into "trust" for tribes. In that last instance the lands might be deeded to the U. S. for the tribe, purchased by the BIA, or purchased by the tribe itself.

OREGON RESERVATIONS, 1853-1990

NAME	DATE CREATED	LOCATION
Table Rock	September 10, 1853	Rogue River Valley
Cow Creek	September 19, 1853	Council Creek
Umpqua and Calapooia	November 29, 1854	Umpqua Valley
Umatilla	June 9, 1855	Eastern Columbia Plateau
Nez Perce	June 11, 1855/ June 16, 1873	Northeast Oregon
Warm Springs	June 25, 1855	Western Columbia Plateau
Siletz (or Coast)	November 9, 1855	Central Coast
Grand Ronde	June 30, 1857	South Yamhill Valley
Klamath	October 14, 1864	Klamath Basin
Malheur	March 14, 1871/ September 12, 1872	Harney Basin
Coos	February 11, 1941/ October 14, 1984	Coos Bay
Siuslaw	June 1, 1948	Florence
Burns Paiute Indian Colony	1935/October 13, 1972	Harney County
Siletz	September 4, 1980	Lincoln County
Cow Creek	September 15, 1986	Canyonville
Grand Ronde	September 8, 1988	Yamhill County

"CIVILIZATION" PROGRAMS

The Bureau of Indian Affairs planned for the transformation of Oregon Indians into sedentary, agricultural, English-speaking Christians. For a century—from 1855 to 1956—it promoted these goals. First, the Bureau designed the reservation as an isolated place where cultural and linguistic change could be fostered. In addition, it worked on the assumption that farming was the highest "calling" and that Indians would benefit best if they mastered the techniques of crop production and livestock management.

Some tribes, such as the Umatilla and Cayuse, which possessed great herds of horses and had acquired gardening skills from their contact with the Whitman Mission, received high marks in agent reports for their march toward a "civilized" state. By contrast, the Northern Paiutes, dedicated to their traditional lifeway and determined to maintain their seasonal round and usual foods, were bitterly denounced in BIA reports as savages and barbarians. Most

Once they were placed on reservations, Indians were forced to give up their seasonal rounds, abandon traditional villages, and surrender to the authority of the Bureau of Indian Affairs. Although Indians had some limited legal authority, represented here by an Indian police force at the Grand Ronde Agency (upper left), they were subjected to control of the U.S. Army which established forts at the reservations. The Klamath Fort shown here (lower left), had counterparts at the Siletz, Grand Ronde, Warm Springs, and Umatilla reservations. Men, women, and children were expected to wear "civilized" dress (upper right) and to learn to be farmers or tradesmen. The agricultural scene (lower right) is from the Warm Springs Reservation.

Opposite. *Civilization programs were driven by a desire to transform Indian children. Most reservations had day schools and some had boarding schools, where children could be isolated from their parents and extended families. These schools enforced a strict "English only" policy and students were punished for lapsing into their native tongues. Native dress was forbidden and uniforms were often issued. The curriculum at these schools was oriented toward manual trades for the boys and domestic science for the girls. The best and brightest students were often sent to Indian Training School, first at Forest Grove (upper left) and later—when local residents protested the youngsters' presence—at Chemawa, near Salem (upper right and bottom row). Today, Chemawa remains the nation's oldest boarding school. Scenes in the center row are from Warm Springs (left) and Umatilla (right).*

Indians, however, had a mixed press in the BIA annual reports. Usually the new agent in his first year spoke of wretched conditions on the reservations: crop failures, hunger, poor housing, lack of understanding about sanitation, broken tools, and inadequate sawmills, grist mills, or numbers of livestock. Within a year or so, however—in order to look "good"—the agent wrote glowingly of the progress of his charges. Then the cycle was repeated again, for the turnover of agents was constant and each seemed to fault his predecessor.

Oregon Indians were the victims in this brutal system of enforced civilization. Thousands died needlessly because of concentration of people, while many others perished of malnutrition because of crop failures. A number of tribes received no annuities because of the

Senate's failure to ratify their treaties, and other Indians suffered because of the agents' malfeasance or corruption. Finally, the administration of President Ulysses S. Grant attempted in the 1870s to reform Indian affairs nationally with its "Peace Policy."

This policy parceled out the reservations among the Christian denominations which, through various sects, were to secure a monopoly for staffing and running them. The Methodists gained Siletz, the Presbyterians Grand Ronde and Klamath, and so it went. The assumption was that people of high principles would deal fairly and humanely with the Indians.

At Siletz, however, agent Edmund Swan, a lifelong Methodist, found otherwise. In 1881 he lamented to the Secretary of the Interior how the Oregon Methodist Conference dictated whom he should employ and from whom he was to buy supplies. Writing of the agency employees, he observed, "I have found it necessary to remind them that Reservations were not formed for the benefit of them, as a class, but rather for other and higher purposes. . . ."

While a number of selfless missionaries like the saintly Adrien Croquet (who ministered from 1859 to 1898 on the Grand Ronde Reservation) devoted their lives to the Indians, many BIA employees proved corrupt and bigoted. With the Indians under the control of denominations, the prospect of forcing attendance at church was enhanced. Parents were informed there was no clothing for children who did not attend the Sabbath School. Others found their interest in messianic religions such as the Ghost Dance, Earth Lodge Cult, or Dreamer Religion challenged by BIA officials on religious grounds. The potential for coercion was increased by this policy until the 1890s, when the federal government abandoned it and put the BIA under the civil service.

On many reservations the civilization programs were driven by a desire to transform the children. While most reservations had day schools, some—either by treaty or special appropriation—secured funds for boarding schools. These latter institutions were of highest priority, for there the isolation of the child from the parents and grandparents was most complete. The schools enforced a strict "English Only" policy and punished children for speaking in their native languages. This requirement went far beyond the classroom and included conversation in the dormitories and at meals. The curriculum was heavily oriented toward manual labor: carpentry, blacksmithing, shoemaking, and farming for boys; needlework or sewing, beadwork, house cleaning, washing, ironing, and cooking for girls. At best, the BIA saw Oregon Indians becoming cheerful, thrifty, hardworking common laborers and did little to prepare them for leadership roles or for higher education.

The brightest and best students of the reservation schools from the 1870s through the 1940s were tapped to attend Chemawa Indian School. Founded by the U. S. Army in 1881 in Forest Grove, this regional boarding school elicited bitter complaints from the local citizens about the presence of Indian children in town. In 1885 the bureau selected a rural, agricultural site five miles from Salem and there the students helped build Chemawa School. The boys mastered brickmaking and carpentry and helped construct the campus, while the girls cleaned the buildings, cooked, and did the

In 1887 the federal government further eroded Indian tribes by passing the General Allotment, or Dawes, Act—a measure designed to divide up reservations into individually owned plots. Because the Siletz Reservation contained rich stands of virgin timber, eager white speculators hovered nearby and offered to assist in the land surveys. At the end of the process, Congress declared 191,798 acres to be "surplus" and turned over 75 percent of the Indians' land to settlers and timber buyers.

laundry, and both boys and girls worked in the surrounding fields to produce food for the facility.

Occasionally, graduates of Chemawa went on for more education, attending Haskell Institute in Kansas or even Carlisle Indian School in Pennsylvania. This system of education segregated the most able students and removed them farther and farther from family and tribal life. The BIA worked on the mistaken assumption that this system would produce a new generation of tribal leaders. Instead it often so transformed the students that many left tribal life and moved into the non-Indian community, never returning to the reservations, where they no longer knew the language or even recognized family members.

To be sure, some returned to the reservations, but these individuals were changed. Each generation had less knowledge of traditional lifeways, and by 1900 the number of speakers of western

Oregon languages was dropping rapidly. By the 1920s some languages were entirely extinct, and in the 1930s linguists scrambled to record the vocabularies and voices of the "last" speakers of the Galice Creek dialect, Takelma, Hanis and Miluk Coos, Tillamook, and Kalapuyan.

The impacts of the civilization programs were evident. The Bureau of Indian Affairs had largely succeeded in destroying many elements of Indian identity. The reservation system and the schools had partly achieved their goals.

ALLOTMENT, 1887-1934

As early as the Rogue River Treaty of 1853, the federal government raised the prospect of dividing up reservations among the Indians. With the passage of the General Allotment Act of 1887, this idea gained national endorsement. Sometimes known as the Dawes Act, the allotment program sought to destroy tribes by dividing their communal land base. Individual Indians—men, women, and children—would receive acreage held in "trust." When they had proven their "competency" or had waited for 25 years, the BIA would issue a deed or "fee-patent" for the land. To accelerate the process, Congress passed the Burke Act in 1906, eliminating the 25-year waiting period and permitting local agents to determine "competency."

For most reservations the allotment program proved a nightmare. First, the Indians had to hold a conference, a meeting staged by the BIA, to agree to accept the law. Once this was done, the process began with the selection of lands. Some people received valuable acreage; others got tracts that were nearly worthless. Some lands were inaccessible, isolated, densely forested, or lacked water. While the agents generally tried to help the Indians make good selections, the competition for prime pieces sometimes pitted families against one another. Powerful individuals obtained cleared, fenced, or otherwise improved lands; children, the aged, and others had to be content with lesser lands.

The allotment process was sometimes surrounded by an almost circus-like atmosphere. Such was the case at Siletz, where in 1892 the Indians agreed to the program. Although reduced by executive order in 1865 and act of Congress in 1875, the Siletz Reservation yet contained nearly a quarter of a million acres, most of it virgin timber or rapidly replenishing coniferous forest. Not surprisingly, eager speculators in timberlands hovered nearby. Indeed, some even volunteered to assist in the surveys to speed up the process. Their interest was rewarded by a compliant Congress, which threw open to entry 191,798 "surplus" or unallotted acres. The allotment program allocated 44,000 acres to individuals, reserved 3,000 acres for the tribes, and turned over more than 75 percent of the lands to non-Indians.

The scramble for Indian lands, some of them highly valuable even at the turn of the twentieth century, became part of the widespread land frauds of the era. After his conviction as "King of the Oregon Land Fraud Ring," S. A. D. Puter wrote in his jail cell *Looters of the Public Domain*. An important chapter in Puter's account focused on the "The Story of Siletz" and "How the Indians Were Robbed of Their Homes for the Benefit of Pale-faced Looters,

Under the Guise of Treaty Rights."

The allotment program consumed some reservations. By 1904 all of Grand Ronde was allotted except the tribal cemetery and lots where the Catholic Church and the agency headquarters stood. Future generations had no prospect of securing land, nor did the confederated tribes have a land base for economic development. At Warm Springs, prime properties passed from the tribes to individuals and often—almost as quickly—to non-Indians. Fee patenting bestowed citizenship on Indians, but also the obligation of paying taxes. Within four years, many lost their allotments, as the counties foreclosed for non-payment of taxes. Thus, at Umatilla the reservation took on the appearance of a gigantic checkerboard made up of tribal lands, individual trust lands, and alienated lands in non-Indian ownership.

While allotment may have facilitated citizenship, it also accelerated the destruction of tribalism and horribly complicated reservation administration. Where allotments remained in trust, there developed complicated heirships of several, sometimes dozens, of owners. Decisions on rights-of-way, reforestation, and land-use planning became almost impossible. Non-Indians acquired key properties such as the hot springs on the Warm Springs Reservation. Some allotments remained in ambiguous status when the BIA lost contact with heirs who had moved away. Neither the tribe nor individuals could acquire the land without a lengthy, often confusing, process of tracking down heirs or waiting for the BIA to probate Indian estates.

Some Indians, however, liked the allotment program. They gained land, secured citizenship, and gradually left tribal life. For them, the allotment provided a way to move into the majority culture that had surrounded the tribes in the nineteenth century. Off-reservation Oregon Indians found the allotment era even more appealing, because amendments to the General Allotment Act and the Indian Homestead Act (1875) permitted them, for the first time, to

In 1938, the Klamath won a lawsuit against the federal government and were awarded $5.3 million in compensation for their lost lands. Here, they gather before a vote to prorate the settlement among tribal members. Claims by other tribes were dismissed by the courts, vetoed by the president, or "satisfied" with paltry settlements based on the value of the land when it was taken from them decades earlier.

secure land. When granted under these laws, the land was in "trust" and therefore exempt from taxation.

After 1887 several thousand Indians in Oregon obtained public domain allotments. These included 11,014 acres to Northern Paiutes in the Harney Basin and over 10,000 acres to members of the Coquille, Coos, Lower Umpqua, and Siuslaw tribes along the southern Oregon coast. Some Indians obtained allotments in the western Cascades of Douglas County and others along the south bank of the Columbia River near their age-old fishing sites at Five Mile Rapids and Celilo.

Too often, however, non-Indians manipulated the Indians and plundered their lands. In the 1950s, in fact, employees of the Portland Area Office of the BIA were charged, tried, convicted, and sentenced to jail for stealing hundreds of thousands of dollars in timber monies from allotments on the lower Rogue River. The disabilities of the allotment era were so evident that Congress abolished the program in 1934 and extended "trust" indefinitely on all individual and tribal lands.

INDIAN REORGANIZATION, 1934-1946

A growing sense of reform hit America in the 1930s. John Collier, named Commissioner of Indian Affairs in 1933, had voiced strong criticism of the BIA and federal Indian policy for nearly a decade. Occupying a key position in the New Deal government of President Franklin D. Roosevelt, Collier attempted to change directions in policy. As a reformer, he believed Indian civilization had intrinsic values. He championed Indian art and music and forbade BIA schools to subvert traditional Indian religions. He also viewed the allotment program as a disaster, destroying tribes and foreclosing their future.

Collier played a pivotal role in helping secure the Indian Reorganization Act (1934). This law ended allotments, extended trust, and encouraged tribes to form modern governments with written constitutions. It set up a revolving loan fund; called for sound conservation of land, water, and mineral resources on reservations; and permitted tribes to form business corporations. Acceptance of IRA was mixed. Some tribes saw it as their opportunity to build for the present and future, while other leaders denounced it as another trick from Washington, another program that would come and go. These conflicting voices greeted the proponents of IRA when they assembled Oregon tribal leaders at Chemawa School in 1935 to discuss the new law.

Some Oregon tribes ignored IRA and did not vote on it. The Klamath and Confederated Tribes of Siletz rejected it. The Grand Ronde Indian Community adopted IRA and organized a corporation under the law, as did the Confederated Tribes of Warm Springs. Whether tribes accepted or rejected IRA, only a few found much change in Indian policy. The Great Depression and then World War II created economic circumstances that assumed there was never enough money to fund the revolving loans or the land acquisition programs adequately. The Confederated Tribes of Coos, Lower Umpqua, and Siuslaw, however, while not voting on IRA, benefited from the changed atmosphere of the 1930s. In 1941 the Bureau of Indian Affairs accepted into trust a 6.1-acre reservation for these Indians, erected a fine tribal hall on the land at Coos Bay, and for the first time provided modest medical care—a once-a-month clinic—through the Indian Health Service.

LAWSUITS AND CLAIMS—1899-1984

In 1869 Congress invoked sovereign immunity to protect the United States from suit by Indian tribes. After that date any tribe with a grievance had to mount a campaign that would convince a congressman to introduce and secure passage of a jurisdictional act permitting the tribe to sue the United States. For most tribes this process was complicated, costly, and almost impossible. In spite of its challenges, however, Oregon Indians displayed great tenacity and tried to use this system.

In 1899 the Clatsop, Kathlamet, and Tillamook bands—signatories to treaties negotiated in 1851 by Anson Dart—joined Chinookans from the Washington shore of the lower Columbia River to sue in the Court of Claims. Silas Smith, whose mother was the daughter of Clatsop chief Coboway, served as legal counsel for these Indians. Although Smith did not live to see the suit settled in 1912, the tribes won a judgment and in 1913 received some modest compensation for their lands. They were the first Oregon tribes to use this system.

In 1920 the Klamath, Modoc, and Yahuskins gained permission to sue for the loss of 86,418 acres from their reservation in a wagonroad grant. They lost the case in 1935, but a subsequent act permitted another lawsuit which led to a claims award of $5.3 million, confirmed in 1938 by the Supreme Court.

In 1929 the Confederated Tribes of Coos, Lower Umpqua, and Siuslaw obtained an act to permit suit over the appropriation of all of their homelands in southwestern Oregon without ratified treaty or compensation. Sadly, after the Tribes labored for 12 years to get into court, the claims court rejected, as proof of ownership, all oral testimony and their unratified 1855 coastal treaty. The court concluded in 1938 that the tribes had no "right, claim, or title to any part of the coast of Oregon whatsoever," and the Supreme Court denied an appeal.

Other tribes lobbied, secured favorable action by Congress on their bills, and then—as in the case of the Cow Creek Band of Umpqua in 1932—lost their opportunity when the measure was vetoed by the president. To "clear the nation's conscience" and—it was believed—end once and for all these lawsuits and petitions for jurisdictional acts, Congress created the Indian Claims Commission. Established in 1946, this special court was to receive complaints for five years, act informally to settle the claims, and go out of business in 1956. Thirty years later, its work still unfinished and virtually all original plaintiffs dead, Congress abolished the commission and passed its still pending cases to the claims court.

Between 1946 and 1951, almost all Oregon tribes responded and filed complaints with the Indian Claims Commission, some securing what at the time were perceived to be substantial judgments. (The Nez Perce, for example, were awarded $9.2 million.) Other tribes, however, obtained only token sums, and some found their com-

Oregon's Indians are dual citizens, owing allegiance to their own people and traditions while participating as American citizens. Indian men have volunteered for service in every war the United States has fought in this century. Eddie Ned, Coquille (left), is shown in uniform. At the annual roundup in Pendleton, an Indian rider bears the American flag. Each year at Warm Springs, Indians stage a Veterans' Day Parade.

plaints dismissed. All worked under a terrible burden to use this "window of opportunity" to file suit. The rules were that—except in highly unusual circumstances—the tribes could obtain no interest; the settlement would be only financial (no tribe could settle its claim with land); and the price of the tribal land was to be fixed at the "date of taking," the year when the Indians lost it through warfare, removal, treaty, or other factors, rather than at the land's current value.

In spite of these rules and the tacit acknowledgment that by participating in the process they were abrogating aboriginal title, tribes from across the country stepped forward. Many had fought vainly for their day in court and saw the work of the claims commission as their only opportunity. Unfortunately, when the cases reached the claims commission, they dragged on and on. Tragically some of the judgments were then consumed in "offsets"—deductions that included attorney fees, and "benefits" the BIA had paid out to the tribes over the preceeding century through reservation programs. When the Indians protested that they had been unwilling beneficiaries of such programs, their pleas were unheeded. The process moved inexorably but slowly forward.

In 1981 the Cow Creek Band of Umpqua Indians obtained a jurisdictional act and brought its land claims case to the claims court. The case resulted in a 1984 negotiated settlement of $1.5 million. Having observed the impact of per-capita payments to other Oregon tribes, the Cow Creeks voted to vest their judgment fund in an endowment. The BIA, however, rejected the tribal plan, demanding a payment to individuals—in spite of the Indian Judgment Fund Act, which had rejected that unwise and discredited program. Congress

then intervened and mandated the tribal plan. The Cow Creeks thus preserved their legacy from the past and banked it. Today their endowment provides annual interest for education, housing, and economic development.

TERMINATION, 1956-1989

The sentiment to reverse the policies of John Collier mounted steadily in the 1940s. Following World War II some in Congress decided to get the federal government out of Indian affairs. They argued that economy and efficiency dictated cutting back, perhaps even eliminating, the Bureau of Indian Affairs. Indians, they observed, should move into the mainstream. They should be "set free" from the disabilities of second-class citizenship and life on isolated reservations. These views accorded with those held by a number in President Dwight Eisenhower's cabinet, among them Douglas McKay, secretary of interior and former governor of Oregon. Presiding over the BIA, McKay concluded that Oregon should be a showcase for the new era of Indian policy. McKay saw the termination of "government-to-government relationships" with Oregon tribes as being "in line with the established policy of our state." He argued that Termination would bring Oregon Indians "full and equal citizenship."

Several members of Congress introduced bills to speed the transition of Indians into mainstream American life. In February 1954 joint House and Senate committees heard debate on the "Termination of Federal Supervision Over Certain Tribes of Indians." McKay's assistant, Orme Lewis, led off by stating:

It is our belief that the Indians subject to the proposed bill no longer require special assistance from the Federal Government, and that they have sufficient skill and ability to manage their own affairs. Through long association and intermarriage with their white neighbors, education in public schools, employment in gainful occupations in order to obtain a livelihood, and dependence on public institutions for public services, the Indians have largely been integrated into the white society where they are accepted without discrimination.

Even in 1954, however, Oregon law continued to prohibit the marriage of an Indian and a non-Indian and provided for fine and imprisonment of both the officiating minister or public official and the couple. At that time none of the Oregon tribes met the standards laid down by William Zimmerman, former acting commissioner of Indian affairs, as a measure of readiness for immediate termination of federal services. Clearly other factors were at work.

One was the desire by timber companies to gain access to the vast resources of the Klamath Reservation in south-central Oregon, where thousands of acres of virgin timber stood. If the Klamath were "terminated," some argued, their timber could be logged and they could find gainful employment in the timber industry.

Coercion became another factor. Although the Klamath had been awarded a judgment of $2.6 million against the United States, Senator Arthur Watkins, one of the primary proponents of Termination, held up approval of the appropriation until the Klamath agreed to terminate. The bill he rushed to pass was ill conceived and made little assessment of social or economic consequences for the Klamath people or for the Oregon timber industry. "The committee members' only desire," wrote Vine DeLoria, "was to get the termination of the tribe over with as quickly as possible. If it meant cutting every tree in Oregon, they would have so authorized, simply to get on to another tribe."

In 1956 Congress, in its exercise of plenary power, terminated every tribe and band west of the Cascades and the Klamath in south-central Oregon. As quickly as possible, the Bureau of Indian Affairs issued deeds to allotments, sold off tribal lands, ended health benefits, and declined to admit Indian children from the affected tribes to BIA schools. For some tribes it prepared Termination Rolls, in part to have a list for disbursing the modest assets resulting from

Opposite. *The last traditional Indian fishing grounds at Celilo Falls on the Columbia River were destroyed by the construction of Bonneville Dam. In the 1950s years of court battles concluded with the Indians' reluctant acceptance of an agreement to let the federal government buy out the great fishery.* **Top.** *Warm Springs representatives sign the settlement agreement.* **Bottom.** *Part of the settlement agreement allowed Indians to afford such modern amenities as running water.*

the sale of communal holdings. In some instances the BIA turned over tribal land and buildings to non-Indian trustees. When tribes objected, demanded an accounting, and charged fraud, they were ignored.

The impact of Termination was disastrous. For tribes like the Klamath it meant substantial, one-time-only cash payments on a per-capita basis. Many Oregon Indians had never had so much money at one time before and few were prepared to manage the windfall of claims payments or the checks received for the sale of tribal lands. A number lost everything in weeks or months, to the delight of car dealers and others. For families in which a dozen or more heirs suddenly owned an allotment outright, the requirement was to pool resources and pay the taxes. The land had never before been taxed and many were unable to persuade their cousins, brothers, and sisters to contribute. By 1960 Oregon counties began foreclosure.

Several hundred Klamath put their assets in a trust managed by a Portland bank, a decision that permitted their assets to grow under careful management. Eventually they disbanded the trust and all but one, Edison Chiloquin, took substantial per-capita distributions. For the western Oregon tribes the assets were modest—a few hundred dollars, sometimes a check for a few cents.

For 20 years Congress ignored Oregon's terminated Indians, as did the Bureau of Indian Affairs. These people may have looked like Indians, affirmed their Indian identities, maintained their tribal governments, or even retained their languages, but they were no longer Indians in the eyes of the federal government. Finally in 1976 the Joint Congressional Commission on the American Indian held hearings in Salem, Oregon. Among those who testified were the Klamath, Grand Ronde, Coquille, Cow Creek Band of Umpqua (Upper Umpqua), Lower Umpqua, and Willow River Benevolent Association (Coos, Lower Umpqua, and Siuslaw).

At hearings, tales of deprivation, poor treatment, and discrimination poured out from witnesses, many of whom challenged the BIA's handling of assets at Termination. Merle Holmes of Grand Ronde, for example, described the fate of the tribe's handsome community building:

That hall at termination time, Bureau of Indian Affairs had a value of $6,689 for this building and almost ten acres of land. And now this land, under the stipulation with the trustee—he was not to even lease that building to anyone else without tribal consent—now he then, in turn, sold it. But now the price he got for it, as per this trustee, he sold that land and the building for $800, and he no more than sold it for the $800 and he turned right around and the white man bought it, turned right around and sold it for $8,000 plus land equity, and Mr. Fuller yet today says the land was worthless over there. But only when we had it, it was worthless. As soon as the white man got it, it was valuable.

Termination hung like a cloud over other Oregon tribes, as well as those in other parts of the country. When tribes became assertive, congressmen or Bureau employees raised the spectre of more Termination legislation. The Termination era only made Indian prob-

Employees of the Inter-Tribal Fish Commission are helping to restore salmon runs destroyed by Bonneville and other Columbia River dams. Here, Mike George and Troy Matheny are catching largemouth minnows (northern squawfish), predators that consume large numbers of young salmon.

lems invisible; it did not ameliorate them. Low income, poor health, early death, and limited educational opportunity did not go away with Termination. The record by 1976 proved that the situation for the terminated tribes had only worsened.

RESTORATION AND SELF-DETERMINATION, 1977-1991

In the 1970s Indians increasingly asserted their rights and federal responsibilities. A new generation of Indian leaders, many of them college educated and supported by able legal assistance, called for redressing the problems of Termination. These currents in Indian affairs, which included the Red Power Movement and the American Indian Movement, were felt in Oregon. In 1977 Congress responded to a carefully developed campaign by the Confederated Tribes of Siletz by passing a bill restoring the tribes to "recognized" status. This bill was followed by others, on a case-by-case basis, for the Cow Creek Band of Umpqua; the Confederated Tribes of Coos, Lower Umpqua, and Siuslaw; the Confederated Tribes of Grand Ronde; the Klamath; and the Coquille Tribe.

Not only had these tribes, through tremendous effort, secured the restoration of their federal relationships, other Oregon tribes had successfully staved off the efforts of the states of Oregon and Washington to abrogate their treaty-reserved fishing rights on the Columbia Plateau. The Confederated Tribes of Warm Springs, the Umatilla, and the Nez Perce waged a spirited battle in federal court to uphold the guarantees of the treaties of 1855, which assured their right to fish "at usual and accustomed grounds and stations."

The states raised many objections to the Indian fishing rights. They argued that the Indians were not conserving the resource. Some argued that the treaties were negotiated "a long time ago" and presumed that because they were old they were no longer binding. The

Indians pointed out that they had not built the dams which spanned the Columbia and transformed it from a free-flowing river into a series of great reservoirs. They noted that they had not poured sewage into the rivers, nor had they logged the hillsides and altered the habitat which had diminished the runs of anadromous fish. In fact, they pointed to their reluctant acceptance in the 1950s of the federal government's buying out their great fishery at Celilo Falls and Five Mile Rapids. They and the River Tribes, those Indians who had steadfastly refused to remove to the reservations, kept pointing to the assurances of the treaties or the hollow promises of the law creating the Bonneville Dam project, which called for the identification of "in lieu" fishing sites.

The "fish wars" of the 1960s and 1970s ultimately led to adjudicated settlements before judges Robert Belloni in Portland and George Boldt in Seattle. The decisions of these judges affirmed the tribes' treaty rights. Boldt's landmark decision was affirmed in 1977 by the Ninth Circuit and in 1979 by the Supreme Court. Judge Belloni, a peacemaker, compelled the state and federal fisheries interests and agencies to sit down with the tribes to negotiate fishing periods and determine the size of the catch, fishing days, and standards for gear. The tribes approached the matter through their Columbia River Inter-Tribal Fish Commission, an organization representing all of the treaty tribes on the Plateau.

Increasingly in the 1970s Oregon Indians found reasons to work together. As tribes they participated in the Affiliated Tribes of Northwest Indians and the National Congress of American Indians. On the state level they sat down several times each year in meetings of the Oregon Commission on Indian Services, whose membership included two members of the Oregon legislature, to discuss issues of common concern and to have a voice in the state capitol. Through Indian education programs, usually financed with federal monies, they coordinated curriculum development, teacher training, culture camps, tutoring, and related activities. Dozens of Indian parents served on advisory committees to assist their local school districts in multicultural education.

In the 1970s and 1980s some tribes obtained special funding through the Comprehensive Employment Training Act (CETA), the Indian Education Act, Housing and Urban Development (HUD), and development grants from the BIA or from the Administration for Native Americans (ANA). These resources, tribal monies, and able leaders encouraged a number of Oregon Indian tribes to launch economic development programs. The Confederated Tribes of Warm Springs became a national model for this work.

CONCLUSION

The history of federal-Indian relations in Oregon is a complex story of tension, warfare, treaties, brutal removals, miserable conditions of death and forced cultural transformation on reservations, and shifting federal policies. There are elements of pathos, moments of heartrending contradiction. In spite of the many turns, the Oregon tribes have survived.

7

MISCONCEPTIONS
ABOUT INDIANS

BY DAVID H. FRENCH

*The statements in boldface type below represent some of the misconceptions
that people have, or have had, about American Indians.*

*These misconceptions range from beliefs that most readers will recognize
as "obviously incorrect" to assertions that seem—on the surface—to be reasonable.
All the misconceptions and responses to them apply to Oregon Indians.*

Indians were noble savages.

This idea flourished in the eighteenth and nineteenth centuries, thanks in part to the writings of French philosopher and writer Jean Jacques Rousseau. Embracing the apparently contradictory elements of "savage" and "noble," the idea meant for some that Indians led untamed, idyllic lives, untouched by the complexities of an expanding industrial society. These idyllic images have been perpetuated by some novelists and others. Today, the film industry, which originally portrayed Indians as enemies, has come to present them as either noble savages or—rarely—as human beings with all the complexities of character and motive the human state entails. Most readers of this publication already know that no Indians are or were savages. They have indeed been successful human beings, whose cultures have a richness and sophistication that non-Indians do not fully appreciate.

Indians belong to a distinct race.

The term "race" has had various meanings, including the widespread American belief that humankind is subdivided into distinct biological groups that can be recognized by visible traits such as skin color and facial characteristics. Psychological traits, such as amount of intelligence, are also attributed to "races." Individuals are often thought of as "belonging to" or "being members of" such genetically derived "racial groups."

"Races" cannot be precisely defined and lack definite boundaries. Of course, specific physical characteristics do differ from population to population. For example, blood types—some of them little known—are not randomly distributed but have a certain statistical frequency within geographic regions. However, genetic similarities among humans far outweigh the differences.

Despite the similarities, there are historical and cultural reasons for people to classify themselves—while also classifying certain others as "different" from themselves. In today's world, there exist many culturally driven ways in which this classifying is done, with language and nationality (or ethnicity) being common. Czechs and Slovaks have a sense of being members of their own ethnic groups, and (as of late 1991) members—citizens—of the Czechoslovakian state as well. In the U.S. some of us belong to the Polish-American or Korean-American ethnic groups. Similarly, Indians can be defined as belonging to one or many ethnic groups. This is more useful than the bad biology of "racial" classification. No human being *belongs* to a "race."

Indians are one large group with the same language and customs.

Movies, television, and novels portray American Indians for us in a way that causes us to forget the hundreds of languages and dialects they speak. Those who lump all Indians together are likely to say or write, "The Indian does such and such." (Those same people might also say, "the Jew" or "the teenager.") Oregon itself was once home to a large number of native languages and cultures, so diverse that anthropologists assigned them to three or four "culture areas" (described at the beginning of this publication). The movie/TV stereotype of "the Indian" is usually based on another culture area: the Plains.

It's obvious who is an Indian and who is not.

Proving that one is an Indian can be difficult for individuals who must establish their heritage for legal reasons. A common criterion from the point of view of Indian authorities is the percentage of Indian "blood" (ancestry) a person can establish. Another criterion is the "tribal" identities of one's ancestors. Local regulations exist by which to decide uncertain cases. A related question is, "What is a valid tribe?" When a group that lacks a treaty tries to establish its

Photographs can lead to misconceptions, too. These Indians appear to be excluded from a rodeo, but it is likely that they have merely paused before entering the arena and finding seats from which to view the events.

identity as a tribe, the Bureau of Indian Affairs and appropriate courts can become involved in finding the answer. These are not simple matters and have frequently been handled badly on the federal level.

Oregon Indians were originally organized as tribes with chiefs.

The term "tribe" has often been applied to linguistic groups and has been used in other misleading ways. Very few of the Indians west of the Rockies had political units with territorial boundaries, internal organization, and the capability for extended collective action. Along the Oregon Coast, and up the Columbia River beyond The Dalles, villages with headmen were the largest "organized" units, and elsewhere winter villages functioned in a somewhat similar manner. However, summer could be a time when medium-sized groups moved away from the village and when—under special circumstances—people from diverse localities would come together.

When reservations were established, organizational structures more like tribes or confederated tribes developed, chiefs and other officers were chosen by various means, and long-range collective activities became common. Today, these arrangements are so well

established that some Oregon Indians believe their ancestors always had "true" tribes.

In earlier times, Oregon Indians lived principally on fish and game.

Both such animal foods were important in the area, but—with the possible exception of some fish-rich Columbia and Willamette River groups—plant food provided a higher percentage of the total diet. Most of the "hunters and gatherers" of the past and present world might better be called "gatherers and hunters."

Oregon Indians were completely democratic (or they were thoroughly undemocratic).

It is true that important decision-making involved participation by many members of the communities. In overall terms, the Paiutes, who valued achievement over ancestry, were probably the most democratic. In early times, various other groups had a class system— and even a slave caste; upper-class people, especially village headmen, had more influence than others, and men and women often did different kinds of work and had different roles.

More recently, decision-making among Oregon Indians has become increasingly democratic. Two indications of change within reservations are the existence of constitutions and the fact that major decisions are reached by voting. Women are quite often among the leaders.

A universal Indian curing system called shamanism could benefit all humans.

Shamanism or its equivalent was once found throughout Oregon and persists today in some communities. It includes healing with supernatural aid, especially that of personal spirit powers. However, practices differ so much in the Americas that it is questionable whether they should all be subsumed under one name. Sincere misunderstandings, bad books, poor lectures, and outright fraud have also cast shadows over the concepts and practices called "shamanism". Non-Indians may be disappointed if they seek benefits from such practices.

Columbus discovered America.

"Aha!" some Euro-Americans say, "that's wrong—it was the Norsemen who first made the discovery." Either assertion strikes some people as being one of the most public examples of racist or culture-bound thinking.

Some who attribute the "discovery" to Europeans, however, are not racists. They simply forget that Indians, Eskimos/Inuits, and Aleuts were the first humans in the Americas. Others use a culture-bound definition of "discovery"—a definition in which that term means "discovery by Europeans."

Whites had to "conquer" the "wilderness," particularly in the West.

Such thinking ignores the fact that Indians were living full lives in the "wilderness" and in fact tends to see Indians as being part of the wilderness. These ideas have troubled Indians, while serving as a justification for destroying environmental balances. Today, "conquering" and "subduing" are expressed as "developing" the land.

Treaties between the U.S. government and Indians are no longer valid because they are outdated.

This belief is a simple fallacy. The treaties are still being upheld in courts and have no expiration dates. Changes in governmental relations with Indians have occurred, but these changes— when relevant and legitimate—have been within the frameworks of the diverse treaties.

The government gave the Indians land for reservations.

On the contrary, the land was originally occupied and utilized by Indian populations with varying densities. Later, most of the land was occupied by Euro-Americans, and the Indians—under pressure—had to move to reduced areas of land, often far from the regions they had originally inhabited. In short, it was the Indians who provided land for non-Indians.

Fishing and hunting rights were granted to Indians by the federal government.

In fact, the Indians, who had been fishing and hunting freely, were able to retain some version of their right to do so in the nineteenth-century treaties (see "Federal-Indian Relations" beginning on page 39).

Indians are forced to live on reservations.

This is an old fallacy. Many Indians have become farmers on their own, non-reservation lands or have moved either temporarily or permanently to urban areas.

Indians receive payments from the government simply because they are Indians.

A few Indian groups in the U.S. may receive token checks or commodities on the basis of treaty provisions; reservations have received payments to rectify early, unfair treaties; and other, sparse governmental benefits exist, based on legislation. Without providing their own sources of income, however, Indians live at the poverty level. Over the years the government has not been benevolent.

The term "Native Americans" should be used instead of "Indians."

The term "Native American" distinguishes American Indians from inhabitants of India or the East Indies. In addition, it is a term that covers Indians, Aleuts, and Eskimos/Inuits alike (though "Indigenous" or "Aboriginal" Americans might have been more appropriate). Today, most Indians call themselves Indians, and "Native American" is being used less frequently than in the recent past. The latter term remains available but might seem "dated" to some.

Indians live in tipis (teepees).

Tipis were once used only by Plains Indians but were introduced into Oregon many decades ago. They have since been used mainly as temporary tents for special occasions. Many non-Indian adults know that tipis are not in daily use, but some children cling to the stereotype. All the more reason to give them ample opportunities to learn about the contemporary lives of the world's peoples so that commonly held misconceptions can be eradicated once and for all.

Author's Note: *Thanks to Rochelle Cashdan, Kathrine French, Wendell Jim, Christopher Roth, Floy Pepper, and others for suggesting items to include in "Misconceptions About Indians." A good source of information on the subject is* History of Indian-White Relations, *Vol. 4 of the Smithsonian Institution's* Handbook of North American Indians, *published in 1988.*

The grand entry opens the 1991 Grand Ronde Restoration Powwow. This powwow, celebrated by the Confederated Tribes of the Grand Ronde Community of Oregon near the coast each August, commemorates the restoration of the tribe's legal status in the 1980s by Congress, which had terminated this and numerous other tribes in the 1950s.

8

OREGON INDIANS TODAY

BY FLOY C. PEPPER

The Indians of present-day Oregon live in two worlds.
Like non-Indians, they compete in the economic realm and are often
indistinguishable from their fellow citizens. But Oregon Indians are also
keenly aware of the need to maintain their heritage through tribal governments,
celebrations, powwows, and other forms of cultural expression.
In both ways, they continue to enrich the state in which they live.

OREGON'S INDIAN POPULATION

According to the 1990 census, the Indian population of Oregon was 38,496, an estimate that is probably low due to the unresolved question, "What is an Indian?" and the fact that since Oregon tribes were terminated in the 1950s, the state's Indians have been highly mobile. As the tribes were terminated, many Indians were relocated and moved to urban areas, where intermarriage caused many to identify with more than one Indian tribe or with other ethnic groups such as Hispanics, Asians, African-Americans, and Caucasians. Today, in addition to Oregon's federally recognized tribes, over 100 different tribes from around the United States are represented in the state. Moreover, many Indians travel from urban centers to reservations and back again, which has resulted in a unique blending of values and customs.

According to information in the *1991-93 Oregon Directory of American Indian Resources*, Indians fall into three groupings:
- Urban/Rural
- Reservation/Non-Reservation
- Recognized/Unrecognized.

Urban/Rural

Surprisingly, urban Indians comprise approximately 89 percent of Oregon's Indian population, compared to about 50 percent nationwide. The majority of urban Indians live in Portland, Salem, and Eugene, although most towns in Oregon have some Indian people. Urban Indians come from tribes in Oregon and other states and move to the city for many reasons—for example, to seek employment or education. Rural dwellers—the remaining 11 percent of the state's Native American population— live either on or off reservations.

Reservation/Non-Reservation

Reservation Indians live on or in the vicinity of Oregon's five reservations—Burns Paiute, Grand Ronde, Siletz, Umatilla, and Warm Springs. Each reservation community is made up of indi- viduals enrolled in the reservation's tribe or tribes and members of other tribes who took up residency later on. Oregon reservations vary widely in size, climate, and topography. For example, the Siletz tribe has 3,666 acres, an enrollment of 2,084, and a lush wooded site near the rainy coast. Warm Springs, on the other hand, occupies 641,035 acres, has a tribal enrollment of 3,278, and is located east of the mountains in a sunny, dry desert area.

Recognized/Unrecognized

Non-reservation Indians can be either "recognized" or "unrec- ognized." The Coos, Coquille, Cow Creek, and Klamath tribes are examples of recognized tribes that do not have reservations. "Rec- ognized" Indians are enrolled in tribes acknowledged by the federal government and include urban, rural, reservation, and non-reser- vation people. Unrecognized Indians come from tribes that were terminated by Congress or were never federally recognized.

RELATIONSHIP TO THE LARGER SOCIETY

Today's Indians are described by William H. Hodge in *The First Americans—Then and Now* as having three kinds of rela- tionships to the larger society and to one another. While no particular individual would fit a single description, most are oriented toward one or the other.

Some Indians have a long, successful relationship with whites, view the world as offering opportunities to gain the good things in life, feel capable and complete in all areas of work, and use their Indian heritage to compete with the white society and to improve their positions in it. They are usually middle aged and well educated, have politically and socially prominent white friends, work hard, use their abilities, manipulate politics to achieve their ends, and reflect Western European traditions.

Other Indians avoid white people and the dominant way of life, are uncomfortable with white society, and feel that whites are not to be trusted. These Indians do not marry whites; take a somewhat militant stance; and seek wealth, power, and prestige only to gain a permanent escape from the evils of the larger society—evils such as arrest and imprisonment, poverty, and federal paternalism. These Indians want to live a blend of traditional, tribal, and pan-tribal life. They usually lack high levels of formal education and have as heroes political and military leaders of the past such as Chief Joseph and Sitting Bull. They use lawyers, lobbyists, courts, and communication media to gain their own ends.

A third kind of Indian sees white society as neither friend nor enemy, does not consciously seek friendship or competition with whites, and usually prefers Indian spouses. These individuals often leave the reservation, but do not want to become a part of the city slums and express their Indian identity by organizing or attending urban-based Indian activities. They accept, without rancor, the reality of the white society and do nothing to change it. They believe they must live in a white world to obtain wages, pensions, and Social Security but make frequent trips "home" to the reservation. For these individuals, cities are places to camp while earning wages and attempting to create a comfortable niche on the reservation to which they can retire.

All three kinds of Indians are found in all parts of society—in tribes, on reservations, and in communities around the state. All are trying to define contemporary American life and their place in it.

GOVERNMENT BY AND FOR THE TRIBES

Indians are citizens of the United States as well as of their own tribes. As U. S. citizens, of course, they have the same rights and are

A fifty-hour vigil was held at Bonneville Dam in August 1987 to call attention to issues, such as the decline of salmon runs and broken promises for alternative fishing sites, being ignored at the fiftieth anniversary celebration of Bonneville Dam, which was sponsored by the U.S. Army Corps of Engineers and Bonneville Power Administration. In the front row (from left) are Tim Wapato (Colville Tribe), then director of the Columbia River Inter-Tribal Fish Commission(CRITFC); John Platt, representing the Oregon Wildlife Federation; Bernice Mitchell (Warm Springs) and Kathryn Brigham (Umatilla), then both CRITFC commissioners; and drummer Art Mitchell (Warm Springs).

The handsome modern community center on the Burns Paiute Reservation is the site of a variety of tribal meetings and ceremonial occasions.

subject to the same laws as all other Americans. However, the tribes can govern their own people and lands and have the power of sovereign governments, except where limited by an act of Congress.

After hundreds of years of persistence, Indians in Oregon are succeeding in making the federal government and the public aware that they were once free, self-sustaining nations. In developing their own forms of self-government, they are assuming their rightful place in American society.

Tribal Government

As sovereign nations, tribes have the power to:
- choose their own form of government;
- make their own laws;
- keep their own forms of judicial and governing bodies;
- regulate trade within their borders, among their members, and with other nations;
- determine the use of their property and other resources;
- tax property and resource use;
- determine their membership;
- govern the conduct of members and non-members on tribal lands; and
- exercise the many rights of an independent government.

Today, Indian tribes in Oregon maintain a level of control over their own affairs on reservations through their tribal governments, or councils. In most tribes these governing bodies are elected by all the people, and in some the councils decide on courses of action by unanimous, rather than majority, agreement.

The tribal council, in turn, may choose tribal members to be on committees that decide resource use or manage tribal law and order, health, welfare, education, and culture. Most committee members serve three-year terms.

Federal and State Laws

When one adds to tribal governance the plenary power of the United States Congress and state laws and regulations, the picture becomes complex indeed. Over the years the federal government's exercise of plenary power has varied in scope and intensity, and federal policies and laws affecting Indian activities have changed according to the political and social situations of the time.

During the early days, state laws and regulations had little effect within the boundaries of Indian reservations, but as Congress allowed non-Indian settlement on reservations, state laws began to be factors to consider. Today, there are no rigid rules to determine whether a particular state law may be applied to an Indian reservation or to tribal members. However, the assertion of state regulatory authority over Indian activities can be pre-empted by the federal government's broader powers.

The Court System

The courts that have jurisdiction over activities in Indian country are divided among tribal, state, and federal authorities. A court's jurisdiction in any particular situation depends on what issue is at stake, where an action takes place, and who is involved.

Tribal courts are created by their tribal governments and obtain their jurisdiction and structure from the tribe, whose laws apply to non-Indians to the extent that those laws regulate hunting, fishing, zoning, and land use within the reservation. However, the U. S. Supreme Court has ruled that non-Indians are not subject to tribal criminal laws. Tribal police are generally deputized by both tribal and local police agencies and coordinate with county and state agencies.

ECONOMIC DEVELOPMENT

Indians in Oregon earn their livings in as many different ways as non-Indians, engaging in the full range of trades, professions, and occupations. Many Oregon Indians have overcome enormous social and economic hurdles to adapt to the larger society. Some maintain high positions in government agencies and private industry and take part in many ways in the life of their community, county, and state. Others remain adrift between the two cultures, seeking to participate in the mainstream without forfeiting their own cultural values.

The Role of Indian Values

Change and economic success in the mainstream society have been inhibited by a number of Indian cultural values:

- The concept of generosity and sharing—whatever Indian people have, they share.
- The extreme importance of family, which extends two or three generations and includes aunts, uncles, cousins, and other significant individuals.
- The belief that children should participate in adult activities.
- The belief that the kin group, or extended family, is responsible for childrearing.
- The tradition of respecting elders for their wisdom, age, and experience.
- The belief that cooperation is necessary for family survival and that the basic worth of any individual is judged in terms of family and tribe.

The First Salmon ceremony is an important one for Oregon Indians and is held over the first catch of each species at any place where the salmon run is heavy. The ceremony consists of formal speeches extending greetings to and honoring the salmon. For the occasion, the salmon is prepared in a cermonial way. A Salmon Feast is held each spring at Celilio Falls and is open to the public.

The root of the bittersweet plant (known as *Piaxi*) is the first named at traditional Root Feast ceremonies. It is especially valued by the Indians of Warm Springs and has long been a staple in the diet of these Indians. The plant is usually found in dry rocky soil native to much of central Oregon. The Indians have always been careful not to overuse their natural food supply. Conservation measures are now being taken to increase the supply of bitteroot.

Other roots honored at the Root Feast are the *lu'ks* and the *xa'us*. Special people are selected to dig the roots. Prayers are offered, a bell is rung, and these individuals dig roots at the same time. The elders take several days to peel and prepare the roots. On Sunday, they are cooked, and worship dances are performed until dinner is ready.

The table is set and everyone stands to sing a song. A prayer song is offered and a blessing given. The food is eaten in a certain order: fish, deer, *piaxi*, *lu'ks*, *xa'us*, celery, moss, and fruit. The elected leader names the first food and the people take a bite of it. The leader continues to name all the foods in order until a bite of each has been eaten. The leader then says "cuus" and everybody sips holy water. After that, people may help themselves to whatever food they wish to eat.

Teryl Florendo is one of the Unity Dancers from the Warm Springs Reservation. She performed at the 1991 Salmon Festival at Oxbow Park along the Sandy River east of Portland.

- The practice of basing relationships on equality and mutual respect, of recognizing individual differences.
- The importance of land, which gives the Indians their identity and religion.
- The belief that land is not to be sold or owned but used by all.
- The view that nature is a part of life.
- The tendency to live in the present; to view time as the passing of mornings, nights, days, moons, or seasons; and to believe that the time to begin is whenever people are ready—when everyone arrives.
- The belief that tradition is important, even in the here and now.
- The tendency to judge people by their actions, not their words.

These values are inconsistent with the values of competition, hierachy, material success, and achievement that the white society tends to hold.

BARRIERS TO ECONOMIC DEVELOPMENT

For the Indian tribes of Oregon, there are other barriers to economic development: commercial resources are quite limited; the distances from major population centers often increase transportation costs; energy is expensive; roads are often bad; and sanitation facilities, energy services, and electrical power are often inadequate. In addition, limited fire protection adds to insurance costs, and local investment capital may not be available. Moreover, some of Oregon's reservations do not have enough land to permit development.

While one major strength of the reservation is the availability of a labor force, most workers there have low-level job skills and little formal education. Traditionally, Indians have not learned business skills, are inexperienced in management, know little about marketing, and tend to be unrealistic in their planning—all of which contribute to Indian business failures.

Despite these impediments, the vitality of reservation economies has increased. Individual reservations have taken over management of many of their own programs, and several reservation enterprises are operating successfully. The strongest resources remain timber, water, land and—especially—people. As the reservations create healthy, growing economies, the benefits extend as well into the non-reservation areas that surround them.

The Tribes and Economic Development

Today the nine federally recognized Oregon Indian tribes or confederations are establishing their own businesses to improve their economies and to provide jobs for tribal members.

Confederated Tribes of Warm Springs. Warm Springs, with a tribal enrollment of 3,364 and a reservation of 641,035 acres, is probably the leader in developing its own tribal enterprises. The tribes built Kah-Nee-Tah resort in a scenic valley on the Warm Springs River, on land they had previously lost but repurchased. Originally, Kah-Nee-Tah Village consisted of eight Indian teepees for overnight camping and four motel units. In 1967 the tribes also purchased a sawmill on the Warm Springs River, built a plywood plant, and began to process timber cut from the reservation. In 1972

a modern convention center, Kah-Nee-Tah Lodge, was opened on a hill above the original "village." And in 1977 the Warm Springs Indians completed a new power plant that generated electricity for the sawmill and added monies from the sale of surplus power. Later, a home-building corporation was set up to provide good housing for tribal members and a community center was built in the town of Warm Springs, along with a garage and automotive repair shop.

Six years ago a new venture, the Warm Springs Clothing Company, was opened on a contract basis to produce sports clothes. In the spring of 1991, this company began to develop its own designs, as well as continuing to manufacture sportwear. The designs, which are found on sweatshirts and coats, feature Indian beadwork. The coats include denim and Pendleton wool creations, which sell for $120 to $900.

These activities have generated jobs, produced income for tribal members, enhanced pride, and inspired other tribes to work to determine their own futures.

Confederated Tribes of the Umatilla Reservation. The Confederated Tribes of the Umatilla Reservation own approximately 20,000 acres and have a tribal enrollment of 1,425 members. However, a total of 157,982 acres is included in the reservation, which resembles a checkerboard of Indian and non-Indian ownership and includes a non-Indian population of approximately 2,000.

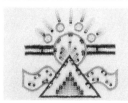

The Warm Springs Clothing Company, a venture begun six years ago on the Warm Springs Reservation, offers a handsome line of fashions designed by Bernyce Courtney (right). The company offers three clothing lines— "Tradition," "Spirit," and "Legend." All feature traditional or original beadwork designs.

Until recently, the Umatilla had some difficulty developing enterprises for their tribe. In the 1970s they had no tribal economic structure, and neither per-capita payments nor revenue from timber sales was reinvested with the idea of developing a self-sufficient economy. Sadly, the money left the reservation, never to return.

Today the Umatilla can boast an economist, an updated economic development program, and a capital improvement program. In addtion, they have several tribally owned enterprises. One—the Indian Lake Campground—was developed late in 1960 and covers about 42 acres. Another—a Bingo parlor—is open one night a week. The Umatilla lease a grain elevator to Pendleton Flour Mill and realize some income from wheat acreage and grazing. They also lease Mission Market, a small convenience store and gas pump. The Confederated Tribes also act as a holding company to purchase land and re-lease it and have acquired 159 acres to relocate a pheasant farm for the 1000 Hills Chukar Farm. Other projects include a museum gift shop, a hunting enterprise, and an interpretive center on the reservation for the 1993 Oregon Trail celebration. The tribe has also purchased and improved the Link Trailer Court.

The Burns Paiute Reservation. The Burns Paiute Reservation includes 11,786 acres and a tribal enrollment of 356. In 1976 the Paiutes implemented a Home Construction Program and in 1977 built a community center. Because of the reservation's remote desert location, economic development has been a major source of frustration to the tribe, which has found the cost of shipping, the isolation, and the lack of local customers for its products to be barriers impossible to overcome.

Now the tribe is contracting with the Department of Defense to distribute French fries and is assessing the feasibility of opening a Bingo parlor that could produce revenue for tribal purposes.

The Confederated Tribes of Grand Ronde. The Confederated Tribes of Grand Ronde have 9,811 acres and a tribal enrollment of 2,943. Each year they net about $3 million from timber sales on the reservation. Individual Grand Ronde Indians own a variety of small businesses, and the tribes are hiring an economic development specialist and organizing an economic development plan. The Spirit Development Company runs the tribal businesses, which include metal fabrication, electronics, and special forest products (floral greens, botanical products, and Christmas greens, which are shipped across the country and overseas. The tribes are also working with Oregon State University on a tourism master plan.

The Confederated Tribes of Siletz. The Confederated Tribes of Siletz have a total acreage of 3,666 and a tribal enrollment of 2,111. The Siletz Tribal Council has set up the Siletz Economic Development Commission, which has responsibility for making money for the tribe, as well as developing job opportunities. The Siletz also have several tribal businesses, including a Timber Market Organization that brings in revenues of about $2 million per year; their Evergreen enterprise, which distributes minor forest products such as moss, salal, ferns, Oregon grape roots, and herbs; rental property; and a Bingo parlor. Another enterprise, the Siletz Tribal Smokehouse, produces smoked salmon,

In the Umatilla basin, dipnet salmon fishing is again open to tribal members, thanks in part to a fish restoration program undertaken by the Confederated Tribes. In addition to affording tribal members the opportunity to fish as their ancestors did, efforts to restore salmon runs are vital to the ecological and economic well-being of the region.

black cod, shrimp, and other seafood.

Other Tribes. The **Klamath Tribe** has an enrollment of 2,688, employs an economic developer, and is preparing an economic self-sufficiency plan.

The **Cow Creek Band of Umpquas** has an enrollment of 806 and has purchased 29 acres of commercial property on Interstate 5, with plans for commercial development of an adjacent 17 acres. The tribe, which has been restored, also has a detailed five-year business plan.

The **Confederated Tribes of Coos, Lower Umpqua, and Siuslaw**, with a 464-person enrollment and 6.1 acres, have contracted for technical assistance and research to determine the feasibility of establishing a Wood Pellet Mill. The Confederated Tribes also have plans to restore their reservation.

The **Coquille Tribe** has an enrollment of 630 and is working on an economic plan.

Joe Coburn, a Klamath Indian, heads a program at the Northwest Regional Educational Laboratory in Portland that seeks to improve Indian education. Coburn and his staff cooperated with 16 Northwest tribes to develop a series of readers featuring authentic Indian stories and legends from the region. The series and accompanying workshops for teachers have proven extremely popular. Coburn, a former tribal chair, continues to play an active part in Klamath tribal affairs, while maintaining his professional activities at NWREL.

URBAN INDIANS

Many Indians, of course, have left the reservation, and in so doing have faced a very special set of problems. Some were moved by the government and left without resources to draw on.

Transition to urban life puts a strain on individuals with a traditional Indian heritage, plunging them into other cultures and environments where they may not even know their next door neighbors. Urban Indians have a sense of losing "who they are" and seek to hang on to their Indian identity, while attempting to adjust to a different and often frightening way of life. They encounter a physical environment, social organization, impersonal behavior, attitudes, and values that are foreign to them. The sense of an Indian community, with extended family and elders who pass traditions on to their children and grandchildren, is usually disrupted or undermined.

Alcohol is the main social and medical problem of the Indian population. In Oregon, one out of nine Indians dies as a result of alcoholism. The Native American Rehabilitation Association (NARA) is successfully using elements from traditional Indian culture as the basis for a treatment program.

Why People Leave the Reservations

Many factors are involved in an Indian's decision to migrate from the reservation or to return. The advantages of living on the reservation include the opportunity to serve in a decision-making capacity, to be selected as a member of the tribal council, and to live among tribal members. There, the extended family provides security, traditions are passed on to new generations, and natural resources such as wood, game, fish, roots, and berries are often available. In addition, housing and health-care services are usually provided and there are no property taxes. Individual freedom and respect for others are paramount.

However, reservation life has its disadvantages, one of the most important being poverty, economic depression, and unemployment. Moreover, the reservation is a close-knit community, where everybody knows everybody's business, privacy scarcely exists, and some complain that certain tribal leaders practice nepotism or show favoritism.

For young people, reservations lack excitement and recreational activities, and alcoholism and suicide rates among young tribal members are high. Unfortunately, city life doesn't solve the latter problem, because in urban areas those who seek alcohol and drugs find them in abundance.

For some, however, the city provides a way to avoid disadvantages temporarily imposed by reservation or rural living, offers a good standard of material comfort, and affords access to commercial entertainment, including professional sports. Although jobs are hard to find, they promise the chance of "a future" and make Social Security possible.

Those who leave the reservation often seem to be younger and better educated than those who stay. Those who return to the reservation usually come from depressed circumstances and give housing, rather than lack of employment, as their reason for moving back.

Adjusting to Urban Life

For many, adjustment to the urban world is made by seeking out fellow Indians and relying on one another. This may mean that older people improve their housing prospects by living with young relatives or that friends develop elaborate systems for sharing goods, services, and emotional support.

However, urban Indians have limited means of communicating with one another and of making their needs and demands heard by non-Indian society. The result for all too many is dependence on alcohol—the Oregon Indian's main social and medical problem, which in the 15- to 44-year age range, results in a death rate 12 times that of any other race.

Urban Indians are also keenly aware of the need to maintain their culture and find numerous ways to do so. Trips back to the reservation and to powwows and other ceremonies are common,

Opposite. *Liz Cross, curator for the Middle Oregon Indian Historical Society, is surrounded by artifacts that form the core collection for the new museum on the Warm Springs Reservation. A special feature of the museum is interpretation of the Indian culture from a tribal perspective.*

Urban Indians are keenly aware of the need to maintain their culture. One way to do so is by attending powwows and other traditional ceremonies.

and though 89 percent of Oregon's Indian population is found in urban areas, many see city living as a temporary condition and long to return to their reservations and families.

Of course, not all urban Indians want to return to the reservation. Many, especially those who migrated to the city in the 1950s and 1960s, have little or no inclination to return. They are stable in their jobs or professions and are often leaders in their fields. They represent the "successful" Indian in a modern world. However, many of them keep their ties to their Indian heritage through attendance at powwows and committee meetings, service on various boards, and participation in one or more Indian organizations.

Dwindling Urban Programs for Indians

Today the Indian population is less likely than other urban groups to have social programs to assist them. Two of Portland's best—the Urban Indian Council and an Urban Indian Center, both offered by the City— were forced by financial problems and internal disagreements to disband. Both agencies helped Indians find employment; offered increased educational opportunities to Indian students; and provided special services to elders, as well as emergency help, counseling, Indian health, and other programs. When the organizations went out of business, they left a significant void in social services that was felt throughout the Indian population.

The newly organized American Indian Association of Portland (AIAP) is trying to help fill this void. While recognizing that Indians' trust and loyalty are not won easily, AIAP has begun to serve as a vehicle through which diverse groups can acquire information, coordinate their efforts, communicate, and become advocates for social, cultural, and economic improvement. The AIAP board represents a number of Indian organizations, as well as the community-at-large, and keeps abreast of local issues, needs, and resources. The organization publishes a semi-monthly newsletter, *Portland American Indian Community*, and an information and referral publication, *Portland American Indian Community Resource Directory*, as well as maintaining a speakers' bureau and acting as a liaison with the Portland community.

Social service needs are addressed through a variety of resources in Oregon towns and cities. In the state's largest city, the Portland Indian Health Clinic offers a limited health-care program for the family, acute and long-term care, disease prevention/health promotion, and mental health services; the White Buffalo Center for Homeless and Runaway Indian Youth is a drop-in center for young people on the streets; and the Bow and Arrow Club provides a vehicle for Indians in the area to participate in cultural activities. Other agencies like these are located throughout Oregon.

The Northwest Indian Child Welfare Association, incorporated in 1987, serves Idaho, Oregon, and Washington and promotes the well-being of Indian children and families. It does so in part by placing Indian children in Indian homes.

CONCLUSION

The world of Oregon Indians today is extremely complex and, for many, thoroughly "modern"—facts that are rarely appreciated by the larger population. Yet for the state's Native American population as a whole, the ancient lifeways, traditions, and values provide a source of inspiration and point the way to a stronger, more self-assured future.

9

SPEAKING FOR THE TRIBES

BY ROCHELLE CASHDAN

*"We have listened to all you have to say, and we desire you to listen
when any Indian speaks."*

—PEOPEOMOXMOX [1855], WALLA WALLA CHIEF

*"They came through council, and it was discussed through council, and
it will finish through council—or it will not finish."*

—BILL BRAINARD [1978], COOS, LOWER UMPQUA, AND SIUSLAW

Indian-style diplomacy is alive and well in Oregon. The tribes maintain a presence at the Oregon Commission on Indian Services in Salem, federal hearings in Oregon and Washington, D.C., intertribal meetings, and other important settings. These diplomats, who live in both the tribal world and the world surrounding it, must understand well, listen well, speak well.

Oregon Indian speakers are following a wellworn path. Like the Iroquois speaker Kiosaton, who spoke for his tribe in 1645 ("Give ear—I am the mouth of my nation"), a representative of a Northwest tribe today may still need to explain that he is the official voice of his council. Like Peopeomoxmox, a woman representing her tribe may find herself explaining that tribal government is like any other government. Although tribes now use English as their common political language, the purpose, theme, and even style of formal statements are not necessarily different from those of statements that were interpreted at Champoeg, Oregon, in the mid-nineteenth century.

A tribe, like any other organization, may find its members do not agree. Yet the idea of the council as sovereign—as being the voice of its tribe—is basic. A council's membership may change, but not its authority. On official matters, the council speaks for the tribe.

In this spirit, each tribe sends to the commission or other body an instructed member—whether its chairman or a member of the council or staff. This practice is reminiscent of one that anthropologist David French has reported for Indians along the Columbia River—expressing the headman's speech to strangers through a delegated speaker.

As diplomats, tribal spokespeople often sit and listen when it is more appropriate to take information back to the tribe than to express a position. When tribal spokespeople make a statement, they carry on a tradition of morally infused political speech that depends on recognizing situations fraught with danger.

Because of differences in reservation and urban Indian lifestyles,

As in earlier days, committee members on the Burns Paiute Reservation sit in a circle as they consider matters affecting the tribe.

speaking styles, and authority, Indian spokespeople have many ways of speaking. Some have distinctive accents; more sound like their mainstream neighbors. Nevertheless, common patterns exist—in the hospitable acts and greetings they use, in their way of expressing consensus, in their patterns of turn taking and repetition, in the use of a joke.

In light of their history, Indians are masters of the rhetoric of separateness—the language of drawing a line between "you" and "us." A running theme expressed by Indian speakers is the difference between superior force and superior morality. As a nineteenth-century member of the Klamath Tribe said to an armed federal soldier who called him a son of a bitch, "I am not a dog. Speak to me as a man." His remark also shows the concrete way an Indian speaker is likely to express what others might generalize.

Speakers for tribal councils take the act of speaking seriously. A young member of the Siletz Tribe expressed his admiration for the competence of a former Commission on Indian Services chairman, saying, "He has the experience of talking to Indians and non-

Charles "Pete" Hayes, chairman of the Nez Perce Tribe, listening to speakers at a Columbia River Inter-Tribal Fish Commission (CRITFC) meeting. CRITFC is the technical fisheries agency for the Nez Perce, Warm Springs, Umatilla, and Yakima tribes.

Indians, important people and "'low' people." The man who made that comment added that sometimes he himself had spoken without knowing what was in him until the moment. He said that at such times, part of what he said came from his mother, part from his father, and part from their mothers and fathers—a concrete expression of the sense of being one in a long line before and to come.

Non-Indians listening to Indian speakers may notice differences in the way the talk is structured. Although English is now the language of Oregon tribal politics, traditional features of arrangement and style persist when Indian people speak in public. For instance, out of respect, a speaker may express the same idea in several ways to accommodate the diversity of words used by members of the community.

Although nowadays a person may bring a tape recorder to a meeting, talking so that people remember is still part of being Indian. In the days before writing, of course, exact reporting was vital. Even now, traditional speakers may use pointer phrases to highlight each new section of a statement. An occasional formulaic phrase like "Open our ears" is deliberately brought to bear to remind people of continuity. The still relevant art of expressing or evoking consensus rests on careful listening, precision, and political savvy.

When making an authoritative statement, older speakers may use the phrase, "I think." The speaker uses "I think" to mean both "here comes my next point" and "take this seriously"—defining the type of statement and cuing the memory. An Indian speaker may also want to emphasize differences between his own position and that of an outsider—using the same organization but inserting his own terms and ideas for the ones expressed earlier.

Indians are experts at uncovering assumptions in non-Indian words and at drawing analogies. On the radio a Sioux woman explained her religion by saying, "The eagle is our Bible." At the Commission on Indian Services, another woman noted that "putting a building over our burials would be like building a McDonald's over a churchyard." Her mixed audience responded with quiet laughter and comprehension. A joke like this shows a keen awareness of audience and, like much humor, captures the listeners' emotions and intellects with a single cast.

Indians notice details of speech. Most speakers use short words sprinkled with many-syllabled government jargon. But when one Indian considered another's views as not being Indian

A commission member prays at the opening of a Commission on Indian Services meeting in the 1980s:

Grandfather,
Great Spirit,
We ask you to help us today
As people come before us and tell us
What they are trying to do for the people.
We are here to help people,
Grandfather.
We ask you to give us the knowledge to do this.
Open our ears, Grandfather,
So that we can hear what is said.
We ask you for that power.
We pray for all the people that are on the streets,
Grandfather,
And that are having a hard time.
Help them.
Help the people that are in the hospitals
And that are locked up in the prisons.
Give them the power and the strength to carry on.
Then we ask you for the powers
from the four directions to guide us. Amen.
  —Used by permission of Clayton Schultz, Klamath

enough, he said that speaker used "too many long words—too many *uhs* and *huhs*."

With Indians making up only a small fraction of the Oregon population, speakers keep needing to educate non-Indian people—especially about the sovereignty of the tribes. Their tribal diplomats have to continue to be persistent and well prepared.

Times change, and today, although some Indian families maintain their native languages, most don't. But a tribe outlasts its language. The distinctive words and grammar may disappear, the texture of tribal life may change, but the native speakers' descendants live. Using English, speakers for the tribes continue to talk politics and shape their futures, speaking on themes the great tribal spokesmen of the past would recognize.

"Open our ears," said Meninock in 1915 in a court on the other side of the Columbia. "Open our ears," said Clayton Schultz of the Klamath in a prayer at a Commission meeting in the 1980s. Both men used a traditional phrase and a meaningful one, reminding people to look inward as well as outward in solving problems.

Another day, another meeting.

The people continue to speak.

This essay is dedicated to the memory of commission members Arthur Bensell, Lewis Alexander, and Larry Calica.

Recovering Lost Heritage

In 1988 the Oregon Council for the Humanities invited the state's federally recognized tribes and tribal confederations to propose research projects that would help them recover their people's heritage. In response, some tribes decided to revive ancient languages, while others gathered oral histories from tribal elders, used photographs and videotape to record important data, found rich sources of information in faraway archives, or captured their stories in ways that could be shared with others.

The essays on the following pages touch on each group's history and most describe the projects that were undertaken to recapture it. Each writer or pair of writers has taken an individual approach to the task at hand. Some have focused primarily on the tribe's heritage-recovery projects, discussing only enough history to make clear the reason the project was undertaken. Others have taken the opposite approach.

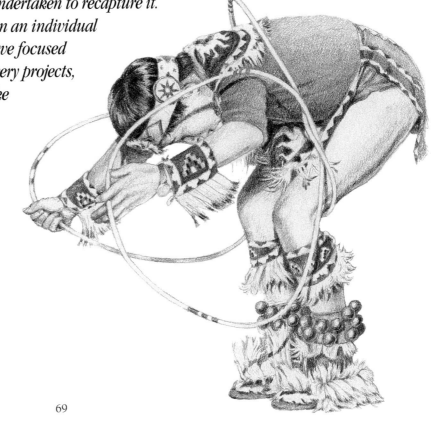

The tribes' efforts and those of the writers do much to enrich the historical record.

This is one of the earliest known photographs of the Burns Paiute people.
Paiute Chief Captain Louey appears in the right foreground.

10

THE END OF A WAY OF LIFE:
THE BURNS PAIUTE INDIAN TRIBE

BY MINERVA T. SOUCIE

*The "Wada Tika" band of Paiute Indians, known today as the Burns Paiute Tribe,
is descended from an ancient band of Paiutes that once roamed the length and breadth of
central and southeastern Oregon in search of food to sustain its members throughout the year.
The traditional lifeway of the Paiutes is described in detail in "The Great Basin" (page 21).
Suffice it here to say that for the Wada Tika, the nomadic life was vital to survival,
as each year their band covered great distances to gather food and to visit and trade
with other Paiute bands or with the Klamath, Modoc, or Umatilla.*

THE FIRST CONTACTS WITH NON-INDIANS

The Wada Tikas' first contact with non-Indians occurred when fur trappers came into the Harney Valley in search of beavers. At first, the Indian people avoided the foreigners, but soon they became anxious, as more and more of the strangers appeared in the country the Paiutes had always regarded as their own. At first, the Indians encountered the intruders during their food-gathering travels, but before long they found that their camas fields had been fenced off by the new Harney Valley cattle barons and their traditional way of life was being threatened.

THE QUESTION OF LAND

By the 1860s the Indian people knew that they and the government must try to reach some agreement about the land. With more settlers moving into the country and the military roaming the hills, the leaders knew that they had to make some decisions so that their people could have a place where they would feel safe. Among the Paiutes who negotiated for land were Egan, Oits, Gshanee, Ponee, Tashego, and Weyou wewa.

The bands wanted an area where they could still maintain the old gathering and hunting ways, but the settlers pressured the government to give their cattle more room to graze. On September 12, 1872, by executive order, President Grant established the 1.8 million-acre Malheur Reservation and most of the Paiutes were encouraged to move onto it and start to live like civilized people. The children started school and the men began farming or learning carpentry skills.

However, the boundaries of the new reservation had scarcely been set when they were changed, reducing even more the territory where the Paiutes could roam freely. Those first changes took place between 1872 and 1876 in response to pressure from settlers, who wanted use of the reservation's grazing land. Later, when gold was discovered in the northern portion of the boundary, the reservation was again reconfigured.

After the Bannock War, the Burns Paiute people were rounded up and forcibly sent to Fort Simcoe in Washington. The Officers' Quarters are shown here. During the Paiutes' exile at the fort, their Malheur Reservation was returned to public domain because no Indians were living on it.

LIFE ON THE RESERVATION

Life on the reservation was far from happy, for it put an end to the Paiutes' traditional lifeway. Some of the leaders were dissatisfied because their people were not allowed to wander outside the boundaries of the reservation to hunt and gather food. Oits, a medicine man, was also angered by the inconsistent treatment of his people by various Indian agents. Those agents and the military watched Oits closely because they didn't like his influence with the Paiutes and thought that while he was doctoring his people, he was trying to recruit some of them to go to war against the whites.

When the Bannocks came to the Paiutes and sought their help to rid the land of these newcomers, dissension was already affecting different members of the tribe, and it was easy for them to be persuaded. The Bannocks had decided to act in the belief that if they took action, life would return to normal.

THE BANNOCK WAR

Although most Paiutes did not participate in the Bannock War of 1878, they suffered from it. Many were killed in their sleep or attacked by troops in their camps, innocent women and children were captured and tortured, women were raped by the soldiers, and men were killed or tortured.

During the winter of 1879, the Paiutes' leaders surrendered after one of their number (Egan) was beheaded by Umatillas, who—along with Warm Springs scouts—had been hired to help the U. S. Cavalry. Ironically, Egan had been on his way to ask the Umatillas for help, because the Paiutes had regarded them as friends. To prove that Egan was dead, a Umatilla cut off his head and delivered it to the cavalry in a burlap sack.

News of the death brought the Bannock War to an early end. Though the war had been started by the Bannocks, the Paiute people suffered the greatest losses.

REMOVAL FROM THE RESERVATION

At war's end, the Paiutes were rounded up like cattle and moved to Fort Simcoe, Washington—a journey that killed many. The men walked two by two in iron shackles; the women and children rode in wagons. Babies were born and died on the trail, while old people froze before they reached the Columbia River.

This was the outcome of the Bannock War for the Wada Tika. Those who survived spent many years in Washington, where they were treated badly by the Yakima Indians. Subsequently, many of the Paiutes escaped and made their way back to the Harney Valley, enduring many hardships to reach their homeland.

A PEOPLE WITHOUT A HOME

In 1883, while the Paiutes were still at Fort Simcoe or at Fort Vancouver, where some like Oits were moved, the government returned their Harney Valley reservation to the public domain, giving as one of their reasons the fact that "there weren't any Indians living on the Reservation." However, even before the land was opened to public use, settlers were running cattle and homesteading within reservation boundaries.

The 1887 Allotment Act gave a few Paiutes land in the Harney Valley, but the poor soil could not support farming. During the 1920s, when the Paiutes lived in dire poverty, Father Huel (upper left) spoke to government officials on the Indians' behalf and secured donations of land and tents to ease their plight. Altar boys Tony Beers and Chester Beers were the author's uncles. To help support their families, many Paiute women worked as washer women in the town of Burns.

In 1887, at Fort Simcoe, the Paiutes were asked if they wanted to return to Harney County. Many, being suspicious, opted to remain where they were—or to go onto other reservations such as Warm Springs, Fort McDermitt, and Owyhee in Nevada. Oits was one who went to live at Warm Springs.

Many others moved to Duck Valley and settled in the area of Miller Creek. Of the remaining Paiutes, each head of household received 160 acres, in what was known as the 1887 Allotment Act. In all, 115 Paiutes were given land on which to live and grow their food.

The soil, however, was alkali, and the land was covered with sage and scrub brush. Without any water for irrigation, farming on it was bound to fail. As a result, many Paiutes hired on as ranch hands and as washer women in the town of Burns. People who did not have homes on the allotments lived outside Burns in makeshift tents alongside the city dump. Plagued by poor conditions, without a land to roam on, and living with people who looked down on them, the Paiutes felt hopeless.

HELP FROM AN UNEXPECTED SOURCE

A Catholic priest, Father Huel, became interested in the Paiutes' plight and agreed to speak on their behalf to government agents at Warm Springs. The Paiutes regarded him as their friend and rightly so. One result of his intervention was the donation of army tents and a total of 10 acres in 1925. The previous year, the Paiutes had been included in the Indian Citizenship Act, which had given them

status as American citizens. Soon homes were built and a school was erected at the "Old Camp"—the area into which many of the Paiutes had gone from the allotments.

In 1935 the Paiutes finally were moved to a more permanent home, the "New Village." This 771-acre area had been purchased from the Brown Land and Title Company by the federal government and held in trust for the Paiutes by the Bureau of Indian Affairs. The tribe also adopted the Indian Reorganization Act and created a business committee consisting of five members who met and considered issues of concern to the tribe. However, title to the land was not received from Congress until 1972, making it difficult to obtain mortgages and to finance development projects.

During this time, many of the Indians still worked for ranchers and some got jobs with sawmills. Others piled brush for the U. S. Forest Service, and some women still washed clothes for families in Burns. These women went home at night and sewed buckskin gloves by the light of kerosene lamps, to trade for groceries the next day. For most of them, life had begun to improve.

WORLD WAR II AND ITS AFTERMATH

During World War II several Paiute men enlisted in the army and fought in lands they had never heard of: Germany, Africa, the Philippines, Japan, and France. Many Paiutes came back from the war highly decorated.

Meanwhile, Indian children at home were still not allowed into

Despite repeated attempts to eradicate their traditional lifeways, vestiges remained. Although rifles replaced earlier weapons, some Paiutes continued to hunt and trap. In the 1940s, Ada Smoke Capps (center) was photographed tanning buckskins. In a scene from The Earth Is Our Home, *Nepa Kennedy demonstrates how she makes chokeberry cakes in the old way.*

the Harney County Public Schools because, authorities reasoned, they had eye disease and were not healthy. It was not until 1948 that Indian children were allowed in the schools.

When the Korean War broke out, some Indian men were again at the front of the enlistment line. Paiutes were also sent to cities like Los Angeles under the Relocation Act of 1953. There, Indians who didn't have plumbing or electricity at home in Harney County became secretaries, factory workers, welders, and plumbers.

In 1968 the Paiutes finally were fully recognized by the Bureau of Indian Affairs when they adopted the tribal constitution and bylaws. However, they still didn't own the land they lived on. On October 13, 1972 the Burns Paiute Tribe finally acquired title to its 771 acres and the reservation was created. Although this was a fraction of the land they once called theirs, it was at last and once again their home.

Today, the tribe is engaged in various economic development efforts, described on page 63 of this publication.

THE TRIBAL RESEARCH PROJECT

The Burns Paiute people have felt a strong need to recover a tribal identity that was displaced as a result of their ancestors' forced relocation in 1878 and 57 years of governmental delay in ratifying their reservation authority. Despite the fact that the Burns Paiutes have the highest percentage of native speakers in Oregon and are the least intermarried with non-Indians, it is safe to say that we don't yet know our full history.

Since 1972 an effort has been made to call tribal people back to the area, and in 1980 a film about the lifeway of the Burns Paiutes, called *The Earth Is Our Home*, helped draw attention to ancient Paiute traditions. Now the goal of a new tribal research project is to recover a tribal identity and to recapture information about the tribe's history and culture, particularly for the period of displacement (1878 to 1935). To do this, the Culture and Heritage Committee and I are recording and videotaping the oral histories of the elders. Those working on the project are Connie Hawley, Lillian Maynard, and Betty Firstraid. Also assisting in the project is Marilyn Couture, the principal advisor for the film *The Earth Is Our Home*, for which I was a tribal advisor.

The methods used to recover tribal history involve videotaping oral histories of the elders, relating the oral responses to written records, retrieving historical photographs and records, researching and preparing an annotated bibliography, and organizing and editing transcriptions of oral material for the purposes of archiving and publication.

One early oral account concerns Captain Louey, a Burns Paiute chief, who was born at the muddy-dance place (Diamond Valley), lost his family when he was a boy, was subsequently captured by white soldiers in the course of fighting at Rock Fort (Barren Valley), and at a young age was made a scout for General Crook. In that capacity, Captain Louey was present during the Modoc War and offered the following eyewitness account, taken from an unpublished manuscript, "Notes on Paiute Ethnography," by Alfred Kroeber and W. L. Marsden (University of California, Berkeley). The account was probably recorded in the 1920s, shortly before Captain Louey died at approximately 100 years of age.

Captain Louey's Account:

In the early fall we were at Fort Bidwell and the stage was bringing us reports. The papers in Sacramento were saying that in three weeks many soldiers were going to come up. We heard that General Canby was going to come. They were also coming from the other side from Camp Warner to Fort Bidwell. Two companies of cavalry and two companies of infantry arrived with a cannon. Three days later a Captain Kisto came. He was talking to General Wheaton and said that we were going to go to the Modoc lava beds. Then the Lieutenant said that he was going too, and he liked to see that we had a cannon. Then we all had lain down, and General Wheaton had come and said to me, "We are both going to go, Louey Crook. The soldiers are coming from over yonder with ten of the Umatillas and fifty of the Warm Springs. You are going to meet them there. Donald McKay and Buck the Warm Springs' chief who is a very tall man will be there too." Eight companies of soldiers left the fort and marched from there to Yainax Agency where we camped. We went off in the morning and climbed up Modoc Mountain about a quarter of a mile. There were a lot of us there, and we stood there without moving when the captains told us to. While we stood there we were told to eat a few crackers and a slice of bacon with it. Then we climbed this good mountain peak nearby. General Wheaton, the Lieutenant, and Major Perry went with us on foot. Major Perry got his spyglass and looked down and stood looking for a long time. He said, 'I see the smoke. Yes, there are many white soldiers' tents.' Then we march quickly down into the valley. I could see about five miles with just my eyes, and looking there I could see many, many soldiers. Some captains were coming and saw us. One of the soldiers' captains took off his hat and beckoned to us with it. It was Captain Curry, and he told us where to pitch our tents. After we pitched our tents we lay down to rest. There were about five hundred soldiers from San Francisco and Sacramento. They were very good soldiers, very fine in appearance. There were five companies of soldiers plus sixty Warm Springs.

We could see the Modocs about one and a half to two miles away; with that field glass I could see women, boys, and girls; some just looking at the soldiers for a long time. They were piling up rocks to form a barricade as tall as a person. Captain Perry, General Wheaton, General Canby, the white men's leader, Thomas, and Olliver built a large cloth tent one mile away. After four days they called to Captain Jack, "Come! We are going to talk." General Canby gave tobacco to Captain Jack as he said, "Yes, you see that we are here." Captain Jack said, "Yes." Canby warned Captain Jack, "You had better be good people, because Washington tells you to be good." General Canby was a very large, tall man, and he said, "You had better be good people. I am telling you, but it is Washington's word that I am giving you. All of our people, all the way to the Atlantic coast in Washington are saying this to you. I am telling it to you, Captain Jack. It will be well after awhile. Washington is telling your people that you must not desire to make war. It is your Modoc people that these five hundred soldiers have come to see. Your men must not shoot at these soldiers, says Washington. Just pretend to

Burns Paiute Chief Captain Louey

have a battle and after awhile all will be good."

I Louey was there listening to that letter language that General Canby was talking, and Commissioner Thomas, Olliver, Meacham, and two white interpreters were there too. All of us were in the big cloth tent. Later we were lying in the soldiers' tent over there, and Canby came in. I wasn't with them at that time. They only had that white man interpreter, Shack-Nasty Jim, with them in the tent talking to Captain Jack. Captain Jack was saying that he didn't like these soldiers, and he didn't like that Indian reservation. He didn't like them at all. He said, "I, Captain Jack, say this to you, General Canby: I am going to die here. I cannot go to the reservation. My people would not like that." General Canby said, "You are talking of bad things; I am talking of good things for you. I am going to give you blankets, cloth for houses, flour, coffee, sugar, things that you will like, crackers, and bacon. I am talking of good things." Captain Jack arose saying, "Not I! Indeed, not I!"

Then a man wearing a long coat for concealment came up close to the tent and went inside. The man came up close to where General Canby was sitting and shot him in the forehead. He also shot Commissioner

Thomas in the armpit and Meacham in the suboccipital depression. Olliver dropped to the ground and rolled out of the tent so the man's pistol shots didn't hit him. Then the man ran off towards the other side of the stream. They shot at him many times, but they didn't hit him. At that time I was at the packtrain packing those crackers on a mule about a half mile away when I heard the guns. The big cloth tent was about a mile from the Modocs' camp. There was no fighting for a day because General Canby had been killed.

Two days later the soldiers surrounded the rock fort, and there was a battle. Sixty of them and one of the soldiers were killed that day. After the sun set they shot the cannon into the sky, and when it came down again, the bomb shell burst, and it rent the rocks. For four nights almost until daylight they fired the cannon, and during the day they fought. Every day the soldiers were dying. They had made loopholes in the rocks and were shooting at the soldiers through them. The soldiers fired whenever they saw a face in the loophole; they shot them in the forehead. By this time the soldiers were so weary that they said they had had enough, and the captain allowed a rest of three days before the fight continued. I marched with the Warm Springs and fought in the afternoon. I was nearly killed then. I was shot through in the neck, in the inside of my thigh, in my body, and also in my shoulder blade. By that time the soldiers had killed many people, about five hundred in one day. I was running around with a pistol and shooting very well. . . .

We scouted the Modocs on horseback with General Wheaton. We were on the outside when the fighting began twelve miles away, and I fought with these soldiers. I killed two Modocs then and dragged them back to the camp. When the fighting ceased, nine of the Warm Springs were dead; and Sacramento Charley, the one with black whiskers, was also killed. Six hundred of the cavalry and fifty Warm Springs were engaged there, and many horses were killed. A Modoc without any clothes on came at me aiming his gun. I wasn't scared, and I whipped my horse and was able to hit him under the throat before he could shoot me. He fell, and I saw the blood that he vomited out as he died. He had dropped his gun, and I saw it lying over there. It was a very bad, old gun. Then the fighting stopped, and we were sitting there without fighting for a week.

The paymaster was paying money to the soldiers and the Warm Springs, and at that time I was paid sixty dollars. I was angry there. I went to Yainax, to Camp Warner, and to Chief Hutzihu's country very slyly. I got some good horses, the one marked with the white spots and Captain Jack's yellow mare with it. Two were good horses of the men of Captain Jack's Modocs. They were standing guard over them, and I trotted in there with my knife and cut them loose and drove them out to that rocky trail. I took them back to our camp to show them to the others. Then when the paymaster was giving the money to the Indians, General Wheaton said that he was going to give the horses to the Warm Springs chief for a present. I said no, that they were mine. General Wheaton said, "No, you are my soldier. Give them to the Warm Springs chief!" Then the sergeant gave them to him. I was very angry, and I took those two mares early in the morning. One of the mares died here on Scarface Charley's Ranch. It was the yellow mare, and she had two colts here before she died. That is why my horses continue to look like Modoc horses.

Author's Note: I learned the Paiutes' history as a little girl, when it was told to me by my grandmother's sister, Marion Smoke Louie, and my grandfather, George Beers. They talked about the old ways the Paiutes lived, the hard life on the Reservation, the Bannock War, and the way my ancestors were made to suffer.

11

CAPTURED HERITAGE: CONFEDERATED TRIBES OF COOS, LOWER UMPQUA, AND SIUSLAW INDIANS

BY STEPHEN DOW BECKHAM AND DONALD WHEREAT

In 1990 the Confederated Tribes of Coos, Lower Umpqua, and Siuslaw mounted a project,
funded by the Oregon Council for the Humanities, to try to recover their "captured heritage."
Their goals were to identify sources of tribal culture, history, and material culture and recover—
through photocopies, microfilm, or audio tapes—the legacy of their past.

The Confederated Tribes of Coos, Lower Umpqua, and Siuslaw regained federal recognition in 1984.
The tribes include some 460 members who live primarily in Coos, Douglas, and Lane counties.
The tribal reservation is 6.1 acres, taken into "trust" in 1941, and is the site of the community building
erected in 1942 and restored in the 1980s. The tribes maintain administrative offices in Coos Bay
and are presently at work on plans for a reservation and interpretive center.

VOICES FROM THE PAST

In many ways the federal programs of enforced "civilization" mounted by the Bureau of Indian Affairs succeeded. Over decades of forced cultural transformation, the BIA eradicated aboriginal languages and changed the lifeways of western Oregon's Indians. Fortunately, however, elders survived with a store of useful information about the past. The Confederated Tribes have identified those "voices" from their past and tracked the materials Indian informants shared with patient linguists and anthropologists who cared enough to spend part of their professional lives recording the information. That enterprise was one of mutual interest. The elders were eager to share and preserve; the scholars were committed to recording and, in some instances, to publishing the information.

The record is impressive. It includes dozens of hours of wax cylinder recordings of Coos, Lower Umpqua, and Siuslaw songs, oral literature, and language. It also includes extensive collections of basketry, a few pieces of clothing, and hundreds of pages of manuscript field notes on many aspects of traditional culture. This is "captured" material, however, for it is hundreds—sometimes thousands—of miles away in distant archives and museums. It is a legacy from the past largely unknown to present tribal members. It is the wisdom and ways of the ages stored in archive boxes, dusty notebooks, museum cases, and basement storage rooms. The materials once represented a thriving lifeway. Today they document what once was. The tongues of present tribal members no longer say the old words; their minds no longer calculate the numeral systems, the traditions, and the ancient lore. The tribal culture is held "captive" and in the hands of curators; few, if any, know what they have or care about its import.

This chapter traces the work of those whose research captured the traditions and heritage of the Confederated Tribes. It also honors the informants whose memories and language skills made the research possible.

INITIAL WORK, 1855-1884

Dr. John J. Milhau

Dr. John Milhau was one of the earliest to record information on the tribes. While fur trappers and explorers had noted the presence of the "Kakoosh" (Coos), "Ompqua" (Lower Umpqua), or the "Sayonstla" (Siuslaw), Milhau penned the first detailed accounts. Serving as U.S. Army surgeon at Fort Umpqua on the North Spit at the Umpqua's mouth in 1856-1857, Milhau was prodded to writing by George Gibbs. Gibbs was a linguist and ethnographer who chose

One of the earliest observers to record information about the Coos and Lower Umpqua Indians was U.S. Army surgeon Dr. John Milhau. He wrote his brief "Observations" in a letter to linguist George Gibbs from Fort Umpqua, where some of the Indians were imprisoned. Milhau made his notes in 1856 and 1857—at about the same time Vollum and Lorain photographed the post blockhouse.

Leo Joaquim Frachtenberg of Columbia University began his field work in western Oregon in 1909 and returned several times to work with Indian informants. His published work is a major contribution to our knowledge of coastal lifeways, language, and oral literature. He is shown here with his Indian wife, to whom he was married at Siletz.

the Pacific Northwest as his special field of study from 1849 to 1860 and developed a questionnaire, largely focused on language, which he dispatched to would-be assistants.

Milhau, an educated officer, was one who received Gibbs' questions and wrote descriptively about the Coos and Lower Umpqua. He discussed their population, impacts of recent outbreaks of illness, material culture, including canoe and house types, subsistence, dress, and a few elements of world view. His brief "Observations," a letter penned while the army held the Coos and Lower Umpqua imprisoned at Fort Umpqua, provides useful glimpses of the traditional culture. Milhau's letter is in the National Anthropological Archives of the Smithsonian Institution.

> They state that within the last twenty years, a great many have died all along the coast of the 'Doctor's sickness.' Their idea of the disease is that the medicine man or woman wishing to destroy an individual performs certain incantations, upon which a small insect with a very hard shell and numerous legs, penetrates into the vitals of the victim and feeding upon the tissues increases in size, while the sufferer loses all appetite, coughs, becomes emaciated & dies.

Bissell

A man of unknown origin named Bissell filed in 1881 a Lower Umpqua vocabulary with the Smithsonian Institution based on a word list developed by the first director of the Bureau of American Ethnology, John Wesley Powell. Presumably Bissell interviewed a Lower Umpqua Indians in western Oregon, but no further information is available.

J. Owen Dorsey

In 1884 J. Owen Dorsey worked at the Siletz Reservation to record linguistic and cultural information of the Indians of coastal Oregon. While most of his labors focused on the Athabaskan-speakers from Curry County, he met a Miluk-speaker of the Kusan (Coosan) language family who had lived on the lower Coquille River but been removed to the Siletz Reservation in 1856.

Dorsey recorded language identical to that spoken by the Miluks on lower Coos Bay and collected short vocabularies in Lower Umpqua and Siuslaw. Dorsey's papers, including lists of village sites by name, are in the National Anthropological Archives.

EARLY TWENTIETH-CENTURY LABORS, 1903-1922

Henry Hull St. Clair, Jr.

In 1903 Henry Hull St. Clair, Jr., collected oral literary materials from the Coos—probably from Jim Buchanan (a Coos man born in the 1840s) and Tom Hollis, both of whom he encountered while visiting the central Oregon coast. St. Clair's notes included such topics as the traditional Coos "naming feast," an event which occurred when an infant was five or more days old:

> First guests agreed on a name, which was submitted to the mother of the child for approval. The name being satisfactory to the mother, two men sitting on opposite ends of the group of guests, and appointed by the nearest relatives of the parents, called out in a loud voice the name given the child. Then the whole audience repeated it, and the ceremony was over.

Leo Joaquim Frachtenberg

During the summer of 1909 Leo Joaquim Frachtenberg (1883-1930) of Columbia University began his field work in western Oregon. He, like Henry Hull St. Clair, Jr., found Jim Buchanan an excellent informant. Buchanan then resided at Acme, a small community east of Florence on the Siuslaw River. When Frachtenberg prepared St. Clair's data and his own field notes for publication in 1913, he observed of Buchanan: "He is at the present time the only member of the Coos tribe who still remembers and can relate coherently some of the myths and traditions of the bygone generations." Frank Drew, a Coos who had an excellent command of English, assisted in the work. His familiarity with Miluk and Hanis languages was good, but so mixed that he was frequently unable to differentiate the two tongues. Frachtenberg depended primarily on Buchanan for information, while Drew assisted him as an interpreter.

Jim Buchanan had much to say. He laid out many elements of the traditional culture, a world which was intact during his childhood. Religious practices were a subject of considerable interest to Buchanan and he told Frachtenberg, for example, about traditional curing:

> The cure of a patient was very simple. The doctor, attired in his official garb, chanted powerful songs supposedly received from the spirits. He then applied his mouth to the sore spot of the patient's body and proceeded to extract the 'pain'—in accordance with the belief that the 'pain' was a small, animate object sent through the air by some hostile medicine-man. The standard of a doctor's efficiency was the number of his songs. The more songs he knew, the more powerful he was.

Buchanan had perfect command of the language and sufficient understanding of its structure to assist Frachtenberg in recording the nuances of Coos grammar and usage.

Frachtenberg returned to western Oregon and from March to May of 1911, while residing at Siletz, began work with Louisa Smith, a Lower Umpqua woman then over 70. Her age and illness made her a "poor, though willing informant," noted Frachtenberg. William Smith, her husband and an Alsea by birth, had, however, lived among the Siuslaw as a child and had secured a good knowledge of the language. "His services proved highly valuable," noted Frachtenberg. This scholar also worked with Spencer Scott, Louisa's son; Louis Smith, a Lower Umpqua; and Hank Johnson, a man of mixed Lower Umpqua and Alsea ancestry. Frachtenberg explained that these three younger men "were employed solely for the purpose of settling questions that pertained to phonetics" and in sorting out translations.

Frachtenberg's labors produced fairly extensive field notes on traditional lifeways, detailed data on language (his primary interest), and literary materials. In 1913 E. J. Brill, Ltd., of Leyden in The Netherlands published *Coos Texts*, a volume containing nine creation myths, ten miscellaneous tales, and a dozen additional tales obtained in 1903 by St. Clair. Frachtenberg provided interlinear translations of Coos and English and also gave complete English versions of each tale across the top of the page. The following year

(1914) Brill published *Lower Umpqua Texts and Notes on the Kusan Dialects*, another result of Frachtenberg's labors. This volume included seven creation myths, five miscellaneous tales, five narratives on traditional culture, and five fragmentary tales. Frachtenberg further provided vocabularies of Lower Umpqua-English and English-Lower Umpqua.

In 1922 Frachtenberg returned again to these studies with large contributions to Part 2 of the *Handbook of American Indian Languages*. He wrote 132 pages on the "Coos" and 196 pages on the "Siuslaw." Although Frachtenberg returned to Siletz to work in 1915 and 1916 and used a battery-powered recorder to prepare wax cylinders of his informants' speaking and singing, none of his surviving work includes material from the Coos, the Lower Umpqua, or the Siuslaw.

MAJOR FIELD WORK, 1932-1942

Melville Jacobs

In the 1930s Melville Jacobs (1902-1971), an accomplished linguist and anthropology professor at the University of Washington, sensed that the last Indian generation firmly grounded in the traditional culture of coastal Oregon and Washington was passing. Jacobs knew that in many instances ages-old languages were then remembered by but a handful, perhaps only a single informant. With desperation he rushed to record information—assisted by a series of small grants from Columbia University, where he, like Frachtenberg, had studied with Professor Franz Boas.

Working with Frank Drew as interpreter, Jacobs secured notes and made wax cylinder recordings of Jim Buchanan in 1932. Buchanan, the last survivor of the 1855 treaty council with Superintendent of Indian Affairs Joel Palmer, died June 18, 1933. The following year, Jacobs found an even more able tri-lingual Coos: Annie Miner Peterson. Born about 1860, Peterson spoke both Miluk and Hanis, as well as sufficient English to provide her own translations. Jacobs journeyed to Charleston at the mouth of Coos Bay and began a concentrated period of collecting the Miluk language. Although Hanis was then spoken by several Coos, Jacobs solicited textual materials from Peterson in that language as well.

Jacobs wrote a candid assessment of his informant:

> She spoke both Hanis and Miluk as a child, Miluk until about fifteen years of age, Hanis until twenty and frequently later. Her translations were rapid though hampered by broken and infelicitous crudity of English vocabulary and idiom; she learned most of her English when past twenty years of age.

Much taken with Mrs. Peterson, Jacobs concluded:

> A very great deal is owing her for her delightful cooperativeness, humor, intelligence, and her considerable sensitivity for language; no little of whatever good qualities of workmanship this recording may exhibit is due not only to her adroitness and clarity but to the pleasantness of working with her.

Part of the treasure preserved by Peterson and Jacobs includes hours of wax cylinder recordings. Annie Peterson participated fully in the traditional culture of her people, even in the terrible dislocation to Yachats, where she resided on the southern edge of the Siletz Reservation in the 1860s and early 1870s. Peterson, in fact, was probably the last Coos girl to go through the traditional puberty rites, a series of rituals of prescriptive behaviors which marked the onset of menstruation and adulthood. Peterson sang dozens of songs and confirmed her able memory. She recalled some 30 "dream-power" songs, the verses gained during "spirit quests" of tribal members at puberty and shared with the village upon the return from the vigil. Peterson also recalled the musical elements that punctuated or enhanced oral tales. She shifted from narrative voice to music in the recordings, singing the old songs the raconteurs employed when presenting oral literature during times past.

Peterson's command of the culture and its nuances was extensive. Jacobs' breadth of vision, interest, and ability to elicit responses were equally impressive. Their joint efforts led, in 1939, to the publication of *Coos Narrative and Ethnologic Texts*. This volume of Hanis-English and Miluk-English texts covered many elements of traditional culture. Peterson discussed, for example, "The Kind of Wife to Select," "Marriage Negotiations," "Children Had to Be Inside at Dusk," "Seeing a Person's Spirit Double," and other usages. She provided biographical sketches of a number of her contemporaries and revealing accounts of the impacts of settlement, dislocation, alcoholism, and rootlessness. The consequences of acculturation resounded clearly through her honest discussions of the lives of "Kitty Hayes" and "Cissy," as well as in her own autobiography.

The following year, Peterson and Jacobs produced *Coos Myth Texts*. In the preface to this volume, Jacobs explained part of the reason why his informant had such a store of knowledge:

> Mrs. Peterson pointed out to me that the reason she knew so many more stories than Mr. Drew, and could tell them as well as she did, was because she enjoyed going out with the older people when they went root digging, berrying, camping out; she liked to accompany the older people in all of their out of door activities, during the Yachats Reservation period of Coos life.

During those outings the elders passed the time recounting their oral literature. Peterson further explained that in former times the children were expected to repeat each tale line-by-line. In that way they got it correct. When an adult audience listened, only one person responded verbatim. This repetition of what the other person said was a conversational etiquette among the Coos. "The person spoken to usually if not always repeated verbatim what was said to him," Jacobs concluded.

Jacobs also worked with Frank Drew in October and November 1932 at Florence, Oregon. One of Drew's texts, "The World Fire," perhaps recounted the great forest fire that swept through Oregon's Coast Range in the 1840s prior to Drew's birth:

> One time long ago there came from the west, in the daytime, five gusts or layers of fire, from the ocean; they swept across the land. It seems as if the people knew just what to do to save themselves. Everything burned. One sheet of fire came east quickly. Seeing it coming the people all went into the river and mud flats, crawl-

Frank Drew (left) and Jim Buchanan (standing) were important Coos informants for several researchers. Drew acted primarily as an interpreter, while Buchanan provided information about a culture that had all but disappeared. Buchanan, the last survivor of the 1855 treaty council with Superintendent of Indian Affairs Joel Palmer, died in 1933. Also shown here is Eli Metcalf (right), who was half Coos-Coquille.

> ing into the wet mud and water until the sheet of fire had passed over them. Only the mud did not burn. Four more sheets of flame were evaded the very same way. The people had taken sealion paunches and put into them the infants that could not run. The people could not explain what made the fire come that way, but maybe it was to purify the earth.

Homer G. Barnett

During the summer of 1934, Homer G. Barnett worked at the Siletz Reservation to record "culture elements" from Indian informants from tribes the length of the Oregon seaboard. Working with a list of 1,901 "elements," Barnett solicited information on tools, basketry, house types, lifeways, political systems, and other aspects of traditional culture. Spencer Scott served as the Siuslaw informant, while Agnes Johnson was his Coos informant. The field studies resulted in *Oregon Coast: Culture Element Distributions, VII* (1937).

Annie Miner Peterson (born about 1860) spoke Miluk and Hanis, as well as English. Her invaluable work with linguist and anthropologist Melville Jacobs in the 1930s was preserved on wax cylinder recordings and in Coos Narrative and Ethnologic Texts *(published in 1939) and* Coos Myth Texts *(1940). Here, Jacobs is shown recording Peterson's testimony.*

Barnett's personal papers are today housed in the National Anthropological Archives of the Smithsonian.

John Peabody Harrington

Another anthropologist came to the members of the Confederated Tribes in 1942. John Peabody Harrington (1884-1961), field ethnographer for the Smithsonian Institution, was a true eccentric. Carobeth Laird, Harrington's ex-wife, wrote a biography of him in her old age and appropriately entitled it *Encounter with an Angry God.* The foreword to this book noted: "The Indians who worked with him appear to have regarded him with great affection and amused indulgence toward his idiosyncracies." Such was the case among his western Oregon informants. Marge (Drew) Severy, a tribal elder today, recalled that in 1942 Harrington boarded with her family while he worked with Frank Drew, her father. Each morning at dawn, Harrington waded through the mudflat to swim in the North Fork of the Siuslaw River. He said that this "Indian method of bathing" would preserve his health. The Drew family found this quite

strange; they never bathed in the river or waded around in the mud, except to dig clams!

Harrington worked with a number of informants. Notably he was able to interview Lottie (Jackson) Evanoff, a daughter of Old Jackson (Doloose) and a cousin of Annie Miner Peterson. Lottie and her Aleut husband, Alec Evanoff, seemed to enjoy the sessions and poured out a flood of data, much of it linguistic. Harrington also worked with several Coos informants: Martha Johnson at Florence; Annie Peterson's daughter, Nellie Assen, at Coos Bay; the Wasson sisters—Laura (Lollie), Nellie, and Daisy; and John Waters. Clayton Barrett, Howard Barrett, and Spencer Scott, who provided Siuslaw and Lower Umpqua language information.

Harrington pursued his favorite topic—ethnogeography—and elicited place names and meanings as he filled hundreds of pages of notes. Unlike the meticulous Jacobs, however, Harrington scrawled his notes across the page, sometimes entering only a few words or a line or two. And he appeared to obscure the identity of his informants. He wrote a cryptic "Lot" (for Lottie Evanoff) and other shorthand for his informants which, with the passage of time, almost persuaded scholars at the Smithsonian, the depository of his notes, that no identification would ever be possible. In the late 1970s Elaine Mills of the Smithsonian tried to ferret out who was whom. (In doing so, she worked with co-author Stephen Dow Beckham, because he knew a number of Harrington's informants, and was able to secure firm identifications for most.)

Harrington graduated from Stanford and carried out graduate study in 1905 and 1906 at the universities in Berlin and Leipzig. Harrington's fascination with language led him, like Jacobs, to record the voices of his informants. However, unlike Jacobs, Harrington made his recordings on aluminum cylinders. John Paul Marr, Harrington's assistant, probably did the actual recording. The 17 Coos language tapes, material transferred from the cylinders, are dated June 1941, suggesting that Marr preceded Harrington in a search for informants. The materials, dictated by Frank Drew, included data on religion, cosmology, vocabularies, and rehearings of linguistic information published by Frachtenberg on the Coos language in 1922. The cylinders and tapes are in the National Anthropological Archives of the Smithsonian Institution.

THE LAST FIELD WORK, 1950s AND 1960s

Morris Swadesh

The next scholar to study the tribal languages was Morris Swadesh (1909-1967), a specialist on Penutian linguistics, who worked along the Oregon coast in the summer of 1953. He collected 575 items or an hour of material from Martha Johnson in Hanis Coos; and about 50 minutes or 300 items from Lolly (Hotchkiss) Metcalf and Daisy (Wasson) Codding in the Miluk Coos language. The latter recordings he made at Charleston, Oregon; a foghorn and occasional buoy bell sound in the background as these aged informants talked with Swadesh in their childhood language. Swadesh also found three Siuslaw informants: May (Barrett) Elliot, Clayton Barrett, and Billy Dick. He led these people through a 200-word list and concentrated on pronunciations. Billy Dick, who lived at Winchester Bay, served as a Lower Umpqua informant and provided some song as well as textual material. The Swadesh tapes are held by the Archives of Traditional Music, Indiana University.

Dell and Virginia Hymes

In August 1954 linguists Dell and Virginia Hymes came to Florence, Oregon, to work with Billy Dick and the Barrett brothers on Siuslaw. Dell Hymes' field work led to the publication, "Some Points of Siuslaw Phonology." These linguists were among the last to record data, though Jane Sokolow, a graduate student, interviewed Martha (Barney) Johnson before her death in 1963. The location of Sokolow's notes is unknown.

MATERIAL CULTURE

The surviving examples of the material culture of the Confederated Tribes are widely scattered and incompletely documented. The artifacts include, however, the basketry made by Annie Miner Peterson, Coos, held by the Whatcom County Museum in Bellingham, Washington, and the handsomely ornamented, white deerskin dress of Lottie (Jackson) Evanoff in the DAR's Newell House at Champoeg State Park in the Willamette Valley. The Coos basketry collection of Agnes (Lockhart) Sengstacken, author of *A Legend of the Coos* (1909) and *Destination, West!* (1942), is housed in the Lowie Museum of Anthropology, University of California, Berkeley. A few Coos baskets are in the Sarah Magee Collection of the Coos County Historical Museum, North Bend; and other Coos and Siuslaw baskets and a solitary, woven fishtrap are held by the Siuslaw Pioneer Museum at Florence, Oregon.

CONCLUSION

The "Captured Heritage" project of the Confederated Tribes has identified published and manuscript sources, recordings on cylinders and tapes, and examples of material culture held in museum collections. The tribe has initiated a data recovery plan, securing photocopies, microfilms, and tapes on information so that younger tribal members can pursue research projects. In some cases the present generation can hear the "voices of the past," the recordings of their great or great great grandparents.

A dedication to scholarship motivated individuals like Frachtenberg, Jacobs, Harrington, and Swadesh to devote their energies to recording information about traditional culture and language. A willingness to share what they knew and a sense of history and responsibility persuaded the elders of previous generations to participate. These materials are a window to the past, a set of clues about a way of life now largely gone. They serve as a source of inspiration, a mechanism for understanding.

12

THE MEMORY OF A PEOPLE: THE COQUILLES OF THE SOUTHWEST COAST

BY GEORGE B. WASSON, JR.

*The Coquille people have lived so many generations in their homeland environment
and traditional hunting-gathering territories, the years have become too many to count.*

*As is true with other southern Oregon coastal people, the oldest stories of
the Coquelle (the original name), tell about the creation of the world
and its rearrangement to suit the needs of the People who were to come later.
Mythical beings such as Talapus (Old Man Coyote) told how the land was built
from blue clay scooped from under the water and how that land was protected from wave action
by lining the shores with woven mats and basketry. The old stories relate first-hand accounts
of the great floods and fires that repeatedly swept over the land from the west,
often changing the geography significantly while scattering people and other animals far and wide.*

Coquel Thompson was an important source of information about early Coquille life and myths.

The home environment of these coastal people extended from the ocean, up through the tide flats of the bays, sloughs, and estuaries, to the north-south summit of the Coast Range. The great variety of seafood, roots, berries, deer, elk, birds, and other game was matched only by the Indians' great wealth of clothing, basketry, jewelry, myths, and legends. This rich cultural milieu was unsurpassed in the West.

To complement the formal written accounts that so often form the basis for an understanding of Pacific Northwest history, Coquille elders still recount stories and legends that previous generations passed on to their children and grandchildren. Thus, the story of the Coquille people is a compilation of information from sources traditional to both the white and Indian cultures.

EARLY MEMORIES

Early memories, it seems, sometimes stretched far back in time. Old Coquille Indians sometimes told about visitors to their area who called themselves "Spañol." In the 1940s Coquel Thompson told ethnologist John P. Harrington that he'd heard of the tribe named Esbanyolla, saying, "These used to come packing into this country long ago." Others said the Spaniards told the Indians, "We'll treat you all right, but the white people will come and they will treat you like slaves."

These comments perhaps give some insight into the dramatic changes in attitude toward newcomers that occurred between 1792 and 1851—changes that have puzzled historians. When Captain Vancouver visited the Oregon coast, he reported the native inhabitants to be "very honest." Describing them as being of medium stature with slender bodies and "tolerable well limbed," he noted that they also seemed to prefer the comforts of cleanliness to the painting of their bodies. By 1851, however, the first settlers were describing the Indians as treacherous, filthy savages. And indeed the Indians were inclined to resist the increasing white encroachment on their homelands.

STRANGE PEOPLE WITH HAIRY FACES

Early in the nineteenth century, white explorers, trappers, and missionaries began to come to the Pacific Northwest and by the mid-1800s much of what is now the Oregon coast was populated with white miners and settlers. An expedition of one early explorer, Jedediah Smith, was later attacked by angry Lower Umpqua Indians. That attack was provoked by an incident that is still a part of Coquille oral tradition.

In the summer of 1828, when the Jedediah Smith expedition made its historic trek up the coast of Oregon, word of its strange light-skinned people with hair on their faces and large four-legged animals that were neither deer nor elk spread rapidly up the coast. (Those animals, it was said, also had curved flat blades of *Chicamin*—iron, in Chinook Jargon—fastened to the bottoms of their single rounded hooves to make them tougher and to help them endure the rough terrain.) The hairy-faced men also carried "rock-throwing sticks," which they didn't have to swing, but merely pointed at a target, causing fire and smoke to explode as the stick threw a metal stone harder, faster, and farther than any of the Indians had imagined possible.

News of the slow and laborious progress of this awesome caravan had been carried up the coast to every village headman. One group, the Nasomahs, had sent word up to their Miluk relatives on the south slough of Coos Bay. Those living at the mouth of the Coquille River were relatively few in number, and as the expedition finally approached the main village, most of the people had gone across the river to the northside village.

Smith must have posed a formidable spectre to the last of the fleeing villagers, for they had paddled furiously to the other shore, smashed their highly prized *thlahkhoosah* (canoes) to pieces, and hid among the trees to watch in awe as the white men tore up the Indians' plank houses to make a raft on which to cross the tidewater.

What Smith and his men did next must have truly puzzled the Indians, for instead of following the well-established trail that led directly to South Slough, Smith took his weary group through the sand hills along the coast and led them into the worst terrain they had yet encountered in their long journey. At this, the Nasomah people rushed to tell Kitzenjinjn (Kitzn jinum, Kitznjenen), a respected Miluk headman who—it was said— was so tall and robust

The origin of the name "Coquille" is uncertain. However, the traditional pronunciation—"Ko Kwel"—has been well documented by early ethnographers. Many tribal members (including this writer) grew up among old timers who would accept no other pronunciation. It has been declared by early residents of the area that the accepted spelling was Coquelle until sometime in the early 1900s, when a group of white business people launched a campaign to change the spelling to the French form, Coquille. Bess Finley Wasson recalls that in the early 1900s, when she was a girl, a group of city supporters organized an annual civic event which they called "The Kokeel Korn Karnival."

In 1942 ethnologist John P. Harrington was interviewing Coquel Thompson, an upriver Coquille, who said, "Mrs. Daisy Codding's statement that Coquille always used to be pronounced by the whites K'ok' wel is correct. Only recently are people changing it to K'o k'il. . . .This name is of Whiteman origin and has nothing to do with the South Slough word for bow."

At the far left in this photograph is the author's father, George Bundy Wasson, who spent his life fighting in the nation's capital to regain lands that had been taken from the Indians in the mid-1800s without compensation. When Wasson was a small boy, his grandmother had predicted that one day he would regain his people's land. Sadly, he died in 1947, before his efforts had borne fruit.

his name meant "elk skin robe would not meet all the way around the middle."

When told of the strangers in their midst, Kitzenjinjn had responded with great military pomp and diplomacy, taking 300 armed men dressed in their finest skins and feathers out onto the coastal headlands near Cape Arago and ceremoniously welcoming the astonished whites. The Indians escorted Smith and his men, along with their several hundred head of horses and mules, to South Slough, where they were duly ferried across to the village site and guided to a suitable place of encampment nearby.

During the next few days, Smith and his party rested and enjoyed the abundant hospitality of the local people. The Indians provided much food, and extensive trading took place. Also, they were introduced to the white method of boiling and eating dried beans—a food that both fascinated and puzzled them and was to lead to a humorous situation years later, when they tried to prepare and eat coffee beans in the same way.

However, during this otherwise amiable interlude, some difficulties were to arise. For one thing, Smith was greatly annoyed by some of the more curious and meddlesome tribesmen, who shot arrows into some of his pack animals, wounding and killing a few. And one other incident that seemed unimportant at the time was to have a disastrous result.

It seems that a man from the Lower Umpqua River who was visiting at Coos Bay could not contain his curiosity about the strange habits of the white men. As was the common practice among European descendants, a cook in the Smith party had hung an elk carcass in a tree to "ripen" until it was suitable for consumption. The Umpqua visitor, however, apparently felt that the meat was turning to a state that decent palates would not find edible and stuck his knife into the flesh to determine its degree of putrification.

Unfortunately, the Indian was discovered by the cook, who thought he was trying to steal the meat and rushed at him with his butcher knife, cutting off an ear and part of his nose. Thus marked, the Indian was disgraced beyond social acceptability, for to his people the severing of an ear or—worse yet—a nose was punishment meted out only to a runaway slave or an unfaithful woman.

When the Lower Umpqua man rushed to Kitzenjinjn demanding that the Indians attack the white men in retaliation for his humiliation, the wise headman responded that the man had trespassed on the territory and possessions of those who were guests of the local people and that those guests had "diplomatic immunity" in their own camp. The Umpqua visitor, he said, would have to suffer the consequences of his bold intrusion.

This response made the wounded man furious and he stormed away from Coos Bay, raving about the hairy-faced intruders and vowing that he would have revenge. When he reached his own people, he related his tale of mistreatment, which seemed to offer proof that the Smith party was not to be trusted and deserved punishment. Thus, the mood was set among the Lower Umpquas for the arrival of Jedediah Smith and his expedition.

History clearly details the events that followed and ended with nearly total destruction of those explorers.

DEFINING THE COQUILLES

In the 1850s, when the U. S. government began to create reservations in Oregon, it defined Indian groups as "tribes." However, as Roberta Hall points out in her *The Coquille Indians: Yesterday, Today and Tomorrow*, the reality was somewhat different. According to Hall:

> *Numerous permanent villages and some camp sites of periodic or seasonal occupation existed along the Oregon coast and social interaction among different villages took place. In order to simplify its relations with diverse people, the government grouped these villages and bands into larger units, whether or not the units reflected existing social patterns. As a result, the Indian population, as well as anthropologists and historians who concern themselves with coastal prehistory and history, have wondered how the pre-contact peoples of the south coast defined themselves.*
>
> *Some twentieth-century observers have attempted to solve this problem by using linguistic classifications, applied geographically, as ethnic indicators. At present, the linguistic consensus seems to be that one segment of the ancestors of modern Coquille people spoke a Miluk dialect of the Kusan language. These people lived from approximately the Whisky Run Creek area along the coast south to Floras Lake, which is just south of Fourmile Creek, some four miles south of the mouth of the Coquille River. The upriver villagers whose descendants now are included in the Coquilles lived along the Coquille River approximately from the present-day site of the town of Coquille to above Myrtle Point. These people are thought to have spoken a dialect of the Athabaskan language*

family, and thus they had linguistic affinities with other southcentral and south coastal native peoples. This is the current majority opinion which is expressed, for instance, in the Atlas of Oregon, *published by the University of Ore–gon in 1976. However, not all linguists agree.*

"A MOST HORRID MASSACRE"

Early on the morning of January 28, 1854, the Nasomah village of the Lower Coquille was brutally attacked and destroyed by a mob of 40 miners from the nearby diggings at Randolph. Two of the main instigators were named Packwood and Soapy. On February 5 of that same year, special agent Smith wrote the following report:

A most horrid massacre, or rather an out-and-out barbarous mass murder, was perpetrated upon a portion of the Nasomah Band residing at the mouth of the Coquille River on the morning of January 28th by a party of 40 miners. The reason assigned by the miners, by their own statements, seem trivial. However, on the afternoon preceding the murders, the miners requested the chief to come in for a talk. This he refused to do.

The report goes on to say that a meeting was held and a courier was dispatched to obtain the assistance of 20 more miners from nearby Randolph.

At dawn the following day, led by one Abbott, the ferry party and the 20 miners, about 40 in all, formed three detachments, marched upon the Indian ranches and 'consummated a most in-human slaughter,' which the attackers termed a fight. The Indians were aroused from sleep to meet their deaths with but a feeble show of resistance; shot down as they were attempting to escape from their houses. Fifteen men and one Squaw were killed, two Squaws badly wounded. On the part of the white men, not even the slightest wound was received. The houses of the Indians with but one exception, were fired and destroyed. Thus was committeed a massacre too inhuman to be readily believed.

End of report. Within less than two years, the people were gone, except for those few women who had taken white men for their husbands. The effect on the culture of the Coquilles and their close neighbors was devastating.

Today, the Coquilles are few in number, yet through all the years of languishing in seemingly total deprivation, tribal descendants have managed to keep bits and pieces of tradition and cultural spirit alive. A few anthropologists and self-appointed historians have recognized the threat of obliteration and have felt compelled to save or write something of the culture, however small the segment might be. Today, there is an active and growing interest among tribal members of all ages in coming together and relearning the old ways, by searching out the hidden pockets of knowledge and recapturing their roots.

STORIES AND LEGENDS

A particularly rich part of the Coquilles' heritage is the wealth of stories and legends that have survived. According to Roberta Hall, these stories fall into several categories: "Coyote" stories, other animal stories about grizzly bear and rhinoceros, canoe stories, legends about the origins of place names, and others. Although the meaning of these tales is often unclear and—as Barry Lopez has suggested—their spiritual significance is often overstated, their importance to the cultural memory is undisputed.

In the 1940s ethnologist John Harrington collected many of these stories from various informants, including Coquel Thompson. Harrington repeatedly questioned several informants from southwestern Oregon, but Coquel Thompson was definitely his favorite; he was most consistent, most prolific, and easiest to understand. Thompson was from an upper Coquille village, which he said was named "Chunch-att-ah-dunn," located at the place where the trail from the upper Rogue River to the upper Umpqua River crossed the Coquille River.

One of the most intriguing stories Thompson and other informants told Harrington in bits and pieces concerns the antics of Tallapus (Old Man Coyote) and how a certain fishing place on the Upper Coquille River came to have the descriptive name "Thet suh-wuh-let sluh dunn" (a place where two large round stones are located on either side of the water). This place, where there was a riffle, lies on the upper Coquille River somewhere around Myrtle Point at a broad stretch. There, the upper Coquilles would build a fish weir and a salmon trap in July or August to catch the salmon, which came in September. This was a notable dam made of willow stakes driven straight down into the gravel bottom, whose immensity spanned the full width of the river. The construction of this dam was obviously a great undertaking and required an extensive communal effort to cut, sharpen, and pound the great stakes into place and weave smaller branches between them to form the secure barricade fence.

Such an enormous salmon weir always seemed to be of special importance to all the people along that river. Each coastal stream with a salmon run had reason to have such a structure, and those people who were dedicated and accomplished enough to build one that reached from shore to shore had reason to be proud of their

Immense fish weirs spanned important streams on the south coast, allowing salmon to be trapped and speared. Shown at right is a smaller weir.

accomplishment. The larger the dam, the more prestige it bestowed on the builders.

No one seems to know where Coyote was coming from on the occasion recounted in the following story, or just why, but he was poling his way upstream in his canoe—along with his current wife, the former Mrs. Fishduck—when his progress was halted by the enormous salmon weir.

Coyote tried to push his way through, but the structure was too sturdy. Of course, true to form he became angry and vowed to smash through. So he went back down stream and loaded two large round boulders into the bow of his canoe and placed his wife at the stern. Even though he was pushing against the current, Coyote was determined to break through the barricade, but his first attempts were too feeble and he failed. Finally in a fit of rage, he poled as fast and hard as he could and broke through. But just as he got to the up-stream side, his pole slipped, he lost his balance, and the current threw his canoe back against the weir, flipped it up on end, cata-pulted the boulders out onto either shore, and dumped Coyote and his wife into the water. Using *Tamanawis*, the magical powers of his mind, Coyote brought the canoe up from under the swift current and quietly took his wife back downstream. That's why the place

was called "Thet" (stones), "suh-wuh-let" (spherical) "sluh-dunn" (on opposite sides of the water-place).

REINSTATEMENT OF A PEOPLE

Just as the history of the holocaust of the Jews in Germany must be accurately and fully detailed, so must the holocaust of the tribes of southwest Oregon. The Coquilles have a proud and important history that can enrich the state. Theirs is a story of the persistence of group memory—reaching far back in time—in the face of nearly impossible odds. Today it serves to empower a small but determined remnant of a vital people.

The Coquille Indian Tribe was restored to federal recognition status by an act of Congress in June 1989. There are presently 630 members on the tribal rolls. A constitution has been drafted and approved by the Bureau of Indian Affairs and the Department of the Interior. At the time of this writing, the constitution is being voted on for adoption by eligible tribal members.

The Port of Bandon has returned to tribal ownership 1.23 acres of land at the sacred site where Tupper Rock once stood at the mouth of the Coquille River. Further land acquisition and development of economic enterprises are the tribe's next high priorities.

13

PATIENCE AND PERSISTENCE: THE COW CREEK BAND OF UMPQUA TRIBE OF INDIANS

BY STEPHEN DOW BECKHAM AND SHERRI SHAFFER

*In the watershed of the South Umpqua River in Douglas County, Oregon,
lives a tribe whose history mirrors the difficult relations between Indians and the United States.
The story of the Cow Creek Band of Umpqua Indians is one of inequity, misrepresentation,
tantalizing hope, deep frustration, and persistence. The tribe's ability to survive is testimony
to the unquenchable human spirit and its determination to shape a better future.*

THE LAND AND ITS EARLY INHABITANTS

The Cow Creeks lived between the Cascade and Coast ranges in southwestern Oregon, along the South Umpqua River and its primary feeder stream, Cow Creek. This homeland was one of mountains, uplands, and valley floors—a place of beauty and challenge that sustained life but demanded work from those who called it home.

The prehistory of the South Umpqua region is only incompletely known, but archaeology confirms a deep time frame for an Indian presence in the interior of southwestern Oregon and suggests a way of life that changed little over the centuries. The archaeological record also confirms a use of the land extending from the margins of streams to the highest ridges, a tapping of both flora and fauna, and the technology typical of that of Indians elsewhere on the Pacific Slope.

LANGUAGE

For centuries, Indian voices floated on the summer air and winter winds of the South Umpqua, and Indian names marked the land. "Lakwal," or Cow Creek as the newcomers called it, flowed past the sleepy villages; the eels surged up the creek to the falls where the young men dived and wrenched them from the rocks; and "Kwenta't," an ancient village, stood on Canyon Creek near the point where it cut out of the hillsides and entered the South Umpqua River. No one speaks these words today. No one thinks in the cadences of words and sentence structures of the time-tested Takelman language, once common in southwestern Oregon.

The term "Takelma" was taken from *Da-gelma*, meaning "those living alongside the river." Collectively these people were called the Rogue Indians, whose kinsmen to the north included the Grave Creeks and the Cow Creeks, bands sharing the same language but living in isolated stream systems to the south and north of the Rogue-Umpqua divide.

The Cow Creeks lived adjacent to people with sharply differing languages. Directly north, below the mouth of Myrtle Creek and in the main Umpqua Valley, resided the Umpqua, who spoke an Athabaskan language, as did the Upper Coquille to the west in the Coquille watershed. The Southern Molalla resided to the east on the uppermost reaches of the South Umpqua River and spoke a language that was part of the Molallan Family. The Chinook Jargon, a *lingua franca* spread during the fur trade, helped tie these diverse people together, as did marriage across language boundaries. In fact, many people were probably bilingual.

An 1841 sketch of an Umpqua Indian, by an American explorer

Cow Creek women wove baskets of wild hazel bark, bear grass, and maiden hair fern stems. Sometimes they dyed the strands by burying them in the earth for several months or rinsing them with a solution made from the bark of the alder tree. These watertight baskets could be used for cooking and food storage.

TRADITIONAL LIFEWAYS

During the first half of the nineteenth century, the Cow Creeks probably lived as they had for the preceding several centuries, following a seasonal round that responded to nature's cycles and food sources. In the spring they hunted along the Umpqua River for ducks and geese, gathered shoots and greens in the meadows, and harvested the first salmon. By April they had access to the first berry crops, and within a month the men and boys began to harvest vast quantities of eels, which the women smoked and sun dried at the falls of Cow Creek above Riddle or at South Umpqua Falls deep in the Western Cascades.

During the late spring and early summer, the women and girls worked their way through the river meadows and mountain uplands to harvest the bulbs of camas and Kitten's Ears and to pick salmonberries, thimbleberries, and strawberries. Meanwhile, the men repaired brush fences on the ridges and anticipated the time when they would drive deer in a frenzied rush into the canyons through the narrow places where they had fixed their prized iris-fiber snares. These snares handily caught the deer, which played an important part in the Cow Creeks' diet and provided hides for their clothing. The men also flaked stone projectile points, hafted them on wood spears and arrows, and carved yewwood bows, which they backed with sinew from the legs of elk and deer. Although these bows were resilient and useful, the snares proved even more efficient during the game drives.

By late summer the families had moved from the uplands to the high country, gathering at Huckleberry Lake, Abbott Butte, and elsewhere along the Rogue-Umpqua divide. There, they picked huckleberries, which they dried for winter use, and the men hunted for elk, deer, and bear. At night the old people sang and told stories, while the young people looked up at the stars and wondered about life. The old ones said that if they spied a falling star it meant the passing of a life and the arrival of a new soul among the humans.

As the nights began to chill and the prospect of rain set in, the people dropped down from the mountains, abandoned their temporary huts of limbs and reed matting, and took up residence in the permanent winter villages in the lowlands. As they returned, the women torched the fields to burn off the globules of sticky tar on the tarweed and, with beaters and funnel-shaped baskets, worked their way over the bottomlands to harvest the seeds. The men made certain that the fires burned out the forest understory, for in that way there would be an abundance of blackberries in another year, as well as good feed for the deer that grazed there.

In preparation for winter, the Cow Creeks constructed semi-subterranean lodges covered with planks or large pieces of bark and stored the gathered foodstuffs—acorns, hazelnuts, cakes of camas, tarweed seeds, smoked salmon, jerked meat, and dried eel. Their supplies also included the amber-colored balls of pitch from the tall "medicine trees" on Jackson Creek and upper Cow Creek—treasures that oozed from scars in the bark of Ponderosa pines and provided "medicine" when the turn of seasons brought colds and chills.

In this manner winter followed summer and summer followed winter in endless progression.

EARLY CONTACTS

During the first half of the nineteenth century, the Cow Creeks probably lived as they had for the preceding several centuries, following a seasonal round that responded to nature's cycles and food sources. However, an early encounter with whites came about 1819, when land-based fur trappers of the North West Company entered the Umpqua watershed and opened fire on the Indians, killing several of them. Then in the 1820s the Hudson's Bay Company inaugurated regular trade in the region and founded the "Old Establishment," a temporary post probably located near the mouth of

Calapooia Creek. In 1836 the same firm built Fort Umpqua at the mouth of Elk Creek, a number of miles north of Cow Creek country. This post assured a steady supply of trade goods to the Indians of the region—goods that included brass kettles, needles and thread, colorful trade beads, clothing of wool and cotton, blankets, and sea biscuits.

While relations between the Cow Creeks and fur trappers were generally good, a new chapter unfolded in 1846 when explorers opened the Applegate Trail and the flow of pioneers began in earnest. Tragically, this north-south trail, which bisected the Cow Creek homeland, soon became an artery of commerce and trouble for the Indians who lived along its margins.

Part of the trouble came with the discovery of gold in the Sierra foothills of California in 1848, an event that sent tens of thousands of miners to the West Coast. In 1851 many of them had shoved north into the Klamath River watershed and begun laying out claims in the Rogue and Umpqua valleys. Then in January 1852 the discovery of gold on Jackson Creek opened a new mining frontier and within months, several thousand men had poured into the Rogue, Illinois, and South Umpqua watersheds in a frenzied search for precious metal.

These events and others combined in the early 1850s to shatter the world of the Cow Creeks. With the gold rush came a rough, lawless element that lay siege to the ancient stream terraces where the Takelman-speakers, including the Cow Creeks, had their villages. Farmers filed for donation land claims on the meadows where the Indian women gathered seeds and dug for bulbs. And travelers passed regularly through the Indians' lands.

These incursions disrupted the Cow Creeks' subsistence patterns

The sweat lodge was an important structure in each village. The men daily steamed themselves to become clean, have luck in hunting, and cure illnesses. These lodges were almost subterranean, constructed deep into the earth.

and cut deeply into their lives. The acorns they had once harvested were now eaten by hogs, and the camas that played such an important part in their diet was cropped by horses and cattle. The pioneers constructed split-rail fences and log cabins and ruthlessly forbade field-burning, for fear that their investments would be destroyed. The miners sent a flood of muddy debris down the rivers to threaten fish runs, and the newcomers' firearms decimated both deer and elk. Before long the Cow Creeks and their neighbors were reduced to starvation.

TREATY AND WARFARE, 1853-1856

In 1848 Congress created Oregon Territory through the Organic Act and acknowledged the validity of Indian land title. In so doing it referenced the assurances of "utmost good faith" first articulated in 1787 when the Continental Congress set up a means for dealing with frontier lands. Between 1849 and 1853, however, the execution of good faith with Oregon Indians faltered, as initial rounds of treaty negotiations led nowhere and the Senate failed to ratify any of the treaties.

The discovery of gold and consequent settlement of southwestern Oregon, however, persuaded Superintendent of Indian Affairs Joel Palmer to try a new treaty program. In September 1853 Palmer headed south to the mining region and stopped on Cow Creek, where he assembled a number of Indians. On September 19 he negotiated a treaty and secured "X" marks by the names of men who headed various villages of the Cow Creeks. In his diary, Palmer wrote, "sealed the treaty with two bushels of potatoes."

The treaty called for the Cow Creeks to cede to the United States their entire homeland, approximately 720 square miles, for a price of 2.3 cents per acre. In return the U.S. promised a reservation, two houses worth not more than $200 each, and a plowed and fenced field of five acres. The Cow Creeks agreed to restore any stolen property they possessed, to remain peaceful, and to bring their complaints to a local Indian agent. This treaty and the one made with the Takelma in the Rogue Valley on September 10 were the first from Oregon Territory to become law. The Senate ratified the treaties on April 12, 1854, and on February 5, 1855 the president proclaimed them.

The tarweed (left) has an attractive flower and produces delicious seeds. The Indians set fire to the fields along the Umpqua to burn off the tar adhering to the seeds. Then women used beaters and funnel-shaped baskets to gather the seeds.

THE WORK OF COW CREEK WOMEN

In the early morning the squaws would be out in the Kamass field provided with a basket—a cone shaped affair wide open at the top, and swung across the forehead—a manner in which the Indians carried all their burdens and which left both arms free. Each squaw would be armed with a kamass stick made of Indian arrow wood fashioned to a point at one end by burning and rubbing the charred wood off leaving the point as hard as steel.

George Riddle, 1921

Treaty guarantees, however, provided no protection for the Cow Creeks, who soon became refugees in their own homeland. Settlers drove them from their villages, bands of self-styled "volunteers" from the mining communities preyed on them, and local soldiers—alleging various wrongs—murdered many and drove others into the hills.

Mi-wa-leta, a tribal leader, attempted to chart a course for his people. "That he always counseled peace and was able to restrain his people from going to war with the whites," recalled George Riddle, "we had ample evidence." Tragically, Mi-wa-leta and dozens of his people perished in a fever epidemic that decimated their numbers.

Terrible times ensued. When Palmer visited the Cow Creeks in the spring of 1854, he noted: "I found many of them wretched, sickly, and almost starving." The severe winter, competition with settlers for food, dislocation because of mining and land claims, new diseases, and aggression had dramatically altered their lives.

As if that were not enough, in the fall of 1855 the volunteers provoked a renewed outbreak of the Rogue River Indian War. When that conflict spread north in October, Cow Creek Tom, a leader, faced the pioneers, reiterated the calamities that had befallen his people, and said that the survivors had decided to fight. The Cow Creeks left the conference and disappeared into the hills.

During the winter of 1855-1856, the volunteers attempted to track down and imprison these Indians. Although they succeeded in assembling a bedraggled group on the temporary reservation in Cole's Valley on the Umpqua, dozens more began their long concealment in the mountains, occasionally coming down to the lowlands to raid for food.

Six months later the U.S. Army entered the region and concluded the conflicts. Although the federal government rounded up over 2,000 surviving Indians for removal to the Siletz and Grand Ronde reservations, scattered individuals and families still held out in the hills. Later, these "outlaw" or "renegade" Indians were hunted down by contractors hired by the Bureau of Indian Affairs (BIA).

In July 1856 the BIA estimated that more than 100 Cow Creeks remained hidden in their old homeland. On April 20, 1864 a small band of these people raided the isolated John Doyle farm on upper Olalla Creek, provoking yet another "round up"—a 40-day expedition to southwestern Oregon that netted the BIA and army over 100 Indians. As late as 1871 Superintendent Alfred Meacham wrote: "Another band is now being oppressed and driven by white men from place to place in a small tract of country about thirty miles by forty miles long, covering the head-waters of the Umpqua River, in southern Oregon." Meacham lamented that "at least, as original inheritors of the soil," these poor Indians had "a 'God-given right' to life, liberty, and the pursuit of happiness."

PATIENT ENDURANCE

The surviving Cow Creeks retained a tenuous hold on parts of their old homeland—mostly those parts that had proven too marginal for farming. Some of the Indians had intermarried with French-Canadian fur trappers who had come to the region in the employ of

In 1858 an army officer photographed a Lower Umpqua Indian lodge near the river mouth. Several Indians, held prisoner by the federal government at Fort Umpqua, stand near the building.

the Hudson's Bay Company and lived on the edge of frontier society in Douglas County. Many of their cabins stood on the margins of small meadows above Tiller on the South Fork, near Drew on Elk Creek, or far up the main course of Cow Creek. There, the men hunted for elk and deer, and the women made leather gloves and jackets, which they sold in Canyonville, Myrtle Creek, and Roseburg.

The Cow Creek families lived close to the land. They planted small gardens, fished, hunted, and persisted in burning the hillsides until the Forest Service curtailed the practice early in the twentieth century. The people also found seasonal work harvesting prunes, picking hops, or assisting in farm labor in the Umpqua Valley, and some of the men became placer miners, packers, and trappers.

Because they did not live on reservations, the Cow Creeks had only sporadic relations with the Bureau of Indian Affairs. However, in 1918 the elders decided to establish a tribal government and began to fight for a program of federal services, including better education for their children. Perhaps the presence of the Roseburg Superintendency of Indian Affairs, an office which operated from 1910 to 1918 in Douglas County, inspired this determination.

Unfortunately, the results of their efforts were limited. Some children gained admittance to BIA schools, and the Grand Ronde-Siletz Agency entered a number of tribal families on the annual Indian Census Schedules from 1918 to 1940. However, the greater challenge was to seek introduction of a bill to permit the tribe to litigate over the taking of its lands in the 1850s.

Five times the Cow Creeks secured such bills, largely through the assistance of Senator Charles McNary, and once—in 1932—their bill passed the House and Senate, only to be vetoed by President Hoover. (The president contended that the United States could not afford Indian claims litigation in the midst of a great depression.)

Twenty years later, on August 1, 1953, their efforts were blocked when Congress adopted House Concurrent Resolution 108, a general statement that Congress would move as rapidly as possible to withdraw from longstanding relationships with Indian tribes. On August 23, 1954 Congress passed the Western Oregon Termination Act, which specified that within two years, the federal government would suspend recognition and services to every tribe and band in western Oregon.

THE LAND CLAIMS CASE AND FEDERAL RECOGNITION

Although no longer federally recognized as a tribe, the Cow Creeks persisted in meeting, planning, and seeking their day in court. In 1979 they secured introduction of a bill to permit them to sue the United States, and on May 26, 1980 P.L. 96-251 passed. The law allowed the Cow Creek Band of Umpqua to file a complaint in the claims court in Washington, D.C., over the value of their lands taken more than a century before. In this litigation, the tribe's counsel was Dennis J. Whittlesey, an attorney in Washington, D.C.

As the Cow Creek case proceeded, the Justice Department filed interrogatories, secured depositions from tribal elders, and sought to discover the nature, extent, and value of the lands in question. In February 1984, before the case came to trial, the tribe and the government reached a negotiated settlement when the tribe agreed to a value of $1.25 per acre, or a total of $1.5 million for their lands as of 1855. By the rules of claims litigation, the tribe could secure no interest and no land. While the claims case proceeded in the court, the Cow Creeks pursued federal recognition and sought to overturn the termination law of 1954. On December 29, 1982 Congress enacted P.L. 97-391.

Once again the Cow Creeks secured a direct relationship with the United States through the Bureau of Indian Affairs, but that relationship proved to be a mixed blessing. When the tribe proposed to vest its judgment fund in an endowment, the BIA opposed the move, demanding instead a per-capita distribution. Although this was a long-discredited manner of handling judgment funds and was contrary to the philosophy of the Indian Judgment Fund Distribution Act, the BIA was adamant. Not only did it refuse to approve the tribal plan, it failed to bring forward its own plan during the 365 days provided for by law. Thus, the Cow Creeks had no recourse but to turn, once again, to Congress. On October 26, 1987, Congress passed P.L. 100-139, the Cow Creek Judgment Fund Act, a

PERSECUTION OF THE COW CREEKS

Although they may not be the possessors of enough political power to secure to them the consideration of local politicians, they, at least as original inheritors of the soil, have a 'God-given right' to life, liberty, and the pursuit of happiness; and no race, however strong, under a Government claiming to be established on principles of 'equal and exact justice,' should be permitted to trample on and exterminate a race whose misfortune is to be 'untutored and untaught'....
Alfred Meacham, 1871

statute that wrote into law the tribal plan. The Cow Creeks vested their entire judgment fund of $1.5 million in an endowment from which they would draw, on an annual basis, only the earned interest. These earnings were earmarked for economic development, education, housing, and elderly assistance.

TRIBAL PLANNING FOR THE PRESENT AND FUTURE

Since the 1850s the Cow Creeks had always been keenly aware of their landless condition. Therefore, one of their most important actions following "recognition" and settlement of their land claims case was their 1984 purchase of 29 acres adjacent to Interstate Five at Canyonville, Oregon. On September 15, 1986, after two years of difficult dealings with the BIA, the Interior Department took the land into "trust." In 1990 the tribe purchased an adjoining 16 acres fronting on the South Umpqua River.

Today the Cow Creeks number over 800, are governed by an elected council, and maintain tribal offices in Roseburg, Oregon. The tribe has chartered the Umpqua Indian Development Corporation (UIDC), which is working on development of the reservation. The tribe has commissioned a business plan which outlines business options and has engaged in site planning, soils testing, and engineering studies for use of its lands to generate jobs. Like more than

a hundred across the United States, the tribe plans to erect a bingo hall on this site. It hopes this investment will create jobs and assist in improving the standard of living of its members.

The Cow Creeks are a modern, federally recognized tribe that remembers it was Oregon's first treaty tribe. That treaty proved costly, but recent events suggest that patience and persistence have paid off. The tribe is working for a better tomorrow.

THE TRIBAL STUDY PROJECT

The tribal study project involved oral histories from 15 elders on uses of the land. These informants discussed many ways in which the Cow Creeks secured foods and maintained themselves into the historic period. The elders identified sites for hunting, fishing, berry picking, root gathering, residency, burial, quarrying of special minerals and rocks, and religious practices.

The study project resulted in a scripted color-slide program of 65 images entitled "Cow Creeks and the Land." The program, which is available for use in Douglas County schools, recounts the traditional lifeways of the only tribe to continue living in the upper Umpqua region.

THE CONFEDERATED TRIBES OF THE GRAND RONDE COMMUNITY OF OREGON

BY YVONNE HAJDA

*The self-study project undertaken by the Confederated Tribes of Grand Ronde
consists of collecting and identifying historical and cultural information
related to pre- and post-reservation times. This information includes
written, oral, and photographic materials and the identification and location of artifact collections.
A bibliography of information pertaining to the Confederated Tribes has been compiled and,
when possible, items have been collected for eventual deposit in tribal archives.
These will be added to records and materials, already in the tribes' possession,
which are also being compiled and archived. Because tribal history is not completely captured
by the written records, elders are being interviewed to record oral history as well.*

A brief glimpse at the history of Grand Ronde shows why this project was needed.

THE FIRST GRAND RONDE PEOPLE

While the ancestors of the people who today comprise the Grand Ronde tribal community came from all over western Oregon and beyond, the majority were from the Willamette Valley and from the upper Rogue River and its tributaries. They included a few Lower Chinook-speaking Clatsops and Chinooks from the lowest few miles of the Columbia River and the adjacent coasts; Upper Chinook speakers, who originally lived along the lower Columbia from the Lower Chinook area up to The Dalles, on the Clackamas, and on the lower Willamette; a few Klickitats, possibly from southwest Washington or east of the Cascades; and Tillamooks from the northwest Oregon coast.

From the Willamette Valley came speakers of three Kalapuyan languages and several dialects: Northern, consisting of Tualatin and Yamhill; Central Kalapuyan, including Santiam, Luckiamute, Hanchuyuk, Chepanefo, Chelamela, Winnefilly, Mohawk, Tekopa, Calapooia, and others; and Southern, or Yoncalla, Kalapuyan. From the slopes of the Cascades came two groups of Molala speakers and from several interior valleys adjoining the Yoncallas came speakers of Upper Umpqua and other Athabaskan languages. In addition, there were speakers of Takelma, a language related to Kalapuyan, who lived mainly in the upper Rogue River and Cow Creek area, with groups of Athabaskan speakers interspersed. From the same general Rogue River area came some Shasta speakers. In addition to their native languages, many of these Indians—especially those from northwest Oregon—also spoke the Chinook Jargon, and a few knew English and French.

Needless to say, these groups' backgrounds were extremely varied. Yet in spite of their differences, the people brought together at Grand Ronde had a good deal in common, including similar political units, social organizations, and marriage customs.

EVENTS THAT LED TO CREATION OF THE RESERVATION

The story of how vast Indian lands in Oregon were appropriated for white settlement is told elsewhere (see pages 39-54). Those actions led directly to the establishment of reservations on and near the central Oregon coast. Joel Palmer, who became superintendent in 1853, proposed that a reservation for all western Oregon Indians be established on the central coast, on land that had not been settled, was seen as poor farming country, and was separated by mountains from the settled Willamette Valley. This plan was approved and in 1854 and 1855 Palmer proceeded with treaties with Willamette Valley and coastal Indians. The United States was to pay annuities in exchange for the land and was to furnish what the Indians might need if they were to learn to live like white people.

The treaty with the Umpquas and Kalapuyas—some of whom had been moved to the upper Umpqua—was ratified in 1854, as was one with the Shastas. The Molala treaty was ratified in 1855, and so was one with the Kalapuyas and Confederated Bands of the Willamette Valley. The treaties with the Tualatins of 1854 and with coastal tribes in 1855 were never ratified, but by executive order in 1855 the Coast Reservation was established in their territory anyway. The new reservation encompassed about a third of the Oregon coastline, 50 miles north and 50 miles south of Yaquina Bay, extending about 25 miles inland and comprising over a million acres. It included 60,000 acres at the northeast corner that became the Grand Ronde Reservation.

The Indians who signed the treaties received no compensation but were forced onto the reservation. While the Rogue River Wars in southern Oregon continued, Indians from the Rogue and Umpqua were marched north by the United States Army, beginning in February of 1856. During their month-long "trail of tears," these Indians suffered from disease, exposure, and attacks by white vigilantes. In June, with the fighting almost over, others were sent north by steamship. These Indians from the southwest part of Oregon were located around the Siletz and Grand Ronde agencies. In 1857 most of the Rogue River Indians at Grand Ronde were moved to Siletz, leaving an official count of 267 Rogue Rivers at Grand Ronde. Peaceful Indians from the Willamette Valley were also moved to the reservation, mainly to the Grand Ronde agency. The Clatsops and Tillamooks of the northwest coast and those already on the central coast were left where they were. By 1858 the population at Grand Ronde was about 1,200.

LIFE ON THE RESERVATION

During the latter half of the nineteenth century, reservation agents tried to keep track of the Indians under their supervision, but this proved difficult because groups were relocated and people moved off and on the reservation to work for whites, to look for traditional foods, to visit relatives elsewhere temporarily or permanently, or—the reservation having proved much less than promised—to return to familiar places to live. At first, fluctuations were especially large, as groups were added or transferred. Later on, in the 1870s, reductions in the reservation lands uprooted many more, with some Indians from the coast and from the Alsea agency moving to Grand Ronde and others trying to homestead among the whites. Some joined small groups that had escaped or managed to avoid being swept off to the reservations; such groups were found even in the growing cities.

Portland newspapers in the 1870s reported on disturbances caused by Indians: one such incident, in 1872, occurred in "the Indian quarters" in Oregon City, where Indians had lived for "many years past." As the agent at Grand Ronde complained in his 1887 report, "There are several hundred Indians that belong to this reservation that are scattered over the country, but I have not any authority to bring them back." The large drop in population reported that year was not due to illness—though outbreaks of disease did reduce the numbers from time to time—but to the agent's decision to re-

John and Hattie Hudson and some of their children are ready to market the baskets made by Hattie and her mother, Martha Jane Sands. Baskets made by women provided welcome extra income for many families.

move from the rolls the names of many people who had left the reservation and not returned.

Life on the reservation was difficult, as people settled down among strangers while trying to learn new ways of life in an unfamiliar land with inadequate means provided to do so. Victoria Howard recounted what she had heard of the move and the first months on the reservation:

> On the following day they [the whites] killed cattle, they killed hogs, they brought them to them [the Indians]. In the same way also sugar, grease, potatoes, wheat flour and all sorts of things they came and gave us. Some of the old people would not eat it. They just cried, and the days following they were still crying. . . .Some of them would not have as their food the meat of cattle, even worse was pig which they would not eat.

> We stayed there [at Dayton] for quite a while. The houses were sail houses [tents] which they constructed for us. They took them farther, where we are living now [Grand Ronde]. . . . The Upper Umpquas, the Shastas, the Rogue River Indians, the Kalapuyas, the Yonkallas, they brought all of them to this place here.

> At first they gave us just sail houses. Speedily we lived in log houses there. They were full of people. . . . Others had no houses, but later on they built small houses. . . .

> It was quite some time before they assigned land to us. They moved some of them [Shastas, Rogue Rivers, Upper Umpquas] across there [to New Grand Ronde]. . . . Then they constructed houses for us [Molalas, Chinooks, Kalapuyas, Klamaths] here on this side [Old Grand Ronde]. . . .

> Now they brought soldiers, they took care of us. Wherever we went, they gave us a paper. They stood on each side

For a time, the reservations were parceled out to various churches to oversee. At Grand Ronde, Belgian missionary Father Adrien Croquet established a Catholic presence in 1860 and arranged for a group of nuns to operate a boarding school.

The first teachers at Grand Ronde had to communicate with their students in Chinook Jargon. Their efforts to discontinue what one called "that barbarous" tongue were reinforced in 1887 when the federal government decreed that English would be used exclusively.

of the road, they held guns. Some ran away, they went back to where their home village was. Such persons got no land.
(Taken from Melville Jacobs, *Clackamas Texts*)

Until the Indians could learn to farm productively, much of their food had to be supplied by the government, or they had to find their own in the traditional way as best they could on the unfamiliar reservation. Only those with ratified treaties were eligible for government help, however, and many Indians on the reservation had no such protection. Because of the unratified treaties, funds were never appropriated on a regular basis, so in lieu of the payments and annuities Palmer had promised, special funds and yearly appeals had to be relied on. Indians were regularly given passes to leave the reservation to get food—by salmon fishing at Oregon City as they used to do or working for white farmers in the neighborhood. The efforts of fishermen and hunters to learn to farm were hampered by disease and weather, land not suited for the crops chosen, bad decisions by agents, and inadequate tools and supplies. The Indians at Grand Ronde, however, were strongly motivated to learn as fast as they could.

BECOMING GRAND RONDE INDIANS

How did it happen that by the first decade of the twentieth century, these people from all over western Oregon had become a community calling themselves "Grand Ronde Indians" rather than Molalas, Clackamas, or Rogue Rivers? This was a long-term process, which started when they were thrown together in one place under a military regime that at first enforced segregation from the surrounding society. The situation made it necessary for people to cooperate in solving common problems, helping to create an "us against them" mentality. Coercive government policies undermined key elements of native society and promoted, if not compelled, the wholesale adoption of Euro-American dress, habits and attitudes, religion, and language.

Just before the reservation period, not only villages but whole tribes had come to have chiefs who acted as their representatives in dealing with government officials and with representatives of other tribal groups. Depopulation, followed by population consolidation and treaty making made "tribes" and their chiefs into salient social units. Those government officials who were responsible for negotiating treaties often directed a group of Indians to select a "chief" to represent them by signing a treaty. If and when native leaders were available, they were likely to be the ones chosen. On the reservation the 13 Grand Ronde tribal groups censused between 1877 and 1899 averaged only between 35 and 50 people, with the largest only about 105. Each group at first had its own location on the reservation, making it much like an aboriginal village. In these local groups, people lived together in households of 10 to 50, as in the pre-reservation extended households. The chiefs continued to represent these groups in dealing with reservation agents and other officials, but within 25 years the native political systems, with headmen and followers, lost much of their earlier significance.

During the 1870s and early 1880s the Grand Ronde Indian Legislature governed the internal affairs of the reservation, choosing chiefs, writing laws, setting up courts, and appointing police. During its first five years this body was made up of 19 representatives of 13 tribes, but in 1878 tribal representation was replaced by a division of the reservation into three precincts, each with three representatives.

The federal policy of allotting land to individual family heads was intended to break down Indian patrilocal extended families and tribes and to destroy the traditional relation to the land. It did so by emphasizing nuclear families, instilling a Euro-American sense of property, and creating self-sufficiency. This process began only 15 years after the reservation was established, and indeed caused residence patterns to become more like those of the whites.

As a result, group activities of all kinds, from native ceremonies to Indian gambling to hop-picking, became keys to uniting the reservation population. Especially important in creating a new identity, however, were the marriages between members of local groups that—before the reservation's creation—had been widely separated. The early tradition of "marrying out" now created ties that helped to make the reservation people into one network of kin.

Indian agents complained about the fragility of Indian marriages and the extension of adoption and other forms of social kinship beyond the bounds of consanguinity. Polygyny—strongly disapproved—disappeared early, but serial marriages and socially defined kin ties continued. However, as the extended families broke down,

marriage became a matter of personal choice rather than the result of a contract between two families as it had been before the reservation was established.

By the early twentieth century, people who remembered life before the reservation were dying off. With them died the tribal languages, which together with attachment to local territories had been the foundation for tribal identities. After the 1950s all that remained was the Chinook Jargon—"The Grand Ronde language"—which had been necessary in the first years of the reservation for communication among people who did not share a common language.

CULTURAL CHANGES

According to the Euro-American views of social evolution prevailing in the nineteenth century, Indians were simply savages who had to be "civilized" before they could fit into the larger society. Accordingly, schools were set up by the agents. At Grand Ronde the

In some ways, hop picking served the same function for reservation dwellers as traditional trade centers like Celilo had before white settlers arrived. Beginning in the 1880s, Indians came to the Willamette Valley from all over Oregon to harvest hops and have the opportunity to visit with distant friends and relatives. This photograph was taken around the 1920s.

earliest schools reflected the geographical division on the reservation between Indians from southwest and northwest Oregon: one school was for Rogue Rivers and Umpquas, the other for Kalapuyas and Clackamas. After many of the Rogue Rivers were moved to Siletz, the arrangement changed.

These early schools were not wildly successful: teachers changed frequently, students were often sick or absent, and many older people viewed the schools with suspicion. A common idea was that they were responsible for outbreaks of disease. In fact, one shaman proclaimed that illness came from the trumpet blown by the teacher at the opening of the school, an act that spread disease over the camp like a mist. The teacher reported, "I was not such a monster as to sound it again, so the Indians 'still live.' "

At first, teachers had to communicate with their students in the Chinook Jargon. English made some headway, but in 1864 the teacher reported difficulties in inducing children to speak it, and in 1866 the new teacher said that although the boys could understand English, "they will use that barbarous jargon, the Chenook." Prohibiting the use of native speech in schools became official government policy in 1887.

Because Christianity was equated with civilization, native religions were regarded by government officials as particularly pernicious, and everything possible was done to stamp them out. In an attempt to stem the tide of poorly trained, avaricious, and badly motivated agents, the reservations were in effect parceled out to the churches, with agents chosen by various religious denominations. In 1860, before the policy went into effect, Father Adrien Croquet, a Belgian Roman Catholic missionary, had arrived at Grand Ronde, where he remained for 38 years, well loved by Indians and respected by whites (except some Protestants).

The year Father Croquet arrived, he wrote the superintendent of Indian affairs for permission to bring nuns to operate a school at Grand Ronde. The boarding school there was under the auspices of the nuns for some 35 years.

Father Croquet also opened St. Michael's Church in 1862. Ten years later, 650 of the 870 Indians at Grand Ronde were at least nominally Catholic. Unlike many officials who spent time at Grand Ronde, Father Croquet had no interest in acquiring land or otherwise profiting materially from his position. His concern for the welfare of the Indians did a great deal to ease their adjustment to Western society.

In spite of the priest's efforts, however, native religions persisted at Grand Ronde, though decreasingly so as the years went by. Especially popular were the Warm House Dance and a variant of the Ghost Dance. The Indian Shaker religion, a Christianized reworking of native elements, also gained adherents, as did several Protestant groups. Shamans, though strongly discouraged by officials, continued to practice to some extent until after the turn of the century, but yearly the agents reported that their influence was declining. As the shamans died, they were not replaced and the old religions died with them. Even today, however, a few old people can remember being warned as children to stay out of the way of one old woman who was reputed to be an "Indian doctor."

In addition to adopting white religions, the Indians were expected to learn Euro-American occupations. Besides farming for themselves and for local whites, the men found an important source of income in logging. The women often made baskets for the white market in styles unique to each maker. Some of the baskets were taken to cities as far away as Portland.

Hop picking also deserves mention, for it offered not only a source of income but a time of celebration rivaled only by the Fourth of July fairs. From the 1880s well into the twentieth century, Indians came from all over Oregon to pick hops in the Valley. To them the games, dances, and opportunities to meet with distant friends and relatives were as important as the pay they earned.

ATTEMPTS TO DISSOLVE THE RESERVATION

Ironically, attempts to isolate Indians on the reservation were matched by attempts of the larger society to appropriate pieces of reservation land. No sooner had the Coast reservation been created than whites discovered the value of Yaquina Bay and the coast generally and began trespassing on the reservation. In 1865 a 30-mile-wide strip running east from Yaquina Bay was returned to the public domain, and almost immediately plans were made to eliminate the Alsea agency and the entire southern part of the reservation. Meanwhile 15 miles of land north of the Grand Ronde agency was being made available for eventual white use by removing the Indians who lived there and taking them to the Yamhill River headwaters. Congress later removed the southern section from the reservation and opened the lands north of Grand Ronde. All that remained were about 600 square miles around the Siletz and Grand Ronde agencies.

The Dawes Severalty Act of 1887 gave individual Indian heads of households title to 160 acres of arable land, with additional grazing land. (Single people and orphans received less.) Allotments were to be accompanied by full citizenship and by the dissolution of tribes, while programs in education, forestry, health, and employment were to be instituted to help Indians become good citizens.

Any "surplus" lands could be purchased by the government and returned to the public domain. By 1904 over 33,000 acres had been allotted, and 26,000 "surplus" acres of prime timberland had been returned to the government. The land was sold to private interests for about one dollar an acre. (Minor children were to receive per-capita payments for this land, but no payments were ever made.)

Although the allotment program did not work smoothly, more plans for "civilizing" Indians and improving their conditions continued to appear. In 1934 the Indian Reorganization Act created major changes by authorizing Indians to form business councils and corporations upon a vote of the tribes. At Grand Ronde the election took place in 1936, with most voters favoring the Act.

After World War II, the BIA adopted yet another policy: to terminate entirely those reservations whose tribes were considered capable of managing their own affairs. By 1950 federal controls were being reduced in favor of state and local controls.

In 1951 the Grand Ronde community in effect accepted termination, but reserved rights to hunt and fish under federal rather than state regulations. However, in 1954, when Congress terminated all western Oregon tribes, no provision was made for the loss of hunting and fishing rights. At that time 597 acres were left in the Grand Ronde Reservation, and just before termination 800 allotments were still held in trust.

The reservations were closed in 1956 and a trustee was appointed to dispose of the remaining land, most of which was sold by 1961. Tribal members received only a pittance, and many discrepancies in the financial records resulted. The question of land ownership was never fully resolved, and the tangled mass of federal, state, and local governments thoroughly confused the question of Indian rights and status. Through all these changes, some Grand Ronde Indians still had no ratified treaties and had never been reimbursed for lands taken from them.

The failure of the termination policy was all too clear. Its impact had not been foreseen by those tribal members who had supported it. Not only was land ownership in question but services were now cut off, allotments were taxed, local jobs were scarce, and some people were forced to sell out and move away. Many Grand Ronde Indians moved to Portland, Salem, and elsewhere in search of opportunities for work, but over 300 people remained on the former reservation. Those who had moved returned when possible to visit friends and relatives and to tend family graves.

RESTORATION

In the 1960s and 1970s Indians across the country who had never given up their tribal attachments worked to restore the reservations in an attempt to mitigate the effects of termination. At Grand Ronde, a tool shed on the remaining 2.5 acres of land became the tribal headquarters, and a newsletter was issued regularly. The Grand Ronde Tribal Council soon reorganized under a state corporation charter and began receiving some federal and private help. Not everyone favored restoration, but a resolution in support was eventually passed.

After nine years of much hard work by many people, the Confederated Tribes of the Grand Ronde Community of Oregon were restored in 1983. At that time, Grand Ronde members had incomes averaging about one-third those of other Oregonians, 68 percent were below the poverty level, and unemployment was three times the state average. "Restoration" meant that treaty obligations were once again acknowledged, making health, education, housing, and other benefits available. In 1988, after several years of negotiating with local, state, and federal organizations and individuals, a reservation of 9,811 acres on BLM-managed timber land in Yamhill County was established by act of Congress. Though the new reservation was a small portion of the former one, income from the timber was intended to provide the people of Grand Ronde with a subsistence base. To allay the fears of their neighbors and local timber companies, the Grand Ronde Tribes also negotiated a plan for hunting and fishing rights with the Oregon Department of Fish and Wildlife and agreed not to export timber or compete in the local timber market for 20 years. The tribes also agreed to set aside 30 percent of timber receipts for economic development and to adopt a 20-year plan of payments to Yamhill, Tillamook, and Polk counties for revenues lost from the land taken for the reservation.

Today, Grand Ronde is concentrating on improving and expanding services for over 2,000 members. The tribal logo shows Spirit Mountain, a sacred landmark, with five eagle feathers denoting the five remaining tribes, symbolizing the secure and functioning community now being rebuilt.

RELEARNING THE PAST: A LANGUAGE PROJECT OF THE KLAMATH TRIBE

BY ANDREA LERNER

"I always wanted to tell my husband in Klamath that I love him.
And now I feel like I am really fulfilled."
—Remark overheard at the first Klamath language class in March 1989

In the fall of 1987, the Klamath Tribe embarked on a journey of self-discovery designed to undo decades of damage to its cultural identity. The project the tribe undertook was a full-scale language-recovery program, aided in part by a grant from the Oregon Council for the Humanities. The story of how the Klamath began their project is an interesting one.

Like many tribes across the country the Klamath had been victims of a series of assiduous and damaging policies that climaxed in 1954 when the tribe was officially terminated. In 1986, just a year before the language recovery project began, the Klamath successfully regained the right to tribal status with the successful passage of House Resolution 3554 through both houses of Congress and the executive branch. This legal victory followed two others: In 1974, *Kimbol vs. Callahan* reaffirmed the tribe's hunting, fishing, and gathering rights, and in 1975 the *United States vs. Adair* (known locally as the Adair case) reaffirmed tribal water rights.

As restoration became a reality, community members came together and began to pose some difficult questions. Their central concern was, "How can we reassert our identity?"

If recognizing the Klamath people's integrity was merely a matter of paperwork for Uncle Sam, it was more complicated for the tribal members themselves. After a century of attempts by the dominant society to obliterate their cultural identity, tribal members questioned just what it meant to be distinctly Klamath again. "In what ways," they asked, "does a minority culture that is totally surrounded by the dominant culture reassert its unique identity?"

As part of a charge of legal restoration, the tribe assembled a comprehensive needs assessment survey which was sent out to enrolled tribal members all across the state as well as to individuals and families across the country. The purpose of the assessment was to help the tribal administration identify those areas of concern that members felt most strongly about.

The survey was completed and returned by approximately 93 percent of those who received it, which demonstrates a phenomenal degree of interest by tribal members. It was clear already that the Klamath themselves were eager to work together and celebrate their identity.

In the area of cultural concerns, the survey item that drew the greatest response was language restoration. Following this lead, the tribe began to develop a language program that would meld a traditional tribal approach to education with the most advanced technology available. In ways, this wedding was symbolic of the tribal situation itself. Wishing to celebrate its past and cultural heritage would not mean a romanticization of the "the way things were." Rather the tribe would struggle to balance the advantages and opportunities of modern life with the richness of its traditional and cultural legacy.

A BIT OF BACKGROUND

How does a language come to the verge of extinction? The Klamath situation, like that of many other tribes, is essentially a result of a history of self-serving, if at times well-meaning, government policies, which are discussed elsewhere in this publication. However, in the Klamath case, two features of government policy stand out.

The first is the belief that the best answer to the "Indian problem" was to make Indians as much like the newer inhabitants of the North American continent as possible—to break down Native American cultures. In terms of indigenous languages, the most threatening effect of this policy may have been the requirement that

Author's Note: I would like to note my special thanks to Mr. Gordon Bettles, culture and heritage specialist of the Klamath Tribe, for his assistance in preparing this report. I do maintain, however, that any errors of a factual or descriptive nature are mine alone.

Indian children of school age be forcibly removed from their communities and sent miles away to boarding schools, where they were denied the right to honor their customs and severly punished for speaking their language. As a result, generations of young Indians did not learn their native languages and as years passed, many families turned to the exclusive use of English in their households so that their children would not have to face further abuse from boarding school officials.

The policy disrupted traditional connections between tribal elders and young people. In Klamath culture, the education of youth had always been the domain of the community's elders. During the boarding school era, even when Indian children returned home on school vacations, many of them no longer spoke their languages. And because many elders did not speak English, the traditions of storytelling and cultural transference did not take place. Not only was language receding, so too were ceremonies and others facets of Native American life that relied on language for cultural transmission.

A second feature of United States Indian policy that jeopardized native languages was the Allotment Act of 1887. Under its terms, Indian peoples were allowed to sell individual land holdings to white settlers. Although the Klamath Tribe fought valiently against the effects of the Act, by 1906 allotment was bringing a steady stream of homesteaders into what was once Klamath land.

The problem of white encroachment was severe. According to Theodore Stern, in 1924 Superintendent Fred Baker reported in his Annual Narrative Report that "whites were acquiring title to Klamath lands at a rate which he estimated would render the Indians homeless in twenty-five years." Again, the government was breaking down traditional tribal values by violating one of the most cherished tenets of native life—communal land holdings. The outcome was a mixed community where English came to be the dominant language. In addition, there was a migration of young Indians to cities like Portland and Seattle in search of jobs.

The final blow to Klamath cultural integrity and the language came in the form of the government's ultimate solution to "the Indian problem": the policy of Termination. The Klamath Tribe was officially terminated in 1954. Lacking a land base, communication between generations, and legal recognition, the Klamath found that their language and sense of tribal identity were in peril. Ironically, it was largely because of such a sustained and systematic assault on the tribe that the Klamath finally challenged the federal government. Following the lead of the Menominee Tribe, which had successfully gained legal restitution and recognition, the Klamath launched a long and bitter struggle with the U.S. government. In part because they came so dangerously close to losing their language and foresaw the resulting loss in cultural terms, the people rallied with unparalled vigor to reassert their identity. Perhaps this experience accounts to some degree as well for the way the community has embraced its current language program.

THE LANGUAGE PROGRAM

In 1987, according to the Klamath Culture and Heritage Committee, only a half dozen elderly people could speak the Klamath language. It is important to note, however, that archival materials about the language existed. These included waxed cylinder recordings of native speakers and scholarly texts that had been produced by anthropologists and linguists throughout this century. In particular, Barker's *Klamath Texts*, published in 1963, proved to be a vital source for scholars of the Klamath language. Yet by 1967 the living language had almost disappeared.

The winter of 1988, one of the coldest on record, dealt the tribe a further blow, when two of the six remaining Klamath speakers died in their homes of pneumonia. The Klamath knew it was time to act.

The language program they devised centered on actual language classes, taught by the tribal elders using traditional Klamath educa-

Klamath life traditionally centered on the importance of families and tribal elders as teachers and transmitters of culture. This pattern was disrupted by federal educational programs that removed children from their homes.

This family, camped near the Klamath Agency, had adopted Euro-American dress and implements—one of the first steps in the gradual process of becoming "civilized." Today, thanks to Klamath language instruction, the people are becoming "Klamath" again.

tional models. Their appeal was overwhelming. Classrooms were crowded with students, ranging from very small children to grandparents. Often whole families arrived and sat in class together facing the oldest members of the community. The classes were conducted weekly, and over the year their popularity forced leaders to seek out new and larger facilities.

The elders' teaching methods varied. Sometimes the class was taught by a single individual, but more often the teachers worked together. Sometimes they taught vocabulary, but they also used stories, legends, and myths. They were teaching more than language, and they knew it. In homes in Chiloquin and Klamath Falls and all around the area, people were not only practicing words, they were telling stories again. Those stories held the values of the people, the mythological and real links to the past.

The people were learning the old names of their surroundings, old words for the lakes and mountains, for the animals and trees. With the words back on their lips, interest sprang up for traditional sites, traditional foods. With the names came more of the stories.

Today, the Klamath language is being spoken again all around the region and has brought with it the strongest elements of cultural identity and pride. As the program continues to grow, one can see incredible changes. In the street and in the schoolyards, in shops, in living rooms, and over the phone lines, Klamath is being spoken and sung again.

While the Culture and Heritage Committee recognized its advances, it constantly sought to expand the range of the program. One of its members articulated the need to have the program reach all Klamath people and as a result, research was undertaken to staff classes in other centers of tribal population throughout the state including Portland, Salem, and Eugene. As well, Modoc and Yahuskan Snake members of the tribal community sought to begin their own language classes.

The most striking limitation program directors noted, however, was the paucity of skilled native speakers. Since virtually all of the teachers were elderly individuals, the tribe sought to shore up the language by developing a set of resources that would be lasting and easy to reproduce and distribute to tribal members. Using grant funds from the Oregon Council for the Humanities, the Culture and Heritage Committee began to produce a series of videotaped language lessons.

Videotapes were chosen instead of audiotapes because the Klamath language is very difficult to master, its sounds hard to reproduce, and its glottal stops uncommon in English. Although audio tapes are a more common and less expensive method of language training, the Klamath teachers felt it vital to see the language being spoken so they might better learn how the lips and tongue must be held to reproduce all sounds correctly. On the videos, students can see the elders demonstrating pronunciation and explaining where in the mouth the sounds actually come from or where in the chest and throat air is held and released.

The videotapes and classes are two components of the Klamath Tribe's wide-ranging program in language training. With the assistance of two noted linguists, Dr. Noel Rude and Dr. Scott Delancey

Elders like Neva Eggsman (seated) are again taking responsibility for teaching young tribal members. In their language lesson, these youngsters are also learning ancient cultural and spiritual values. Culture and Heritage Specialist Gordon Bettles (standing, center) reports that children and adults alike are taking a renewed interest in Klamath customs, festivals, and ceremonies.

from the University of Oregon, and with assistance from the Northwest Regional Educational Laboratory in Portland, the tribe has been able to publish a Klamath phrasebook and distribute it to all heads of households currently on the tribal register. Other resources the tribe has taken advantage of include a collection of language tapes recorded by several ethnologists and linguists, as well as Barker's 1963 dictionary. In addition, the education office has often referred to Gatchet's 1890 ethnography of the Klamath Tribe and to works by Dr. Leslie Spier and Theodore Stern.

PRODUCTS OF THE WORK

The first product of the project is in some ways the easiest to assess. The tribe has on hand approximately 20 hours of videotaped language lessons. The tapes include several hours of rootword instruction, Klamath vocabulary, and pronunciation. The tapes also show the elders sharing oral histories, tribal history, and stories that demonstrate traditional Klamath values. These tapes help younger community members do more than understand their past: The values inherent in the stories point to ways of facing the challenges of contemporary life with integrity and pride in living the Klamath way.

Another concrete outcome has been the training of an all-Klamath video production crew. Using funds from the grant, the tribe contracted with a local video trainer and hosted several training sessions. All of the videos for the project were made by the Klamath crew, overseen by the Culture and Heritage Program. This skilled crew is now in position to record elders' storytelling sessions, oral histories, and other topics of tribal interest. The tribe was also fortunate to enlist the aid of KOTI, a local television station, and to use the facilities and services of the Oregon Institute of Technology in Klamath Falls to help edit the tapes under tribal direction.

Wokas gathering—an ancient fall activity—is now being celebrated in traditional ceremonies. Wokas, the seeds of a water lily found in the area, were once a staple of the Klamath diet. Today thay are considered a delicacy.

A third outcome of the project is the reemergence of several cultural endeavors that seem to stem from the language program. Gordon Bettles, culture and heritage specialist, reports that in the past year his office has received numerous queries from tribal members seeking information on Klamath vocabulary and customs. He also reports that there has been a burgeoning of traditional festivals. Mr. Bettles points out that tribal members have celebrated traditional wokas-gathering ceremonies and the gathering of huckleberries and apos (a kind of root), two traditional foods. Several individuals have also participated in naming ceremonies to acquire Klamath names. As more people study the language, the old songs and ceremonies are being taken up again—a hint that language and culture are closely connected. Bringing a language out of musty textbooks and into the mouths of the community has brought back and will continue to bring back other cultural components, including ceremonies and gatherings.

Finally, the classroom atmosphere itself has reasserted the once-vital connection between Klamath elders and young people. In traditional Klamath culture the elders oversaw the education of the next generations, an education that included cultural, religious, and spiritual values. Aside from the concrete value of language instruction, the benefits of this reaffirmation of family and community among the tribe has only begun to be estimated and appreciated. As one middle-aged tribal member observed, "When we learn from our elders, we are all children again."

Tribal members are coming together in classrooms, in community centers, and in kitchens speaking the language. Ceremonies that have not taken place in years because not enough people knew the words are now being celebrated again. These developments have led to a widespread tribal interest in working on new and related projects. One might say—as they themselves have—that the people are becoming "Klamath again."

The Pulitzer Prize winning Native American novelist N. Scott Momaday has continually referred to the incredible power of language, of the spoken word, in American Indian culture. Perhaps in the activities of the last year, the people have harnassed this power "of the word" as an answer to these lines penned almost four decades ago by a Klamath leader:

We have no power over what has been but we have it in our own power to shape our future and the future of our children. Out of the discouragement, the bitterness of the past, and out of Termination, perhaps something good can be created. It is important that you and I work harder than ever so we can continue to lift up our heads with pride, and if they were living today, our ancestors, too, could be proud of us.

Seldon E. Kirk
Past Chariman , Klamath General Council
Letter to the Klamath People, *The Klamath Tribune*, 1961

16

THE CONFEDERATED TRIBES OF SILETZ INDIANS OF OREGON

BY CYNTHIA VILES WITH TOM GRIGSBY

*Since the restoration of federal recognition of the Siletz Tribe in 1977,
the Siletz people have organized efforts to provide a wide variety of programs
to their community. A cultural program was established by tribal government
in direct response to a growing interest on the part of the general membership.
An important goal of that program was to better understand traditional
Siletz cultural patterns and thereby to reinforce tribal identity.*

First, tribal programs have encouraged the collection of examples of material culture and historical documents to be used for both research and exhibition. Second, coordinated activities have brought elders and youth together to encourage the direct transfer of traditional values. Third, members of the cultural program have contacted elders to help in the documentation of tribal culture, history, and languages as those elders remember them. This oral history project has the added benefit of moving closer to the completion of a written tribute honoring elders whose unique perspectives have provided personal insight into the diverse events that have shaped tribal history.

A BRIEF HISTORY OF THE SILETZ

Prior to white contact, the coast and inland valleys of Oregon were a hodge-podge of linguistic diversity. At least three unrelated language families were represented: Athabaskan, spoken in various closely related dialects from the California border to the Upper Umpqua River; Penutian, represented by diverse, mutually unintelligible languages such as Takelma, Hanis, Miluk, Alsea, Mollala, and Calapuya; and the Salishan languages such as Tillamook. With the establishment of the Siletz Reservation in the 1850s, a fourth unrelated language family—Hokan—was introduced, as represented by the Shasta.

Though cultural practices among these diverse groups were relatively homogeneous, the linguistic situation was complex. The native peoples adapted to this diversity in two ways: through the adoption of a "trade language," Chinook Jargon, and through multilingualism. Because of the mutual intelligibility of the various Athabaskan dialects spoken by the people who were to become the ethnic majority on the Siletz Reservation, Chinook Jargon was never adopted to the extent it was at the nearby Grande Ronde Reservation.

The Indian peoples living along the southern Oregon coast prior to European contact conducted their daily lives in the context of small villages comprised of large extended families. A typical village might have been composed of 100 individuals who were related through the male line. Through the custom of what anthropologists call patrilocal post-nuptial residence, the wife would usually come from a neighboring village and bring her customs, arts, and language with her. In the words of one of John P. Harrington's informants, "when an Indian woman married in a different place, her children talked the language of the new locality. . .also her mother's language." This practice meant that children grew up speaking at least two different languages or dialects. An example drawn from Harrington's notes illustrates this tendency for multilingualism: "His mother spoke Takelma (a Penutian language), his father Gallice Creek (Pacific Coast Athabaskan), he married a Mollala (Penutian), and his grandchildren heard and spoke Chinook Jargon." Moreover, the proximity of villages and trade and visiting relationships would have encouraged multilingualism.

Shellfish were found in abundance in the coastal area where the Siletz Reservation was established.

Grand Ronde & Siletz Reservations

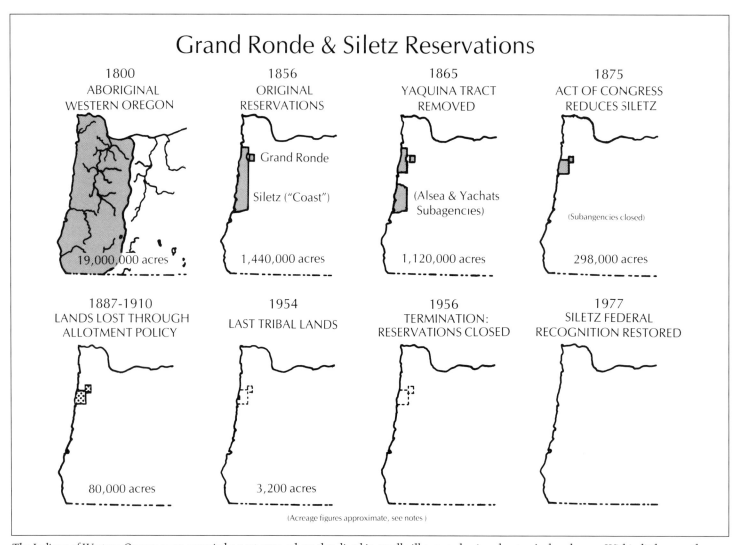

1800
ABORIGINAL
WESTERN OREGON

19,000,000 acres

1856
ORIGINAL
RESERVATIONS

Grand Ronde

Siletz ("Coast")

1,440,000 acres

1865
YAQUINA TRACT
REMOVED

(Alsea & Yachats
Subagencies)

1,120,000 acres

1875
ACT OF CONGRESS
REDUCES SILETZ

(Subangencies closed)

298,000 acres

1887-1910
LANDS LOST THROUGH
ALLOTMENT POLICY

80,000 acres

1954
LAST TRIBAL LANDS

3,200 acres

1956
TERMINATION:
RESERVATIONS CLOSED

1977
SILETZ FEDERAL
RECOGNITION RESTORED

(Acreage figures approximate, see notes.)

The Indians of Western Oregon once occupied a vast area, where they lived in small villages and enjoyed nature's abundances. Within little more than a decade after white settlers arrived, the federal government had reduced the Indians' territory to a narrow strip of reservation land along the central Oregon Coast. In 1865, a portion of the reservation was removed to allow for Willamette Valley commerce and oyster production. Ten years later, the Alsea Subagency was closed and the reservation further reduced in size. Between 1887 and 1910, some plots of reservation were "allotted" to individual Indian families, while white speculators succeeded in securing much of the timber-rich acreage. The final blow to the Siletz came in the 1950s when the tribes were terminated and their reservation closed. Today, following two congressional acts that restored federal recognition of tribal status and set aside scattered timber parcels for a reservation in Lincoln County, the Confederated Tribes occupy 3,666 acres at Siletz. These maps are taken from Oregon Indians: Culture, History & Current Affairs. Acreage figures are approximate.

In all probability each village was politically autonomous, and, in the case of the Athabaskans, had its own slightly different manner of speaking, but the differences from one village to another would have been gradual. The concept of each tribe or band with its own unique and far-reaching political organization is largely a construct of European contact and reservation life. With the establishment of the reservation in the 1850s came rapid cultural genocide.

Nature's bounty soon made Siletz attractive to non-Indians.

Representatives of the U.S. government knew that to control a language is to control a people's culture; the official government policy was to erase any vestige of "Indian" behavior.

Yet groups of elders who had been born into the old way of life gathered at the Siletz Agency store, Upper Farm, Lower Farm, DeLake, and Government Hill and they remembered the old ways: the words, the stories about One-Horn, the trickster Coyote, Salmon, Hummingbird, Big-Snake, and good-medicine and bad-medicine. They taught the listening children about the journey one takes after dying and about the responsibility one has to the dead. The children learned the importance of dancing for personal power and watched the Siletz Indian Feather dances during the Fourth of July celebrations. The children who were to become the elders of today learned and took pride in their heritage.

By the 1930s only a few elders remained as living repositories of the past culture, but the children listened and learned.

Those who were young then remember how logging came to be the main source of employment for men and how more and more white people took up the land and then sold off the timber. They talk about the 12 logging camps right around Siletz and how Indians were the strongest, quickest, and safest loggers. They remember baseball and basketball games between the towns of Siletz and Toledo and that the greatest athletes were always the Indians. For many, the early decades of this century brought summer work in hop fields in the Willamette Valley, where many families would later make their homes.

By the time of federal termination of the Siletz as a confederated tribe in 1954, members of our oldest generation were in their late thirties to mid-fifties. They and their children would experience relocation and the 23-year period of termination. The effect that termination had on the tribal community was to reduce the number of tribal community activities, which in turn accelerated the losses that had taken place four generations earlier.

RECAPTURING TRIBAL HISTORY

The life experiences of the oldest generation provide a perspective on tribal history that spans the generations of Siletz peoples from the time of removal to the present. It is they who hold the knowledge of an old way that their parents and grandparents lived, and of a newer way that their children and grandchildren live. These elders have a foothold in both worlds. To maintain tribal continuity over the generations has been a phenomenal challenge on a *collective*, as

Oral histories provide vital information about tribal history, including methods of gathering food. Well into the reservation period, open-weave baskets and pry poles were used to collect mussels from rocks along the shore.

SOME OBSERVATIONS ABOUT THE LANGUAGES AT SILETZ

The language situation in the latter half of the nineteenth century at Siletz was complex. After removal to the Siletz Reservation in the 1850s, the Confederated Tribes included over 27 bands of Indians such as the Tillamook, Siuslaw/Umpqua, Coos, Coquille, Shasta, Tututni, and Chetco peoples with at least four major language families represented (Salishan, Penutian, Hokan, and Athabaskan). Because of the diversity of languages spoken on the reservation during this period, a trade language (Chinook Jargon) was adopted during the latter half of the nineteenth century and continued to be spoken as a *lingua franca* until the early 1900s. Through surveys conducted by the cultural program, it had been learned that some elderly individuals may have retained varying degrees of competency in these languages. This study attempted to identify the specific languages/dialects retained by the elders.

After the establishment of the reservation, English rapidly became the language of social interaction. No doubt various dialects of the several languages (primarily Athabaskan) continued to be heard, but the prominence of any one form of speech would have depended on geographical location. For example, an analysis of historic records and records of the original allotments shows that there was a tendency for Shasta Costan speakers to settle in one part of the reservation and Tututnis or Mikwunutunnes in another. No doubt to an individual living at Upper Farm (one of the early settlements) *the* Siletz language would have appeared to have been Tututni, to an individual whose allotment was at the Agency, Chetco. These biases may have influenced today's perception of what "our language" is in the minds of many tribal members. In fact, each of the Athabaskan dialects was mutually intelligible and would have been understood by the speakers of the day. Put another way, the differences between these dialects were probably not much greater than the differences between Australian and American English as spoken today. Most differences recognized today are the artifacts of time and social divisions that have grown up since white domination.

Only fragments of Athabaskan (probably a variant of Mikwunutunne or Coquille) and Jargon are remembered and may soon be moribund. Any projected language curriculum will have to take this into account.

All interviews were tape recorded and curated in the tribal archives. These tapes will provide a data base for future scholarly investigations in dialect geography and culture change. Our research also located the existence of previously unknown tape recordings of several Athabaskan speakers. Arrangements were made to provide for the curation of these valuable recordings.

—Thomas L. Grigsby,
Director of a 1987 Linguistic Survey of the Siletz Membership

well as an *individual*, level. For the great grandchildren of the oldest generation, there is a tribal community and a tribal identity.

THE FOCUS OF THE SILETZ SELF-STUDY PROJECT

The focus of the Siletz self-study project has been to finish the process of transcribing previously recorded linguistic material and oral histories and to conduct additional interviews whenever possible. One purpose has been to gather as much information from elders as possible. The method and orientation used in this project has been to incorporate what Henry B. Zenk has called "memory" or "reconstructive" ethnography. A publication of "living" history will be presented to the elders and their families in honor of their lives.

Elders like the two pictured here experienced removal to the Coast Reservation. They are dressed for the Feather Dance. This generation carried forth traditions for those who were to follow.

17

THE MOORHOUSE COLLECTION: A WINDOW ON UMATILLA HISTORY

BY DEWARD E. WALKER, JR.

The Confederated Tribes of the Umatilla Indian Reservation include some 1,425 descendants of the Walla Walla, Umatilla, and Cayuse Tribes, whose traditional territory spanned large portions of both Washington and Oregon. Initially formed through their treaty of 1855, their reservation has been reduced in size and opened to non-Indian settlement by various actions of the federal government.

Through provisions of the Treaty of 1855, negotiated with the federal government, the Confederated Tribes continue to exercise various hunting, fishing, and other rights on lands outside the boundaries of their reservation. Currently, their tribal government is initiating a number of educational, economic, and cultural programs that show great promise of success. Especially noteworthy are their planned participation in the Umatilla Basin Project, the Oregon Trail interpretive center, the fisheries program, the nuclear waste programs associated with the Hanford Nuclear Reservation, and the cultural resource management program.

USING HISTORICAL PHOTOGRAPHS TO PROBE MEMORIES OF THE PAST

Most available ethnohistorical writing on the Confederated Tribes of the Umatilla Indian Reservation emphasizes events of the region's non-Indian exploration, settlement, and development, especially the military and political conquest of the tribes, their concentration on reservations, and the influx of white settlers. However, little attention has been given to the tribes' views of their own culture and recent history. Now, with partial funding from the Oregon Council for the Humanities, an oral history project has been undertaken that will elicit historical knowledge from tribal elders.

The project is unique in that it uses photographs taken by Major Lee Moorhouse during the late nineteenth and early twentieth centuries to trigger the memories of the tribes' oldest members. Moorhouse was the Indian agent on the Umatilla Reservation be-

tween 1889 and 1892 and operated an Indian curio shop and photography studio in Pendleton. At the inception of the project, filmmaker Larry Johnson and I traveled to Eugene and reviewed the original glass plate negatives in the Moorhouse collection, now housed in the University of Oregon's photographic archives. From the collection, we chose several dozen photographs for use in interviewing tribal elders.

In the interviews, the project's staff used a set of open-ended questions prepared in cooperation with tribal leaders Antone Minthorn, Louie Dick, and William Burke and Education Director Marguerite Allman. These questions were designed to elicit information about the identity of persons in the photographs, descriptions of events, and evaluation of Moorhouse's photographic techniques. The responses were full of rich historical detail and tribal elders were able to identify many of their ancestors in the photographs.

As part of the tribal project, information is also being collected on Moorhouse himself and on the photographic techniques he employed. We found that the tribal elders considered some of those techniques to be unrealistic and unfamiliar in their emphasis on classical poses. The elders also noted that the clothing, costuming, weaponry, and other props Moorhouse used were not typical of the Umatilla at the turn of the century.

Despite these shortcomings, the Moorhouse collection has proven to be a valuable device for eliciting memories of the past that might otherwise be lost to future generations. It has helped to reveal important events that normally escape the attention of academic and official tribal historians.

RESPONSES TO THE MOORHOUSE PHOTOGRAPHS

One of the major features of early reservation life remembered by older tribal members is the boarding school. Moorhouse took a number of photographs of the boarding schools on the reservation during the early decades of the twentieth century that revealed the highly regimented life maintained in them. As one tribal elder remarked,

Our homes were the shelter for our culture and traditions. But our children were removed from our homes and put into boarding schools. This prevented them from learning our language and culture. It also weakened our families. Elders were no longer able to teach them as before. A majority of our children entered these schools with no knowledge of English, but came home unable to speak our Indian language. These schools were run like the military. There was no escape. Many of our children died in these schools. They couldn't stand it.

Above. *A major feature of early reservation life was the presence of boarding schools, which imposed military discipline on students.*
Opposite. *The Moorhouse photographs capture the importance of horses on the reservation. One informant called the horse "the high point of our Indian culture." Another recalled that people sometimes rode great distances to hunt, fish, and gather roots. Pictured here is Luke Minthorn.*

During the early decades of the twentieth century, most members of the Confederated Tribes were farmers and still depended on horses. The horse had been a primary form of wealth and pride in the traditional cultures of the Cayuse, Umatilla, Walla Walla, and neighboring tribes. Most contemporary tribal members recall the wealth in horses they possessed and their reputation for quality horses. During the Moorhouse era, horses were beginning to give way to automobiles and the Moorhouse photographs have elicited memories of this transition. Most elders remember the last years of this transition and were often raised with horses rather than cars as their primary mode of transportation. The Moorhouse photographs helped bring to life memories of herding, breeding, riding, and caring for horses, tasks children were often assigned. Were it not for the Moorhouse photographs this historical dependence on horses would not be so evident. As one elder has noted, their central importance cannot be easily exaggerated.

They used to have these horse roundups at Thorn Hollow and up at Telephone Ridge. I think at that time (1940) the horses were still very important to our people. They used them for hunting, fishing, and for root digging . . . . Horses were the high point of our Indian culture . . . . Everything was in terms of horses . . . and when I learned to talk Indian, everything was in terms of horses. It was a big part of our language. Roundups were held at other places like Allen's corral above St. Andrews mission and near Pilot Rock. I believe the last roundup on the reservation was in 1948 or 1949. After that they began to exterminate our horses. They would get in the fields of the farmers, and they would round them up and sell them, just to get rid of them. In the treaty minutes (1855) they say we had 20,000 horses.

Another elder, recalling the days of the horses presented so clearly in the Moorhouse photographs, stated:

We used to round up horses as far south as Starkey (near La Grande, Oregon). The horse had to do everything. They went to root digging on horses; they went up towards Elgin and down towards Hells Canyon, all over. I remember my father in-law telling me that he used to ride from Pendleton to Lapwai (Idaho), three days of hard riding. He would ride on a horse and lead another. At night he would camp and then ride the other horse the next day. Then he would camp the next night and switch again. That way he would always have a strong fresh horse. . . . The people used to ride clear over to Nespelem (Washington). . . . They used to go as far as the ocean (Pacific) and get salmon. . . . My mother was born on such a trip down to Baker, Oregon, where they hunted, fished, and gathered roots.

The Moorhouse photographs have helped a number of elders recall famous tribal personalities, some of whom have been largely ignored in previous writings. On being shown a Moorhouse photograph of an automobile and driver, a tribal elder stated:

This is Parson Motanic. . . . He was one of the successful Indian farmers on the reservation. He had many cattle and pigs. He had a huge combine (wheat) and a new car (Hudson). . . . He was a

One of the most successful farmers on the reservation was Parson Motanic, seen here in his new Hudson. A member of the Cayuse Tribe, Motanic was renowned for his strength.

very successful farmer and extremely strong. . . .He could lift wheat sacks with one in each arm (each weighing 100 lbs) at the same time. . . .He beat Frank Gotch, the first recognized world's (wrestling) champion . . . here in Pendleton. He threw Gotch out of the ring. . . .They had to have the deputy sheriff escort my grandfather (Parson Motanic) out of town, because Frank Gotch threatened to shoot him after Parson threw him out of the ring.

During the Moorhouse era there were still members of the Confederated Tribes living in tipis (teepees) for extended periods of the year. Tipis were also used for storage areas adjacent to the log and frame structures that were appearing on the reservation during this era. One elder states:

They had a teepee there (Thorn Hollow) by their house. When you went inside the teepee there was this place where they had things they were keeping, a storage area . . . .These older teepees were large, larger than most teepees that I see nowadays . . . . You never see them anymore. They were tall teepees. . . .They were also made different. These (now) are more round, but the taller teepees are more full in the front, then straighter down in the back . . . .We used to see them at the Pendleton roundups a lot . . . . I never got to see a teepee made of tule mats (several Moorhouse photographs depict tule mat teepees). They are the oldest . . . .they used to put up a longhouse made of several teepees at Cayuse in the 1930s and in the 1940s . . . .Sometimes they would dig a pit and set the teepee down in it to protect it from the wind especially along the Columbia River where it is so windy . . . .There seems to be more reverence shown by people in a teepee, especially when there are ceremonies. The door used to face east and all the men would sit on the north and the women on the south (during ceremonies).

When viewing a Moorhouse photograph of grandparents with

their grandchildren, another elder remarked about his early childhood discipline:

I remember when I was a boy, my grandfather and I took off from this place out here. We were alone there at the house together, just him and I, and we rode a horse . . . . I rode behind him, and we rode clear up to Cayuse . . . . In those days kids were taught to obey. After he took the saddle off, set it by the tree, and tied the horse, he would tell me to sit there. I wouldn't move, because they had whip men if you did anything wrong. They had permission to whip you. So you didn't do anything out of line.

A surviving tradition photographed by Moorhouse is the sweatbath. It is still in use and the photograph brought the following comment from an elder:

Sweathouses were always close to the teepees and usually close to a creek . . . . The sweatbath could heal people of illness. A lot of people don't take much stock in that, but I do. They keep you healthy.

A very famous medicine man, Charlie Whirlwind, was photographed by Moorhouse. One elder described Whirlwind in the following manner:

He was over six feet. He had sons and one was very tall. Gus Raymond (a Nez Perce) said he was the tallest Indian he had he had ever seen, maybe seven feet . . . .Whirlwind played with rattlesnakes and during a medicine dance he was bitten . . . . He had always used them as a medicine, but that time he was drinking, and that's how he got into trouble. He got bit and eventually died from that bite.

Many Moorhouse photographs depict the missionaries and Bureau of Indian Affairs personnel on the reservation in the early decades of the twentieth century. Tribal police enforced the rules. One elder described them as follows:

They still had Indian Police when I was a boy. One I remember was Galloway, a white guy. Gilbert Conner was a policeman and so was Ike Patrick. There were several others. Captain Sumpkin was head of the police before them . . . . If you didn't do what the agent said, it was like Russia. The police would be on you. In those days the superintendent (B.I.A.) was equivalent to Stalin in Russia . . . . The Indian Police followed his orders. If a person tried to revert back to his older traditions, or if he wanted to leave the Reservation to live at his old home, they would go out and bring him back and publicly flog him, just like he was a kid. It was degrading. If you got caught gambling they would punish you the same way . . . . If some white person had a complaint against an Indian, the Indian Police would go get him and punish him.

The overwhelming influence of the Catholic and Presbyterian missionaries on the reservation during the Moorhouse era is evident in many of his photographs. One elder stated:

One of the things we see here (in the Moorhouse photographs) is that not only were the police used to force the tribal members into following the orders of the agent, but the missionaries were also showing the people how to live a different way. They trained ministers in the tribe, and these ministers were there to force changes on the people too. . . . Presbyterian preachers (Nez Perce) came from the Northern Idaho Reservation . . . . They looked down on our religion. We would have Sunday services in our religion (Washat), just giving thanks for things we have been given like fish, deer, elk, our roots, and our berries. That was looked down on by the missionaries as us worshipping another god . . . . A lot of people have tried to say our religion came from somewhere else. They never stop to think that it came from here and not from anywhere else. The missionaries came here to change our religion and to teach us we would burn in hell. We don't believe that.

Another elder described one such tribal member who had been trained as a preacher by the missionaries:

He had a hell and fire delivery. He would get up there and he would bounce up and down on his toes and holler. He had your attention. If you didn't understand the religion you still got something out of his body movements . . . . They were trying to get rid of the old way .They even had you punished, like if you were gambling — even if you went back in the sticks, and you were gambling there, and they caught you, you would be punished, whipped.

Certain of the Moorhouse photographs awakened memories of intertribal warfare with the Bannock about 1878. These accounts have been passed down several generations as part of the rich oral history of the Confederated Tribes of the Umatilla Indian Reservation:

It is "No Shirts" village in that picture where all the teepees are. The Cayuse caught up with Eagan up here by Deadman's Springs somewhere. The man that shot him, shot him through the arm, and he was helpless . . . . The Bannock wanted allies to fight the white people . . . . They came around through Burns and Long Creek and Ukiah, that way . . . . It must have been in the morning. There were a lot of them. Nobody could kill their chief. He would gallop back and forth to show his bravery, to let people shoot at him to show that he was strong and that nobody could kill him. Finally my great grandfather, Red Elk, ran out and jerked him off his horse and killed him. Then he claimed the war bonnet. That was a prize.

A famous medicine man, Charlie Whirlwind, was remembered as being very tall and using snakes in his ceremonies.

This photograph of Nez Perce preachers elicited memories from elders of "hell and fire delivery" and scorn for traditional ways of worship.

Tribal elders have found the Moorhouse photographs of their ancestors to be of the "Vanishing Red Man" genre, made popular by photographer Edward S. Curtis. Curtis's photographic and ethnohistoric study of the North American Indian, financed in part by J.P. Morgan, celebrated the Vanishing Red Man and stimulated a number of imitators. A primary assumption of the Curtis approach was that the racial extinction and cultural assimilation of the Tribes was inevitable and imminent.

This approach fails to record the devastation of the Tribes' health and cultures that was occurring at the turn of the century, when many of the photographs were being taken, and in no way foreshadows the Indians' ability to develop modern tribal governments that today dominate many aspects of life in the Northwest. In short, the Curtis and Moorhouse photographs are thought by tribal elders to present a fictional and highly selective image of Native Americans — an image that extolled their past but failed to deal with their current state. This fatalistic approach also encouraged viewers to ignore the plight of the tribes and the federal government's role in divesting them of both their culture and their lands.

The Moorhouse photographs depict the growing presence of white people on the reservation. Some were married into the Confederated Tribes of the Umatilla Indian Reservation and one elder noted:

Some of them were Frenchmen from the Hudson's Bay Company days. They came here, a lot of them; they were poor and in rags. A lot of them settled up on Wildhorse and Meacham Creek. They rented and were allotted there sometimes. Some adopted Indian children to get into the tribe . . . . They say that the Walla Walla had the best land and were often married to the whites because of that.

HOW THE INFORMATION IS BEING USED

The rich oral history of the Confederated Tribes of the Umatilla Indian Reservation revealed in the foregoing responses to the Moorhouse photographs will be used for several purposes. As indicated earlier, a video presentation of certain of the Moorhouse photographs is planned. It will contain other photographs and a narrative sound track that draws from the responses of tribal elders.

Other planned uses of these photographs include projected ethnohistorical research concerning the location and other details of buildings that have been destroyed. I am continuing my ethnohistorical research through the Moorhouse and other photographic collections in cooperation with the Tribes, for it has become apparent that much valuable information can still be retrieved from the memories of tribal elders. Further, the tribal impacts of several major events over the last 150 years have yet to be fully described. For example, the impacts of allotment and settlement of whites among the Confederated Tribes of the Umatilla Indian Reservation were profound. The boarding schools also played a major role in

Tribal elder Ely Quaempts and anthropologist Deward Walker (right) review Moorhouse photographs.

the acculturation and assimilation of certain members of the Confederated Tribes. One of the most devastating changes deserving extensive research is the damming of the Columbia River. The Confederated Tribes of the Umatilla Reservation have always depended on the eels and the salmon and steelhead runs as a mainstay of their economy and way of life. The destruction and current efforts to rebuild these runs deserve an extensive ethnohistorical investigation. Future research concerning the tribes will build on the pioneering efforts of Dr. Theodore Stern of the University of Oregon. The Moorhouse photographs will continue to be an important means of involving tribal members in this historical research.

18

GIVING THE PAST A VOICE: THE CONFEDERATED TRIBES OF THE WARM SPRINGS RESERVATION

BY HENRY MORRISON MILLSTEIN

*The three Confederated Tribes of the Warm Springs Reservation in central Oregon
have a rich heritage that spans much of the Oregon country, from the Columbia and its tributaries,
where the Warm Springs and Wascos lived, to the harsh deserts of southeastern Oregon and Nevada,
where the Northern Paiutes roamed. Since the reservation was established 135 years ago,
the Warm Springs people have seen great travail and loss of traditional culture.
Yet they have successfully built a firm economic foundation for their reservation and—
in the process—succeeded in holding onto many of their ancient traditions and values.*

*In the shadow of the sawmill, the modern administration building, and the tribes' two radio stations,
the longhouse still rings with prayer songs handed down for generations. Traditional feasts celebrating
the coming of the sacred foods are also held each year, and many families still perform name-givings
and first-kill ceremonies and observe the rites and taboos surrounding death. Indian languages
are still spoken and the old legends of Coyote and the other Animal People are still told,
though chiefly by the older generation.*

For all their success in the present, the people of Warm Springs realize that they must hold onto their past and bring it into the future if they are to meet the challenges that face them. Mere material well-being is not enough; the spiritual and cultural values that animated the tribes for thousands of years must be maintained if they are to make their unique contribution to Oregon.

Fortunately, the tribes still have older members who can recall and recount their recent history and the traditional culture that was observed when they were children. Furthermore, there is a considerable body of scholarly material, published and unpublished, that pertains to the reservation and its people. With funding from the Oregon Council for the Humanities, the tribes have embarked on a project to record the memories of reservation elders and to locate published and archival sources of information on Warm Springs, with a view to obtaining as much of it as possible for archiving at the reservation.

THE PEOPLES OF WARM SPRINGS

The Warm Springs Reservation is home to three distinct peoples: the Warm Springs (sometimes referred to in anthropological literature as "Tenino"), the Wascos, and the Northern Paiutes. The Warm Springs and Wascos, though speaking entirely different languages, were closely related socially and culturally. Both had what anthropologists classify as a Plateau culture (see pages 8 - 14). Throughout their history, both Warm Springs and Wascos—but particularly the latter—took a leading role in a trade fair each year in early summer near Celilo Falls. There fell the nexus of two of the most important trade routes in aboriginal North America: one connecting the Pacific Coast with inland regions all the way to the Great Plains (providing, among many other items, the dentalia shells that are so prominent a part of Plains Indian regalia), and the other connecting California and the Klamath country with the north, all the way into what is now British Columbia. The Wascos, and to a lesser extent the Warm Springs, were thus experienced both in commercial transactions and in dealing with peoples of differing languages and cultures—experience that would stand them in good stead when they faced the challenge of Euro-American colonization.

The Paiutes' culture and lifestyle were quite different, for they inhabited the harsh desert regions of the Great Basin and won their living in a largely nomadic existence.

Archaeology shows that the ancestors of these groups lived a stable existence, well adapted to their various environments, over many hundreds of years. Starting in the nineteenth century, however, a destabilizing factor emerged that was to disrupt this long-established balance and harmony: Euro-Americans.

At first, the dwellers along the Columbia received white visitors with hospitality, friendly curiosity, and, at times, the commercial shrewdness they had learned from their long experience at the Celilo trade nexus. By the middle of the century, however, as settlers began to pour into the Oregon Country, the Wascos and Warm Springs saw that here they faced a new challenge, for these newcomers arrived not simply to trade but to live permanently in great numbers—and to impose their language, culture, and economic system on those they regarded as "savages."

The Warm Springs and Wascos sized up the situation and quickly decided, with their characteristic realism, that accommodation to the new situation offered the best chance for survival. In fact, by the 1850s some Wascos along the Columbia had already taken up farming in imitation of their new white neighbors. In the Treaty of 1855, they relinquished their claim to one-sixth the land mass of Oregon (comprising roughly the country between the Cascade crest and Willow Creek, east of the John Day River) in exchange for guaranteed retention of a reservation between the Deschutes River and the Cascades (far south of their usual territory) and certain benefits, including government assistance in farming and education.

The land they were allowed to keep for their reservation had little value for farming; indeed, letters of the time reveal that it was precisely the undesirability of the land for white purposes and its inaccessibility that led the government to set it aside for Indians.

For decades, the people of the reservation lived in great poverty, trying to eke out a living from dry, marginal land. To supplement farming's meager returns, they continued to fish regularly in the Columbia. The government attempted to deprive them even of this right, inducing them to accede to a deceptively negotiated treaty in 1865, which signed away the off-reservation fishing and hunting rights they had specifically reserved to themselves in the original Treaty of 1855. Fortunately, this latter treaty was so patently fraudulent that it was not long enforced and was ultimately tossed out by a federal court. Its history still stands as witness to the deep frontier animosity toward Indians, whose seasonal presence in or near The Dalles and other white settlements along the Columbia prompted the fraud in the first place.

Somewhat later in the century, starting at least as early as the 1880s, tribal members worked as seasonal laborers as far away as the Willamette Valley.

The Paiutes entered the reservation population as a result of the

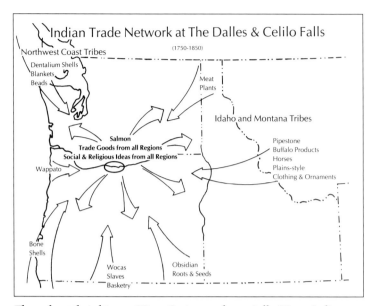

Throughout their history, Warm Springs and especially Wasco Indians took a leading role in the annual early-summer trade fairs held near Celilo Falls. These huge gatherings attracted Indians and trade goods from as far away as the Great Plains, California, and British Columbia. Major trade fairs and their smaller counterparts gave everyone an opportunity to share news, obtain scarce foods (especially salmon), dance, take part in ceremonies, and enjoy a variety of games. This map, taken from Oregon Indians: Culture, History & Current Affairs, *depicts general movements of goods to the Columbia River trade fairs.*

Bannock War. Traditionally, Paiutes ranged over much of what now comprises Lake, Deschutes, Harney, and Malheur counties. The Paiute bands of Oregon were offered the Malheur Reservation, a sizable chunk of land in the southeast Oregon desert. In 1878 some Bannocks in Idaho, close relatives linguistically and culturally to the Paiutes, rose in revolt against the white encroachment on their lands and induced the Paiutes to join them. As a result of the war, even the Paiutes not involved in the uprising fled the Malheur Reservation, which was terminated in 1882. Many Paiutes found themselves prisoners of war. One group, which had originally made its home in the area between Prineville and Bend, wound up interned at Fort Simcoe in Washington. Released from there, they made their way toward their homeland. Finding that the Warm Springs Reservation, not far from their native lands, was still Indian country, they asked permission to settle there. The Indian agent at the time noted with surprise how the Wascos and Warm Springs, traditionally at odds with the Paiutes, had welcomed the newcomers. Most likely, this is testimony to a growing pan-Indian consciousness, as Indians began to perceive themselves more and more as members of a single group standing against the whites.

Over the next several decades, reservation members struggled to eke out a living from the unyielding soil. These were years not only of poverty but also of powerlessness vis-à-vis the dominant society. There existed, at least in the twenties and thirties, a Reservation Business Committee consisting of four men, but it had virtually no authority. The tribes were at the mercy of the Department of the Interior and the BIA superintendent. Indians experienced the power of white institutions early in life, when they went off to the day school in Simnasho or the boarding school at Warm Springs, where they were forced to cut their hair, to dress according to current white fashion, to speak only English in place of their native languages, and in general to abandon any open practice of Indian culture.

Technologically, Warm Springs remained backward. Although the first cars appeared on the reservation in the 1920s, horses and wagons remained the dominant mode of transportation until the forties and even the fifties.

Not until the 1930s did change come to Warm Springs. John Collier, a crusading Commissioner of Indian Affairs, instituted an Indian New Deal. His efforts resulted in the passage of the Indian Reorganization Act (Wheeler-Howard Act), which enabled Indians to set up their own elected tribal governments, to which the federal government would relate on a government-to-government basis. Warm Springs quickly took advantage of the opportunity, voting itself a tribal constitution and charter and electing its first tribal council in 1938. The tribes carefully retained some elements of tradition in their governmental structure, including on the Council three chiefs, one for each tribe, who are chosen for life, generally from among families with a tradition for chieftainship.

The new government was unable to make any immediate change in Warm Springs' economic condition, although as early as the 1940s some profits from reservation timber were distributed to tribal members. In the following decade, however, the reservation's situation changed dramatically, albeit with a terrible ambiguity.

For many hundreds of years, the fishery at Celilo Falls had been central to the lives of the Warm Springs and Wascos, as it was to many tribes of the Columbia Plateau. Before the coming of the whites, the salmon fishery there provided much of the tribes' sustenance; and even after the reservation was founded, fishing at the falls provided many people with the bulk of their livelihood, while many others used the falls to supplement the meager living they gained from other sources. Celilo Falls was, moreover, a central locus of the tribes' culture, the place the Creator had provided for them to take their chief sustenance, the salmon.

In 1957, however, the backwater from the Dalles Dam covered Celilo Falls. The Warm Springs, along with several other Plateau tribes, had previously sold their fishing rights at Celilo Falls. They succeeded in turning this great cultural loss into a tribal economic gain, taking most of the $4 million they received and banking it for tribal use. They first spent this money on a study by Oregon State College (now University) on their economic resources. The researchers pointed out two areas for the tribes to focus on in economic development: timber and tourism. Within a few years, the tribes had bought up the privately owned sawmill on the reservation, so that they owned a whole timber industry, from stumpage to finished board. This industry became the foundation of Warm Springs' economic upswing. Their effort at tourism, centered on the Kah Nee Ta resort, was, until recently, less successful financially; but in the past few years it has begun to break even and, at least at some times, to show a profit.

For a culture whose wealth lay in salmon, access to traditional fishing grounds was vital. In 1909 Edward Curtis photographed a lone Indian fishing in the age-old manner using a dipnet and spring board. Decades after they were confined to the Warm Springs Reservation, some tribal members visited traditional sites on the Columbia River each year (center). In 1957 the Celilo Falls fishing grounds were destroyed to make way for The Dalles Dam. Today, a few Warm Springs Indians still fish from platforms such as these (bottom) on the Deschutes River.

The tribes also have income from rent on dams on the reservation, from the first Indian-owned hydroelectric plant in the nation, and from a number of smaller enterprises. They have used their wealth not only for reinvestment in and expansion of tribal businesses, but also for social services, housing, and education. Warm Springs is thus free of the grinding poverty that oppresses most reservations. This is not to say, however, that it lacks many of the other problems that Indians in this country struggle with: racism in the surrounding community, conflicts between Indian cultural values and those of the dominant society, alcohol and drug abuse. Nonetheless, the tribes are using their resources to confront these problems with energy and determination.

THE POWER OF MEMORY

Such, in brief outline, is the background and history of the Warm Springs Reservation, taken from external history, as it can be discovered from books and documents. But what do the people's own memories tell us?

The tribal Culture and Heritage Department is now engaged in recording oral history interviews with the older members of the tribes. Among them are people who have lived through the important transitions in the life of the Warm Springs community, including the adoption of the tribal constitution, the election of the first tribal councils, the loss of Celilo Falls, and the tribes' way to economic self-sufficiency and prosperity. They have lived through an important and dramatic time of change. Their early years were spent in poverty, in a community where traditional languages and lifeways still dominated; later, they saw this community transformed into one of the most economically successful Indian communities in North America—while its languages and many of its traditions and values fell into disregard or became the province only of a committed few. So they have seen and taken part in a history of both gain and loss. The story of cultural and social transformation that they have to tell is replete with lessons not only for their own tribal posterity but for all who are concerned with the processes of social change that are at the heart of human history. Thus far, we have only scratched the surface of this story. Nonetheless, several themes are already apparent in our oral histories.

Much of our interviewing has focused on the upbringing and education of people whose childhood fell between 1900 and 1930. These people were raised in traditional Indian ways and all attended the boarding school at Warm Springs for at least part of their school careers. Without exception, they noted great contrasts between their upbringing and the methods of child rearing prevalent on the reservation today.

Discipline in Indian families of the time was strict. Children were expected to listen respectfully to their elders, to carry out all requests without hesitation or complaint, and to master practical skills such as food gathering and preparation appropriate to their ages. They were also taught the value of work and sharing. One interviewee told of being made to go berry picking for an elderly man who was unable to pick berries on his own and had no one else to pick for him, and of helping a blind person whom the family had taken in. Children also joined in root gathering, eeling, and fishing—in short, in all the survival and subsistence skills which their tribes continued to practice, even as they were fitting themselves into the white economy and its modes of subsistence. One informant told of being taught to make buckskin gloves at an early age. These gloves were

The old and the new exist side by side in this 1942 photograph taken on the reservation. The new house was built by the Indian Service.

VOICES & MEMORIES

"I'd go to church and then on to the waashat and worship the same God. All and all I think the people of a long time ago didn't discriminate against anything."

"When we teach the young people what they want to learn, if they ask, well, we will translate some of the songs. But you cannot really translate the Indian language into white man's way the way it should sound. But we do try. I'm really glad the young people are trying to learn what these songs mean."

"My dad did talk about his dad being a foreseer and how he saw the white man was going to come—a different kind of people will come, with yellow hair and eyes like stars."

"We took four hours of academic work and four hours of our trade courses. At nights we had study hour. They didn't have time to get into all the mischief that a lot of the children do now."

traded for groceries and other necessities, thus largely obviating the need for money.

Most interviewees (except a few from more acculturated families) told of being disciplined in traditional fashion, not by their parents, but by a person, referred to as "whipman," whom the parents paid for this function (though the children typically did not become aware of this arrangement until adolescence). The whipman would come around at periodic but unpredictable intervals and whip the children for any infractions of discipline since his last visit.

Discipline was similarly strict at the boarding school and the other schools, such as day schools at Simnasho and Warm Springs and Chemawa Indian School in Salem. Students had long school days, consisting at times of four hours of academic instruction and four hours of training in home economics or a trade each day. In addition, boarding school students at Warm Springs and Chemawa were required to help clean and maintain their living facilities; and the boarding school at Warm Springs marched its students off to church every Sunday. The word "marched" is used advisedly; students were made to march, in quasi-military fashion, not only to church but also to a daily Pledge of Allegiance to the flag and to other activities. And matrons in the dormitories might be listening at any time to hear if students were speaking in Indian—an offense for which they were often subjected to corporal punishment.

One might expect that tribal members would look back with resentment on the discipline of their homes and even more on the boarding school, which aimed quite explicitly at extinguishing their language and culture. With a few exceptions, however, our interviewees looked back on their home life and the boarding school with great fondness, some even describing their boarding school experience as the happiest time of their lives. The boarding school is remembered as a place of making new friends, of expanding social horizons beyond the limited range of one's family and its often isolated home (these were, as already noted, days in which horse and wagon was the domi-

nant transportation and cars a rarity). Valued, too, were the practical skills taught at the boarding school, including training and practice in homemaking. When asked what was taught or what they learned at school, our interviewees invariably mentioned only the practical training, not the academic instruction, which clearly is of secondary importance to them—although all of them are literate and clearly make constant use of the academic skills they gained.

Discipline, too, both in the home and in school, they see as positive, particularly in contrast to today's situation, in which they feel children are growing up without any discipline or practical skills. Almost all of our interviewees were grateful to have grown up in a time when discipline was strict and respect for elders expected and enforced, and they regret the passing of those days.

It may be for this reason that they make so little mention of the academic side of their school experience. Children of today receive academic training, probably of a higher grade than the people of grandparenting age who have been interviewed; but today's reservation children are seen as lacking the training in discipline and in traditional skills that our interviewees received as a matter of course. In the interviews, they have pointed out the areas in which they feel contemporary life is deficient.

One may wonder why they express so little resentment toward efforts to suppress Indian language. Most of the people we have thus far interviewed, however, came from homes which were firmly attached to at least a substantial portion of traditional Indian practices and in which Indian language was regularly used. They had, therefore, a firm identity with Indian culture, and the enforced use of English did not threaten their fluency in Indian, which for the most part they continued to use at home.

Memories of elders, interviewed for the tribes' oral history project, often focused on school programs designed to make the Indians conform to white educational practices. Here, an early Warm Springs football team poses for the photographer.

These students from Chemawa were trained for work in the Portland shipyards during World War II.

It is worthy of note that some younger tribal members do express resentment toward the boarding school's efforts to extinguish Indian culture, and that the one person we have so far interviewed who has a negative attitude to the school came from a home in which, apparently, mostly English was spoken.

Although our interviewees look back positively on their own school years and apparently did not find themselves threatened by it in their Indian identity or knowledge of Indian language and culture, they do lay responsibility for the erosion of language, culture, and traditional discipline largely at the boarding school's feet. They attribute the disappearance of the whipman around the 1930s to parents who, raised in the boarding school, did not want their children to go through what they themselves had had to suffer from him. Similarly, many people attribute the decline in Indian language to parents who, having been brought up in the boarding school and punished for their use of Indian language, avoided speaking Indian to their children so as to spare them the harassment they themselves had suffered. This hints at stronger antipathy to the boarding school and its efforts to suppress Indian language than was expressed by those we have interviewed up to this time.

Be this as it may, one senses in our interviews, as in many conversations with older people on the reservation, a deep regret at the loss both of traditional skills and of traditional discipline among the younger generations. Elders often feel that economic prosperity has brought more loss—socially, morally, and culturally—than gain; in the old days, they say, when everyone was poor, people helped and watched out for one another far more than they do today. Some, however, do see signs of hope in the young people who now take interest and pride in their heritage and culture.

THE WRITTEN WORD

As noted above, the scholarly literature on Warm Springs and its constituent tribes is still relatively limited. There exists, however, a vast literature on tribes and cultures closely related to those at Warm Springs. We face the task of sifting through this literature and discovering what is relevant to the people of Warm Springs as they seek to understand their past.

The bulk of the scholarly work directly relevant to Warm Springs is archaeological, much of it originating in the University of Oregon anthropology department, where Luther Cressman so ably pioneered the discipline of Oregon archaeology. Many studies of sites frequented by possible ancestors of the present-day Warm Springs people, or of their close relatives, have been made. Perhaps the chief lesson of these studies is the relative stability and durability of the tribes' cultures over thousands of years. People have been drawing a living from the Plateau and Great Basin environments since long before there was anything resembling a civilization in the Near East and Europe; and while both regions have seen cultural and technological change, the three Confederated Tribes are certainly heirs to a cultural heritage of remarkable longevity and continuity.

Some recent historical and anthropological studies, most notably Miller's *Prophetic Worlds* and Ruby and Brown's *Dreamer-Prophets of the Columbia Plateau*, explore, in an integrated way, the world view and spirituality of the Plateau peoples. Such works, together with older works by Relander, Spier, and DuBois, can help those at Warm Springs anchor their personal knowledge of their people's religion and spirituality in a larger historical context.

Clearly, much is available, both in the memories of individuals and in the written word, to deepen and expand the self-understanding of the Warm Springs people, to help them see themselves as part of a cultural history that reaches as deeply into the realms of the spirit as it does into the vastness of time, and so to prepare themselves to move into a world vastly different from any envisaged by their forebears.

Despite the changes that Warm Springs Indians have had to undergo, their timeless ceremonies and traditions have endured. These dancers were photographed in 1956 at the ceremonies marking a farewell to Celilo Falls.

PRESENT-DAY TRIBAL HEADQUARTERS

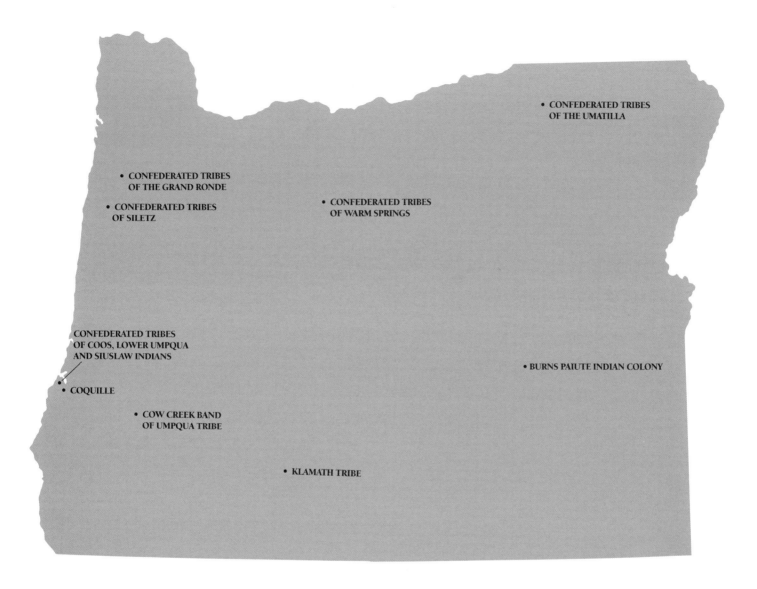

- CONFEDERATED TRIBES OF THE UMATILLA
- CONFEDERATED TRIBES OF THE GRAND RONDE
- CONFEDERATED TRIBES OF SILETZ
- CONFEDERATED TRIBES OF WARM SPRINGS
- CONFEDERATED TRIBES OF COOS, LOWER UMPQUA AND SIUSLAW INDIANS
- BURNS PAIUTE INDIAN COLONY
- COQUILLE
- COW CREEK BAND OF UMPQUA TRIBE
- KLAMATH TRIBE

Approximate locations of tribal headquarters for the nine federally recognized tribes or tribal confederations in Oregon

WRITERS

C. Melvin Aikens is a professor of anthropology at the University of Oregon and has written extensively about the Great Basin.

Stephen Dow Beckham is professor of history at Lewis and Clark College and author of several works on the Indians of Oregon, including *The Indians of Western Oregon: This Land Was Theirs* and *Requiem for a People: The Rogue Indians and the Frontiersmen*.

Rochelle Cashdan is a writer and anthropologist who has recently returned to Oregon from a research assignment for the National Gifted and Talented Indian Education Project in Belcourt, North Dakota.

Marilyn Couture is an anthropologist who teaches for the continuing education program at Linfield College. Since 1974 she has collected oral stories from members of the Burns Paiute Tribe, working in consultation with tribal members Rena Adams, Justine Brown, Ramona Charles, Emma Fox, Alfred Kennedy, Nepa Kennedy, Earl Louie, Marion Louie, Agnes Hawley Phillips, Minerva Soucie, Maude Stanley, and Bernice Teeman, as well as Jesse Williams of the Harney County Museum.

David H. French is professor emeritus of anthropology at Reed College, where he taught for 41 years. His research has focused on Pueblo Indians, Japanese-Americans, and the ethnobotany of central France.

Tom Grigsby received his Doctorate in anthropology from the University of Oregon and has over 20 years experience as a researcher and educator. Dr. Grigsby served as a consultant to the Cultural Program of the Confederated Tribes of Siletz Indians during 1987 and 1988.

Yvonne Hajda is a researcher and consultant in social and cultural anthropology, specializing in the ethnohistory of Northwest Indians. She is based in Portland.

Eugene Hunn is professor of anthropology at the University of Washington. He has been engaged in studies of the Sahaptin language and Plateau enthnography and ecology since 1976 and recently published *Nchi'i-Wana, "The Big River": Mid-Columbia Indians and Their Land* in collaboration with John Day River Indian elder James Selam.

Dell Hymes grew up in Portland, where he graduated from Reed College. He is professor of English and anthropology at the University of Virginia. For a number of years he has worked on Native American narratives and studied Chinookan languages.

Andrea Lerner teaches American literature and Native American literature at California State University, where she also heads the American Studies Program. She is editor of *Dancing on the Rim of the World*, a collection of contemporary Native American writing from the Northwest, published in 1990.

Henry Morrison Millstein has worked for 12 years as tribal linguist for the Confederated Tribes of the Warm Springs Reservation. He is a Reed College graduate and was a graduate student of linguistics and oral literature at Boston University under Dennis Tedlock.

Floy C. Pepper has been an educator for 52 years, serving as a teacher in Indian and public schools, a counselor, consultant, keynote speaker, author, administrator of special education, teacher trainer, and college instructor.

Sherri Shaffer is tribal manager for the Cow Creek Band of Umpqua Indians and a collaborator, with Stephen Dow Beckham, on a new slide program about Cow Creek history and culture.

Minerva T. Soucie is a member of the Burns Paiute Tribe and the tribe's cultural advisor, as well as a forestry technician for the Snow Mountain Ranger District, Ochoco National Forest. She is a consultant, artist, storyteller, basketweaver, and speaker on Paiute history and cultural resources. In 1990 she was named Harney County's Woman of the Year.

Kathryn Anne Toepel received her Ph.D. in anthropology from the University of Oregon and is now co-director of Heritage Research Associates, a private consulting firm in Eugene that specializes in Pacific Northwest archaeology and history.

Cynthia Viles is an enrolled member of the Siletz Tribe and has worked since 1983 in various capacities for tribal government— through work on the tribal court, various committees, and the tribe's Culture Committee. She was born and raised during the Termination era and is currently pursing a liberal arts degree at the University of Oregon.

Deward E. Walker, Jr. is professor of anthropology at the University of Colorado. He has worked with the Confederated Tribes of the Umatilla Indian Reservation since the late 1950s and has many publications dealing with the tribes and the Columbia Plateau. He is also a native of Oregon.

George B. Wasson, Jr. is the great grandson of Kitzenjinjum and Gishgia, grandson of Susan Adulsah and George R. Wasson, and one of five children of George B. Wasson and Bess Finley. He has retired after more than 20 years of service at the University of Oregon in academic counseling and administration and is now a council member of the Coquille Indian Tribe.

Donald Whereat is a member of the Confederated Tribes of Coos, Lower Umpqua, and Siuslaw Indians and serves as the tribes' cultural resource coordinator.

OTHER CONTRIBUTORS

Laurie Causgrove , who produced the calligraphy that appears on the cover and divider pages, is a freelance graphic designer/calligrapher in Portland.

Evelyn Hicks works at the Oregon Historical Society and has illustrated books for the OHS press. Her freelance illustrations have won publishing awards for the Audubon Society of Portland.

Lawrence Johnson is an independent photographer and filmmaker in Portland. He has produced numerous videos on Oregon subjects, including *The First Oregonians*, an overview of the native presence in Oregon, and a forthcoming video documenting tribal experience of the Confederated Tribes of the Umatilla Indians.

Lynn Kitagawa is a medical illustrator and teaches illustration at the Pacific Northwest College of Art. She donates much of her freelance artwork to non-profit organizations. When not drawing, Lynn enjoys flyfishing and skiing.

Victoria Tierney, whose illustrations appear on pages 105 and 106, lives in Bandon and served on the board of the Oregon Council for the Humanities. She is a former art director of *New York* magazine.

Chuck Williams is a member of the Confederated Tribes of Grand Ronde. He has both written about and photographed the Columbia Gorge in his book, *Bridge of the Gods, Mountains of Fire*. His photographs are often seen in Columbia River Inter-Tribal Fish Commission's publications

PRODUCTION STAFF

Carolyn M. Buan is a Portland writer and editor, whose firm, Writing & Editing Services, produces brochures, newsletters, annual reports, and other publications for business and nonprofit clients.

Jeanne E. Galick is a free-lance graphic designer in Portland.She designs corporate identity programs and promotional materials for high techonology firms and many non-profit organizations. She also designs *Oregon Humanities*, the magazine of the Oregon Council for the Humanities.

Richard Lewis has been executive director of the Oregon Council for the Humanities since 1977. He has provided overall coordination of the council's three-year program focus on the native peoples of Oregon.

MAP/ILLUSTRATION CREDITS

FRONT COVER. Portrait of Agnes Hawley of the Burns Paiute Tribe by Evelyn Hicks, based on a photograph by Marilyn Couture and used by permission of the Herbert W. Hawley family.

INSIDE FRONT AND BACK COVERS. Pictographs found in the Pine Creek Watershed of north central Oregon and taken from the booklet, T*he Natural History of Camp Hancock and The Clarno Basin, North Central Oregon* published by the Oregon Museum of Science and Industry;

PAGE VI. Woka gatherers' boats and pole by Evelyn Hicks, based on a photograph from the Smithsonian Institution.

PAGE VIII. Base map provided by Joe Poracsky of Portland State University, produced in the *Oregon Environmental Atlas* by Portland State University and the Oregon Department of Environmental Quality.

CHAPTER 1. Seascape on pages 2 and 3 by Evelyn Hicks; Page 7, forest scene by Evelyn Hicks.

CHAPTER 2. Food round illustration on page 8 by Lynn Kitagawa; Page 10, root digger by Evelyn Hicks; Page 11, Plateau winter house by Faun Rae Hosey, first published in *Oregon Indians; Culture, History & Current Affairs* and used by permission of Western Imprints, Oregon Historical Society.

CHAPTER 3. River scene on page 15 by Evelyn Hicks; Page 16, The Hunter by Patrick Curtis, part of a traveling exhibit produced by the University of Oregon Museum of Natural History.

CHAPTER 4. Page 21, Agnes Hawley of the Burns-Paiute Tribe by Evelyn Hicks, based on a photograph by Marilyn Couture and used by permission of the Herbert W. Hawley family; Pages 22 and 23, food groups by altitude and season by Lynn Kitagawa; Page 24, Paiute headdress by Evelyn Hicks.

CHAPTER 5. Computer map on page 29 by Jeanne E. Galick, based on a map by Jay Forest Penniman, appearing originally in *Oregon Indians: Culture, History & Current Affairs* and used by permission of Western Imprints, Oregon Historical Society; Page 30, language chart appearing originally in *Oregon Indians: Culture, History & Current Affairs* and used by permission of Western Imprints, Oregon Historical Society; Page 69, festival dancer by Evelyn Hicks.

CHAPTER 12. Woman with boat on page 83 by Evelyn Hicks; Page 86, coyote by Evelyn Hicks; Page 87, large fishing weir by Faun Rae Hosey, published in *Oregon Indians; Culture, History & Current Affairs* and used by permission of Western Imprints, Oregon Historical Society.

CHAPTER 13. The Eel-Catcher by Patrick Curtis on page 88 is part of a traveling exhibit produced by the University of Oregon Museum of Natural History; Page 92, tarweed flower by Evelyn Hicks, based on a slide from the Cow Creek Band of Umpqua Indians slide program.

CHAPTER 16. Crab and basket of shellfish on pages 105 and 106 by Victoria Tierney; Page 116, map of disappearing tribal lands by Jay Forest Penniman, originally in *Oregon Indians: Culture, History & Current Affairs* and used by permission of Western Imprints, Oregon Historical Society.

CHAPTER 18. Trading map by Jay Forest Penniman on page 116 published originally in *Oregon Indians: Culture, History & Current Affairs* and used by permission of Western Imprints, Oregon Historical Society; Page 121, base map provided by Joe Poracsky of Portland State University, produced in the *Oregon Environmental Atlas* by Portland State University and the Oregon Department of Environmental Quality. .

PHOTOGRAPHY CREDITS

(Unless otherwise noted, photos credited are from left to right and top to bottom of each page.)

CHAPTER 1. Page 4, Oregon Historical Society Negative #OrHi58495. Page 5, Oregon Historical Society Negative #4465 and #OrHi77340. Page 6, from the collection of Jack L. Slattery, courtesy of Stephen Dow Beckham; from the Bandon Historical Society.

CHAPTER 2. Page 11, Moorhouse Collection Negative #4786, Knight Library, University of Oregon; Oregon Historical Society Negative #OrHi67539. Page 12, Oregon Historical Society Negative #018927. Page 13, Moorhouse Collection, Negative #4020 and #4749, Knight Library, University of Oregon; Oregon Historical Society Negative #OrHi77189.

CHAPTER 3. Page 17, Smithsonian Institution, #76-91. Page 18, Oregon Historical Society Negative #OrHi78079; Cow Creek Band of Umpqua Indians (from the slide program described on page 94). Page 19, Oregon Historical Society Negative #OrHi46193 and #OrHi65927. Page 20, Oregon Historical Society Negative #OrHi21120.

CHAPTER 4. Page 24, Oregon Council for the Humanities. Page 25 and 26, from the film *The Earth Is Our Home*, Oregon Public Broadcasting and Oregon Council for the Humanities.

CHAPTER 5. Page 31, from the film *The Earth Is Our Home*, Oregon Public Broadcasting and Oregon Council for the Humanities. Page 33, *(top row)* Oregon Historical Society Negative #OrHi014710; Oregon Historical Society Negative #OrHi 4322; Moorhouse Collection, Negative #5212 and #4019, Knight Library, University of Oregon; *(second row)* Oregon Historical Society Negative #OrHi61962; Moorhouse Collection Negative #4768, Knight Libary University of Oregon; Bandon Historical Society; Moorhouse Collection, Negative #4993, Knight Library, University of Oregon; *(third row)* Oregon Historical Society Negative #OrHi47126; Coos County Historical Museum; Oregon Historical Society Negative #OrHi78031; Smithsonian Institution, Negative #79-4309; *(bottom row)* Moorhouse Collection Negative #4539, Knight Library, University of Oregon; Oregon Historical Society Negative #OrHi78 and #OrHi67068; from the film *The Earth Is Our Home*, Oregon Public Broadcasting and Oregon Council for the Humanities .

CHAPTER 6. Page 40, Moorhouse Collection, Negative #4812, Knight Library, University of Oregon. Page 42, Oregon Historical Society Negative #OrHi86876 and #624. Page 43, Oregon Historical Society Negative #OrHi44161 and #4472. Page 44, Oregon Historical Society Negative #OrHi5172; Smithsonian Institution Negative #2899A. Page 46, *(top row)* Oregon Historical Society Negative #OrHi0160 and #OrHi36845; *(middle row)* Dan Macy Collection, Warm Springs, Oregon, Courtesy of Central Oregon Community College; Moorhouse Collection, Negative #5473, Knight Library, University of Oregon; *(bottom row)* Oregon Historical Society Negative #OrHi36112 and # OrHi007202. Page 47, Oregon Historical Society Negative #OrHi86917, #CN019267, and #OrHi1677; Dan Macy Collection Warm Springs, Oregon, Courtesy of Central Oregon Community College. Page 48, Oregon Historical Society Negative #OrHi10691-b. Page 49, Oregon Historical Society Negative #OrHi57659. Page 51, Bandon Historical Society; Oregon Historical Society Negative #OrHi010516. Page 52, Oregon Historical Society Negative #OrHi44181 and #OrHi86499. Page 53, Oregon Historical Society Negative #OrHi007237. Page 54, From *Wana Chinook Tymoo*, a publication of the Columbia River Inter-Tribal Fish Commission.

CHAPTER 7. Page 56, Oregon Historical Society #Stout 553.

CHAPTER 8. Page 58, Photograph by Chuck Williams. Page 60, *(top)* Courtesy of Minerva Soucie; *(bottom)* Photograph by Chuck Williams. Page 61, Photograph by Chuck Williams. Page 62, Fashion photographs courtesy of the Warm Springs Clothing Company and Waterston Productions. Page 63, Courtesy of The *Eugene Register-Guard*. Page 64, Photograph by Tony Neidek, Northwest Regional Educational Laboratory. Page 65, Photograph by Steve Nehl, published in *The Oregonian*. Page 66, Photograph by Lawrence Johnson.

CHAPTER 9. Page 67, Courtesy of Minerva Soucie. Page 68, Photograph from Columbia River Inter-Tribal Fish Commission.

CHAPTER 10. Pages 70 and 71, Courtesy of the Burns Paiute Tribe. Page 72, Oregon Historical Society Negative #OrHi86878. Page 73, Courtesy of Minerva Soucie. Page 74, *(top)* Oregon Historical Society Negative #OrHi41248; *(Middle)* Courtesy of Minerva Soucie; *(Bottom)* Photograph by Marilyn Couture. Page 75, Courtesy of Minerva Soucie.

CHAPTER 11. Page 78, *(left)* Oregon Historical Society Negative #OrHi1658; *(right)* Courtesy of Stephen Dow Beckham. Page 80, Courtesy of Stephen Dow Beckham. Page 81, Manuscripts and University Archives/Special Collections Division, University of Washington Libraries, Melville Jacobs Collection, Negative #NA4080.

CHAPTER 12. Page 84, Oregon Historical Society Negative #OrHi015067. Page 85, Bandon Historical Society. Page 87, Oregon Historical Society Negative #OrHi78267.

CHAPTER 13. Page 89, The Cow Creek Band of Umpqua Indians (from the slide program described on page 94). Page 90, The Cow Creek Band of Umpqua Indians (slide program). Page 91, The Cow Creek Band of Umpqua Indians (slide program). Page 92, The Cow Creek Band of Umpqua Indians (slide program). Page 93, The Cow Creek Band of Umpqua Indians (slide program).

CHAPTER 14. Page 96, Oregon Historical Society Negative # OrHiCN22570. Page 97, Oregon Historical Society Negative #OrHiCN022572 and #OrHiCN022603. Page 98, Oregon Historical Society Negative #OrHi65090.

CHAPTER 15. Page 102, The Smithsonian Institution, Negative #28003-B; Oregon Historical Society Negative #OrHi23618. Page 103, Photograph by Jack T. Lee. Page 104, Oregon Historical Society Negative #1416.

CHAPTER 16. Page 107, Oregon Historical Society Negative #OrHi49251; Page 108, *(left)* from the collection of Jack L. Slattery, courtesy of Stephen Dow Beckham; Courtesy of the Lincoln County Historical Society 78-48.2 #83-B1.

CHAPTER 17. Page 110, Moorhouse Collection, Negative #5461, Knight Library, University of Oregon. Page 111, University of Oregon Moorhouse Collection, Negative #5009. Page 112, Moorhouse Collection, Negative #4231, Knight Library, University of Oregon. Page 113, Moorhouse Collection, Negative #4097 and 4548, Knight Library, University of Oregon. Page 114, Photograph courtesy of *The East Oregonian*.

CHAPTER 18. Page 117, *(top)* Oregon Historical Society Negative #OrHi167527; *(middle)* Oregon Historical Society Negative #OrHi81497; *(bottom)* Chuck Williams/Columbia Inter-Tribal Fish Commission. Page 118, Oregon Historical Society Negative #OrHi015298. Page 119, Dan Macy Collection, Warm Springs, Oregon, Courtesy of Central Oregon Community College. Page 120, Oregon Historical Society Negative #OrHi013610 and #OrHi007244.

SELECTED READINGS

Aikens, C. Melvin. "Archaeology of the Northern Great Basin: An Overview." *Man and Environment in the Great Basin*, eds. David B. Madsen and James F. O'Connell. Special Memoirs of the Society for American Archaeology, 2 (1982).

Anastasio, Angelo. "The Southern Plateau: An Ecological Analysis of Intergroup Relations." *Northwest Anthropological Research Notes*, 6, 2 (1972), pp. 109-229.

Barker, M.A. "Klamath Texts." *University of California Publications in Linguistics*, No. 30 (1963).

Beckham, Stephen Dow. Cow Creek Band of Umpqua Tribe of Indians: Occupation and Use of Territory in Southwestern Oregon. Docket 53-81L, Claims Court, Washington, D.C., 1983.

The Indians of Western Oregon: This Land Was Theirs. Coos Bay, Oregon: Arago Books, 1977.

Land of the Umpqua: A History of Douglas County, Oregon. Douglas County Commissioners, Roseburg, Oregon, 1988.

Requiem for a People: The Rogue Indians and the Frontiersmen. Norman, Oklahoma: University of Oklahoma Press, 1971.

Beckham, Stephen Dow, Rick Minor and Kathryn Ann Toepel. "Native American Religious Practices and Uses in Western Oregon." *University of Oregon Anthropological Papers*, 31 (1984).

Boyd, Robert T., ed. n.d. *The Diaries and Letters of Henry K.W. Perkins*. Portland: Oregon Historical Society Press.

Cohen, Fay G. *Treaties on Trial: The Continuing Controversy Over Northwest Indian Fishing Rights*. Seattle: University of Washington Press, 1986.

Confederated Tribes of the Warm Springs Reservation of Oregon. *The People of Warm Springs*. Warm Springs: Confederated Tribes of the Warm Springs Reservation of Oregon, 1984.

Couture, Marilyn D., Mary F. Ricks and Lucile Housley. "Foraging Behavior of a Contemporary Northern Great Basin Population." *Journal of California and Great Basin Anthropology*, 8, 2 (1978), pp. 150-160.

Curtis, Edward S. *The North American Indians, 8 (The Nez Perce, Walla Walla, Umatilla, Cayuse, Chinookan Tribes)*. New York: Reprint by the Johnson Reprint Corporation, 1911.

Drucker, Philip. "Contributions to Alsea Ethnography." *University of California Publications in American Archaeology and Ethnology*, 35, pp. 81-102.

"The Tolowa and Their Southwest Oregon Kin." *University of California Publications in American Archaeology and Ethnology*, 36, pp. 219-299.

Fowler, Catherine S. "Subsistence." *Handbook of North American Indians*, Vol. 11, Great Basin, ed. Warren L. d'Azevedo. Washington, D.C.: Smithsonian Institution, 1986.

Frachtenberg, Leo J. "Coos Notes." MS 1821, National Anthropological Archives, Smithsonian Institution, Washington, D.C., 1909.

"Coos Texts." *Columbia University Contributions to Anthropology*, 1 (1913), pp. 1-216.

French, David. "Wasco Wishram." *Perspectives in American Indian Culture Change*, ed. Edward H. Spicer. Chicago: University of Chicago Press, 1961.

Gatschet, Albert. *The Klamath Indians of Southwestern Oregon*. Contributions to North American Ethnography (1890).

Glover, Richard, ed. *David Thompson's Narrative, 1784-1812*. Toronto: Chaplain Society, 1962.

Gold, Ruben, ed. *Original Journals of the Lewis and Clark Expedition, 1804-1806*. New York: Antiquarian Press, 1959.

Haines, Francis. "The Northward Spread of Horses Among the Plains Indians." *American Anthropologist*, 40, 3 (1938), pp. 429-437.

Harrington, John Peabody. "Coos, Lower Umpqua, and Siuslaw Ethnographic Field Notes." MS, National Anthropological Archives, Smithsonian Institution, Washington, D.C., 1942.

Takelma. MS Field Notes, National Anthropological Archives, Smithsonian Institution, Washington, D.C., 1933.

Hunn, Eugene S. *Nch'i-Wana, "The Big River": Mid-Columbia Indian People and Their Land*. Seattle: University of Washington Press, 1990.

Jacobs, Melville. "Coos Myth Texts." *University of Washington Publications in Anthropology*, 8 (1940), pp. 127-260.

"Coos Narrative and Ethnologic Texts." *University of Washington Publications in Anthropology*, 8 (1939), pp. 1-125.

"Coos Narrative and Ethnologic Texts." *University of Washington Publications in Anthropology*, 8 (1939), pp. 127-260.

Josephy, Alvin M., Jr. *The Nez Perce Indians and the Opening of the Northwest*. New Haven; Yale University Press, 1965; reprinted by University of Nebraska Press, 1979.

Miller, Wick R. "Numic Languages." *Handbook of North American Indians*, Vol. 11, Great Basin, ed. Warren L. d'Azevedo. Washington, D.C.: Smithsonian Institution, 1986.

O'Donnell, Terence. *An Arrow in the Earth: General Joel Palmer and the Indians of Oregon*. Portland: Oregon Historical Society Press, 1991.

Ray, Verne F. *Cultural Relations in the Plateau of Northwestern America.* Publications of the Frederick Webb Hodge Anniversary Publication Fund, 3. Los Angeles: Southwest Museum, 1939.

"Lower Chinook Ethnographic Notes." *University of Washington Publications in Anthropology*, 7, pp. 29-165.

Riddle, George. *History of Early Days in Oregon.* Riddle, Oregon: The Riddle Enterprise, 1920.

Transactions of the Oregon Pioneer Association. Annual Address, 44th Annual Reunion, 1919. Portland: 1922.

Ruby, Robert H. and John A. Brown. *A Guide to the Indian Tribes of the Pacific Northwest.* Norman, Oklahoma: University of Oklahoma Press, 1986.

Indians of the Pacific Northwest: A History. Norman, Oklahoma: University of Oklahoma Press, 1981.

Sapir, Edward. "Notes on the Takelma Indians of South-western Oregon." *American Anthropologist*, 9, No. 2 (1927), pp. 251-275.

Spier, Leslie. *Klamath Ethnography.* Berkeley, California: University of California Publications in Archaeology and Ethnography (1930).

Stern, Theodore. *The Klamath Tribe: A People and Their Reservation.* Seattle: University of Washington Press, 1965.

Stern, Theodore and James P. Boggs. "White and Indian Farmers on the Umatilla Indian Reservation." *Exploration of the Reservation System in North America*, ed. Deward E. Walker, Jr. Northwest Anthropological Research Notes, 5 (1971), pp. 37-76.

Walker, Deward E., Jr. *Conflict and Schism in Nez Perce Acculturation: A Study of Religion and Politics.* Moscow: University of Idaho Press, 1985.

Mutual Cross-utilization of Economic Resources in the Plateau: an Example from Aboriginal Nez Perce Fishing Practices. Washington State University Laboratory of Anthropology, Report of Investigations 41. Pullman: Washington State University Press, 1967.

"New Light on the Prophet Dance Controversy." *Ethnohistory*, 16, 3 (1969), pp. 245-255.

Walling, A.G. *History of Southern Oregon: Comprising Jackson, Josephine, Douglas, Curry, and Coos Counties.* Portland: A.G. Walling, 1884.

Whiting, Beatrice Blyth. "Paiute Sorcery." *Viking Fund Publications in Anthropology*, 15 (1950).

Zucker, Hummel and Hogfoss, eds. *Oregon Indian: Culture, History and Current Affairs.* Portland: Oregon Historical Society Press, 1983.

ABOUT THE OREGON
COUNCIL FOR THE HUMANITIES

*The Oregon Council for the Humanities, founded in 1971 to promote community appreciation
for the humanities throughout the state, is governed by a board of 21 Oregonians.
The Council is an affiliate of the National Endowment for the Humanities.
Through competitive grants, publications, and its own projects, the Council seeks
to enrich people's store of ideas and information about their world, demonstrate the relevance
of the humanities to modern life, and give humanities scholars ways to engage
with other citizens about the things they study and teach.*

*Of special concern to the Council is the multicultural character of our world
and the role the humanities can play in broadening citizen understanding of the many
different histories, forms of culture, and values that constitute our human heritage.*

The First Oregonians *is one way that the Oregon Council for the Humanities
is attempting to focus public understanding on this diverse, collective heritage.
It is but one instance of the OCH program at work.
From year to year, many exhibits, lectures, publications, films, conferences, and other programs
are supported in all parts of the state, so that in Oregon there can be
a continuing exploration of human experience and values, a thinking together
about shared history and different histories, shared values and different values,
a common future and a multiplicity of futures.*

*Anyone wishing to receive more information about the
Oregon Council for the Humanities, to be put on the mailing list, or to contribute
to the support of the humanities in Oregon can write or visit the OCH office
at 812 S.W. Washington Street, Suite 225, Portland, OR 97205
or call us at (503) 241-0543 or 1-800-735-0543.*